PAPER MACHINE

Cultural Memory
in
the
Present

Mieke Bal and Hent de Vries, Editors

PAPER MACHINE

Jacques Derrida

Translated by Rachel Bowlby

STANFORD UNIVERSITY PRESS

STANFORD, CALIFORNIA

2005

Stanford University Press
Stanford, California

Paper Machine was originally published in French in 2001 under
the title *Papier machine* © 2001, Éditions Galilée.

"*Fichus*" was originally published in French in 2002 under
the title *Fichus* © 2002, Éditions Galilée.

This book has been published with the assistance of the
French Ministry of Culture—National Center for the Book.

Printed in the United States of America
on acid-free, archival-quality paper

Library of Congress Cataloging-in-Publication Data

Derrida, Jacques.
   [Papier machine. English]
   Paper machine / Jacques Derrida ; translated by Rachel Bowlby.
      p.   cm. — (Cultural memory in the present)
   Includes bibliographical references.
   ISBN 0-8047-4619-2 (alk. paper)
   ISBN 0-8047-4620-6 (pbk. : alk. paper)
   1. Philosophy.   I. Title. II. Series.
   B2430.D483P3613 2005
194—dc22

                                      2005002882

Original Printing 2005

Last figure below indicates year of this printing:
14 13 12 11 10 09 08 07 06 05

Typeset by Tim Roberts in 11/13.5 Garamond

Contents

Translator's Note

Two terms in particular that recur in these essays need a word of explanation. The first, *sans-papiers*, is directly related to the title. A *sans-papiers* is someone "paperless": "without (identity) papers." The word is parallel to *sans-toit*, meaning a "roofless," hence homeless, person. In U.S. English the equivalent to the *sans-papiers* is the *undocumented person*. This official category does not exist in British English, where *illegal immigrant* is pejorative and the milder term, *asylum seeker* (which can also be), does not cover all the cases of the *sans-papiers*. Because it includes the (lack of) paper essential to the French term, and because it is likewise nonjudgmental, I have generally used *undocumented* for *sans-papiers*, but have sometimes given the French or used the word *paperless*, too, where the connection with actual paper is important.

Another difficult term is *globalization*, for which the French equivalent is *mondialisation*. Derrida often points out that the two are not, however, the same: the geometrical or geographical "globe" of *globalization* lacks the social and historical sense of the "world" (*monde*) that is present in the French word. To introduce a neologism (*mondialization*, say) would not work, since the point is partly that *globalization*, regularly translated as or translating *mondialisation*, has become a cliché. So I have kept *globalization* as the default word, but indicated the places where Derrida is emphasizing its difference from the French word.

Derrida explains in his introduction (Chapter 1) that the essays in the volume were all "occasional" pieces, many of them written for journals or newspapers. ("The papers" in this sense provide an English but not a French resource for the book's questions: the French word *journal*—"daily" [newspaper]—has no paper, whereas the English *paper* has nothing but.) *Papier machine* included a number of texts that are not in the present volume. A long essay, "Typewriter Ribbon: Limited Ink (2)" is translated by Peggy Kamuf, in Derrida, *Without Alibi* (Stanford, Calif.: Stanford University Press, 2002). In *Papier machine* this followed "The Book to Come," as three further lectures given at the Bibliothèque nationale de France. Three articles—"Taking Sides for Algeria," "For Mumia Abu-Jamal," and "'Dead Man Running': Salut, Salut"—are in Derrida, *Negotiations*, edited and translated by Elizabeth Rottenberg (Stanford, Calif.: Stanford University Press, 2002). An additional lecture, *Fichus*, appears at the end of (the English) *Paper Machine*. The most recent piece in the book, this was Derrida's speech in acceptance of the Adorno Prize in Frankfurt in September 2001.

Finally, the French title, *Papier machine*, is not adequately translated by *Paper Machine*. *Papier-machine*—literally, "machine paper"—means typing paper, or any of its more recent equivalents such as printer paper. But the pairing of paper and machine is essential to the book's arguments both about the history of technology and about issues of immigration (the *sans-papiers*), so it did not seem appropriate to use the specific equivalent, which would lose many of the broader connotations of "paper machine."

All unattributed translations are by me. I have occasionally modified published translations to clarify the point being made in the present text.

Rachel Bowlby

PAPER MACHINE

Machines and the "Undocumented Person"

So there's such a thing as *papier-machine*—typing paper, printer paper, machine paper. And what we think we recognize under this name, a French one.

So there's what we normally use, following the "usual" name, *papier-machine*, to the letter, in the strict or the literal sense: the form of a *matter*, *the sheet* designed as the *backing* or *medium* for a *typewriter's* writing, and also now for the printing, reproduction, and archiving of the products of so many word-processing machines, and the like. This then is what becomes a figure here, what a rhetorician would also call a "locus."

Machine paper: so the title gestures toward a place, a figure, in fact more than one figure.

By effectively displacing the normal usage of the expression *papier-machine* to put pressure on its articulation; by juxtaposing, without a hyphen, two nouns of equal stature (paper *and* machine, machine *or* paper: neither is ever the attribute of the other, or its subject), this title is an attempt to name a singular *configuration*, an addition, an ordered set of metaphors, tropes, and metonymies. What then does *paper* mean here? What should we understand by *machine*? What is the meaning of the hypothesis or the prosthesis of their subjectless coupling: machine paper?

There would be no justification for this title unless slowly, laboriously, in the time taken by the texts gathered together here, it awakened, heralded, or prepared something like a "thinking" of "machine paper," a thinking of a hyphen that is visible or invisible, between the machine and the paper. Not a speculative thought, not a philosophy, not even a theory, but an experience of writing, a path ventured, a series of "political" gestures (at the center of this book, we will hear the echoing, for instance, in more than one register, literal and figurative, of the question of the person with no papers, crushed by so many machines, "when we are all, already, undocumented, 'paperless'").

Over a short period, about four years, gestures of this kind recall the attempts arising from an anxious seeking, a modest strategy, in short an effort of orientation in thought, at the point when some are hastening to announce the end of a history constrained not only by the authority of the book but by a paper economy—and therefore the urgency of reactivating its memory and its origin.

From this *place*—a rhetorical topos and an experiential situation—from this historical spot where we are *passing through*, even more or less settled down, we then wonder: What's going on? What's *taking place* between the paper and the machine? What new experience of taking place? What does an event become? What becomes of its archive when the *world of paper* (the world made of paper or what globalization still gets from paper) is subordinated to all these new machines for virtualization? Is there such a thing as virtual event? A virtual archive? Would it be that new? An unprecedented "scene of writing," I would have said in the past, or another "archive fever"? What does that offer us for thinking about the relationship between the act, the actual, the possible, and the impossible? Between the event and fantasy, or the spectral? For what new rights? And what new interpretation of "the political"?

All the texts in this book are *due*—to occasions, to provocations, to opportunities given, sometimes by people close to me, personal friends or political friends. So, taking them as determining *situations*, I thought I should at least indicate the "places" for which these texts were initially written. Always in *reply* to an invitation, a request, or a survey.

All of them institutions (highly national or quite international, if not universal) given over to the machine and to paper, each held to its own rhythm, to the original temporality of its survival.

All of them institutions imposing (as we can tell from writing and reading) their norms, their rules of the game, the memory or the fantasy of their experience, the authority of their assumed competence.

All of them institutions whose names in each case, and just the title (a whole program), would by themselves deserve more than one work, whether or not a book.

1. The *book*, the great archive or the great copyright library of the book: the Bibliothèque nationale de France [French National Library].

2. The *journal*, between the book and the newspaper: *Les Temps Modernes, Les Cahiers de médiologie*, the *Revue internationale de philosophie*.

3. The *newspaper* or magazine, daily, fortnightly, or monthly: *La Quinzaine Littéraire, Le Monde, L'Humanité, Die Zeit, Le Figaro Magazine, Le Monde de l'éducation*.

My warm thanks to all those who have given their agreement for me to collect these texts together, after having given me the chance to respond to their invitations or questions.

2

The Book to Come

A question of "good sense," first of all, and of sense: the meaning of *à venir* in "the book to come" does not go without saying. But the word *book* is as difficult to define as the question of the book, at least if the wish is to grant it a sharp specificity, and to cut it out in its irreducibility, at the point where it resists so many neighboring, connected, and even inseparable questions.

For instance, to go to the closest connection: the question of the book, and of the history of the book, should not be conflated with that of writing, or the mode of writing, or the technologies of inscription. There are books, things that are legitimately called books. But they have been and still are written according to systems of writing that are radically heterogeneous. So the book is not linked to a writing.

Nor is it appropriate to conflate the question of the book with that of technologies of printing and reproduction: there were books both before and after the invention of printing, for example.

And the question of the book is not the question of the work. Not all books are works. On the other hand plenty of works, even literary or philosophical works, works of written discourse, are not necessarily books.

Finally, the question of the book should not be conflated with that of supports. Quite literally, or else metonymically (but we will continually be concerned with these *figures* of the book, with these metonymical, synechdochic, or simply metaphorical movements), it is possible, and this has certainly been done, to speak of books that have the most different kinds of support—not just the classical ones but the quasi immateriality or virtuality of electronic and telematic operations, of "dynamic supports" with or without screens. We cannot be sure that the unity and identity of the thing called "book" is incompatible with these new tele-technologies. In fact this is what we have to debate.

What then do we have the right to call "book" and in what way is the question of *right*, far from being preliminary or accessory, here lodged at the very heart of the question of the book? This question is governed by the question of right, not only in its particular juridical form, but also in its semantic, political, social, and economic form—in short, in its total form. And the question of the book, as we shall see, is also that of a certain totality.

So all these preliminary distinctions are indispensable even though, as we are well aware, the problematic of the book as an elaborate set of questions in itself involves all the concepts that I have just distinguished from the book: writing, the modes of inscription, production, and reproduction, the work and its working, the support, the market economy and the economics of storage, the law, politics, and so on.

I will start again from round about the question of the book with the different but related question of the "support." This is the question that comes to mind when we are interested in the current process, in its future, and in what is transforming the present form of what we call book.

Here and now we are speaking in a place that is still, essentially, a future place that has barely been inaugurated and that we already, or still, call "library," *bibliothèque*.

Even before its proper name, before its national and French proper names (Bibliothèque *nationale de France* and *François Mitterrand*), this precinct bears an ordinary name, *bibliothèque*. This beautiful name is entitled in more than one way to be a title. As we know it means the place where the book (*biblion*) is dealt with. The book is dealt with as a question, and books are dealt with in certain ways—the open history of this treatment and these ways is, we know, immense, complicated, multiple, convoluted. I will say something about this in a moment.

I mentioned the Greek word *biblion* not to sound scholarly, or even—it's too easy—to explain the word *bibliothèque*. I spoke Greek to observe in passing that *biblion* has not always meant "book" or even "work." ("Work" is something else again, which will perhaps take us, in a little while, to the margins of a serious problem, that of the future relationship between on the one hand the form *book*, the model of the book, and on the other hand a work in general, an *oeuvre*, an *opus*, the unity or body of an oeuvre marked out by a beginning and an end, and so a totality: assumed to be conceived and produced, and indeed signed by an author, a single identifiable author, and offered up for the respectful reading of a reader who doesn't meddle with it, doesn't transform it on the inside—in what we now call an "interactive" way.)

But does any oeuvre, be it literal or literary, have as its destiny or essential destination only a "bookish" incorporation? This must be one of the very many questions that await us. *Biblion*, which didn't initially or always mean "book," still less "oeuvre," could designate a support for writing (so derived from *biblos*, which in Greek names the internal bark of the papyrus and thus of the paper, like the Latin word *liber*, which first designated the living part of the bark before it meant "book"). *Biblion*, then, would only mean "writing paper," and not book, nor oeuvre or opus, only the substance of a particular support—bark. But *biblion* can also, by metonymy, mean any writing support, tablets for instance, or even letters: post. A bibliophore (*bibliophoros*) is someone who carries the letters (which aren't necessarily books or works). He's a sort of postman or else a scrivener—the secretary, the lawyer, the clerk of the court.

The extension of these metonymies pushed *biblion* toward the meaning of "writing" in general (in that it was no longer reducible to the support but came to inscribe itself right on the papyrus or tablet, without however being a book: not all writing is a book). Then—new extension—it was pushed toward the "book" form that is what interests us this evening, and which already has a long and complicated history from the *volumen*, the papyrus scroll, to the *codex*, in which notebooks are bound to boards placed over them.

Already in Greek, *bibliotheke* means the slot for a book, books' place of *deposit*, the place where books are put (*poser*), deposited, laid down (*reposer*), the *entrepôt* where they are stored: a *bibliophylakion* is the deposit or warehouse, the *entrepôt*, for books, writings, nonbook archives in general; and the *bibliopoleion* is the bookstore or *librairie*, a name, often given to the *bibliothèque*, and that has been kept, of course, in English ("library").

As to the kinds of treatment these places have in store, let me just stress the traditional words I had to use to describe them, and which are all leads to follow for future reflection. These are the verbs *poser*, *déposer*, *re-*

poser, and *entreposer*. Like the presence of the Greek *tithenai* ("to put") in *bibliotheke*, they all point up the act of *putting*, depositing, but also the act of immobilizing, of giving something over to a stabilizing immobility, and so to the statute, to the statutory and even state institution, which alerts us to all the institutional, juridical, and political dimensions that we must also debate. Setting down, laying down, depositing, storing, warehousing— this is also receiving, collecting together, gathering together, consigning (like baggage), binding together, collecting, totalizing, electing, and reading by binding. So the idea of *gathering together*, as much as that of the immobility of the statutory and even state deposit, seems as essential to the idea of the book as to that of the library. And since the question of the future that we have been asked to consider this evening concerns the book as much as the library, I imagine that there will be no surprise in rediscovering these motifs of the *thetic* position and the collection: of the gathering together that is statutory, legitimate, institutional, and even state or national.

Let me mention in passing that all these motifs are themselves collected together in the question of the *title*. Can we imagine a book without a title? We can, but only up to the point when we will have to name it and thus also to classify it, deposit it in an order, put it into a catalog, or a series, or a taxonomy. It is difficult to imagine, or at any rate to deal with, with a book that is neither placed nor collected together under a title bearing its name, its identity, the condition of its legitimacy and of its copyright. And in connection with titles, it happens that the name of this place, Bibliothèque, gives its title to a place which, as it already does, will more and more in the future have to collect together (in order to make them available to users) texts, documents, and archives that are further and further away from both the support that is paper and the *book* form.

This is in truth the question that we are being asked this evening. "What about the book to come?" Will we continue for long to use the word *library* for a place that essentially no longer collects together a store of books? Even if this place still houses all possible books, even if their number continued to hold up, as I think can be envisaged, even if for a long time books still represented the majority of texts produced, nonetheless the underlying tendency would be for such a place increasingly to be expected to become a space for work, reading, and writing that was governed or dominated by texts no longer corresponding to the "book" form: electronic texts with no paper support, texts not corpus or opus—not finite and separable oeuvres; groupings no longer forming texts, even, but open textual processes offered on boundless national and international networks, for the active or interactive intervention of readers turned coauthors, and so on.

If we still say library or *bibliothèque* to designate this kind of place to come, is it only through one of those metonymic slippages like the one that led to the Greek noun *biblion* being kept, or the Latin noun *liber*, to designate first of all writing, what is written down, and then "the book"— even though at the beginning it meant only the papyrus bark or even part of the living bark of a tree?

Still thinking, under a preliminary head, about titles, or copyright brands, the title chosen for this exchange, as it can be read on the posters, says very precisely: "On the Book to Come." The title does not say "The Book to Come," but "*On* the Book to Come." As you know, the expression *the book to come* has a long history. It was already a book title, hence a title printed on the cover of a book, the book by Maurice Blanchot entitled, in 1959, *Le Livre à venir, The Book to Come.*

Now *Le Livre à venir*, the title, is printed *on* the book, on *Le Livre à venir*, and this *mise en abyme*, a structure that libraries have always favored, takes off once more by itself, when you think that this title, *Le Livre à venir*, printed on *Le Livre à venir*, is also to be found or found again *in Le Livre à venir*, hence within a book, of course, enveloped, gathered up, folded into a book that deals with the book.

More than once, at least three times *en abyme*: for the expression "the book to come," *le livre à venir*, appears inside an article entitled "The Book to Come," which itself gives its title to the book in which it is collected with numerous other articles. Its first subsection is called "*Ecce Liber*," and if there had been time we ought to have read this text very closely, specifically with regard to the questions that concern us this evening. For this quotation *en abyme* is already taking us, at least if we want to follow its genealogy, into a whole French library, from Blanchot to Mallarmé. That is why I would like to insist—only a very little, given the shortage of time— on this quotation of a quotation, even before getting going on the urgent and thorny question we have been asked to consider of the "book to come." A question trembling all over, not only with that which disturbs the historical sense of what we still call a book, but also with what the expression *to come* might imply—namely more than one thing, at least three things:

1. That the book as such has—or doesn't have—a future, now that electronic and virtual incorporation, the screen and the keyboard, online transmission, and numerical composition seem to be dislodging or supplementing the *codex* (that gathering of a pile of pages bound together, the current form of what we generally call a book such that it can be opened, put on a table, or held in the hands). The *codex* had itself supplanted the volume, the *volumen*, the scroll. It had supplanted it without making it disappear, I should stress. For what we are dealing with is never replacements that put an end to what they replace but rather, if I might use this word today, restructurations in which the oldest form survives, and even survives endlessly, coexisting with the new form and even coming to terms with a new economy—which is also a calculation in terms of the market as well as in terms of storage, capital, and reserves.

2. That if it has a future, the book to come will no longer be what it was.

3. That we are awaiting or hoping for an *other* book, a book to come that will transfigure or even rescue the book from the shipwreck that is happening at present.

This word *shipwreck*: before here connoting the abyss, the ghost, or the return of some feared catastrophe, happening now or to come, it plunges us back into a singular work that was and was not a book, Stéphane Mallarmé's *Un Coup de dés* . . . [A Throw of the Dice], around which Blanchot wrote an essay entitled "The Book to Come," inside which one reads the expression *the book to come*, which also happens to be the title of the collection or *recueil*—another word that points in the direction of binding and gathering, but first of all toward welcome or *accueil* (Mallarmé designates the reader as a "guest").

Let me again emphasize the word *recueil*. The linearity with which book writing is so often associated already receives a blow [*coup*], and it wasn't the first, in all the marine, abyssal, ghostly, numerical, or numerological figures of this "*coup de dés*," to the extent that I couldn't read this text out loud, in the linear successiveness of a temporality, without destroying the differentiated sizes of the letters and the typographical distribution of a spacing that no longer respects the division and irreversibility of pagination, and where I'm barbarically selecting a few figures as I would do, and indeed have done, on my computer:

NEVER

[. . .] FROM THE DEPTHS OF A SHIPWRECK

THOUGH IT BE
that

the Abyss [. . .]

corpse by the arm   separated from the secret it withholds

rather
than play
as a hoary maniac
the game
in the name of the waves [. . .]

shipwreck this   pertaining to man

without vessel [. . .]

Nuptials

from which
the veil of illusion sprung up against their haunting
like the ghost of a gesture

will falter
will fall

madness [. . .]

bitter prince of the reef [. . .]

IT WAS   *THE NUMBER*
born of the stars

WERE IT TO EXIST [. . .]

WERE IT TO BEGIN AND WERE IT TO CEASE [. . .]

WERE IT TO BE NUMBERED [. . .]

WERE IT TO ILLUMINE [. . .]

CHANCE

Falls
        the feather
                rhythmical suspension of disaster
                                        to be buried
                                in the original spray
                whence formerly its delirium sprang up to a peak
                                        withered
                        by the identical neutrality of the abyss [. . .]

NOTHING

of the memorable crisis
        or might
                the event   have been accomplished in view of all results   null
                                                                    human

                        WILL HAVE TAKEN PLACE
                an ordinary elevation pours out absence

                                        BUT THE PLACE
                some splashing below of water as if to disperse the empty act
                                abruptly which otherwise
                                by its falsehood
                        would have founded
                                        perdition
                in these latitudes
                        of indeterminate
                        waves
                                in which all reality dissolves [. . .][1]

At the risk of outrageously mistreating the *quotation* or the *presentation*, allow me to insist on *Un Coup de dés . . .* as a way of saluting and paying tribute to Mallarmé, and this unique book, *and* the exemplary respect shown by the old Bibliothèque nationale in the rue Richelieu in its treatment of his manuscript, his original editions, and his very difficult printing.

What account should we take this evening of the meditation that

Blanchot dedicates to Mallarmé in *The Book to Come*? To Mallarmé, which is to say also to the author of *Quant au livre* [As to the Book], which includes "Le Livre, instrument spirituel" (which we should reread closely, especially with regard to folding, meaning the folding of the codex and to this sacralization, the "quasi-religious," as Mallarmé puts it, and which we should have much more to say about).

It's in the text that begins with the famous "proposition": "A proposition that emanates from me. . . . I claim it . . . in brief means, that everything, in the world, exists to end up in a book"; or again "admitted the volume includes no signatory,"[2] and that says so much on the folds, folding, and folding back of paper where it gives rise, gives place, a sacred place, sometimes a place of burial, a dwelling or a tomb:

Now—
Folding is, in relation to the large printed sheet, a sign, quasi-religious: that does not strike so much as its compression, in thickness, offering the miniscule tomb, surely, of the soul.[3]

In the discussion we will surely have to come back to this religiosity, to this quasi sacrality, more precisely to this quasi resacralization that, with all the political issues it involves, has marked the entire history of technologies of inscription and archiving, the entire history of supports and printing methods—as if each stage, in a technological transformation, seemed the one to desacralize, democratize, secularize, defetishize, throughout an interminable history of Enlightenment or Reason (before and beyond the *Aufklärung*); but as though each stage, all the same, was also inescapably accompanied by a sacred or religious reinvestment. For it is obvious, for instance, that if our generation is suffering from seeing the book yield ground in the face of other supports, other modes of reading and writing, this is partly because, inevitably, it has resacralized everything connected with the book (its time, its space, its rhythm, starting from the ways it is handled, the ways it is legitimated, even the body, the eyes, and the hands bent around it, the quasi-priestly sociality of its producers, interpreters, and decision makers, in all their institutions of selection and legitimation); and this, despite the fact that this resacralized and refetishized book has been an element of secularization and democratization, with its phonetic writing, for instance, and then its modes of printing and reproduction.

Roger Chartier's extremely detailed, full analysis in *Les Représentations de l'écrit* makes this point. This democratization/secularization is a process that both Vico and Condorcet, among others, tried to take into account. In *Of Grammatology*, more than thirty years ago, I tried to analyze some other examples of this techno-political history of literature.

Let me leave on one side the questions of fetishization, of sacralization, of surplus value from increasing rareness, in order to return to one of the themes that Blanchot privileges in "the book to come," in *The Book to Come*—in the article on "the book to come" in the book called *The Book to Come*.

This really is about the project of a Book *to come* and not about the book's being-*past* that we have just started speaking about. Blanchot's meditation is inscribed between *Un Coup de dés . . .* and the Book project, the project of the Work (with a capital letter) as Book—it took up a lot of his time and we have his notes for it. In it, Blanchot privileges the double *antinomic* motif of division and gathering (this semantics of the collection, of binding, the vocabulary of *colligere* I was discussing just now). The subtitle of this part is "Gathered Through Dispersion." And that is the beginning of the question of the future, of the book to come. Its past has not yet reached us, we have yet to think it:

I will not assert that *Un coup de dés* is the Book, an assertion that the Book's specifications would deprive of all meaning. . . . It has the essential quality of the Book: present with this lightning-stroke that divides it and gathers it back together, and yet it is extremely problematic, so much so that even today for us, so familiar (we think) with all that is not familiar, it continues to be the most unlikely work. It could be said that we have assimilated Mallarmé's work more or less readily, but not *Un coup de dés*. *Un coup de dés* implies a completely different book from the book that we have: it makes us feel that what we call "book" according to the traditional Western usages, in which the gaze identifies the act of comprehension with the repetition of linear back-and-forth motions, is justified only in the facilitation of analytic comprehension.[4]

What I would like to do here, before concluding, and with a view to setting out for discussion some interconnected propositions, even if this means coming back to them later to back them up, is first of all to formalize a central motif, in Blanchot's *The Book to Come*, concerning Mallarmé. This central, organizing motif is on the one hand a tension, one that is constitutive of *The Book to Come* as Mallarmé projects it. This is the *tension between gathering and dispersion*, a tension which, on the other hand, without being resolved, gets into a circular form, into the circulation of the circle.

Here are some lines on the subject of this motif of putting into circulation a dispersal that is gathered together or linked to itself:

Un Coup de dés orients the future of the book both in the direction of the greatest dispersion and in the direction of a tension capable of *gathering* infinite diversity, by the discovery of more complex structures. The mind, says Mallarmé, following Hegel, is "*volatile dispersion.*" The book that collects the mind thus collects an extreme capacity for rupture, a limitless anxiety, one that the book *cannot contain* [my emphasis: the book contains what it can't contain, it is both bigger and smaller than what it is, like any library in fact], one that excludes all content from it, all limited, defined, and complete sense. It is a movement of diaspora that must never be repressed but instead preserved and welcomed as such into the space that is projected from it and to which this movement only responds, a response to an indefinitely multiplied void where dispersion takes on the form and appearance of unity. Such a book, always in movement, always on the verge of scattering, will also always be gathered in all directions, through dispersion itself and according to the division that is essential to it, which it makes not disappear, but appear, maintaining this dispersion so the book can accomplish itself there.

Un Coup de dés was born from a new understanding of literary space . . . [5]

To this insoluble tension (for what can a dispersion be once it is gathered together as such? what can be the "as such" of a division that gathers and assembles and links division itself?), Blanchot brings a formulation, if not a solution, that, even if the word dialectics is not actually mentioned, remains dialectical—and it is no accident that the name Hegel, as you have heard, enters in at this place and at this time.

This Hegelian formulation is that of a *circle*, a *circular becoming* whose effect would be not to annul tension but to displace it and bring it into a becoming full of meaning: "The Book is thus, subtly, affirmed in the *becoming* that is perhaps [the word *perhaps*—the last word in the chapter—will play a role that I cannot dwell on here] its meaning, a meaning that might be the very becoming of the circle. The end of the work is its origin, its new and old beginning: it is its possibility opened one more time, so that the dice thrown once again can be the very throw of the masterful words."[6]

Well, if I may mention it, that is the point some thirty years ago where I thought I had to make a diagnosis or could make a prognosis, in *Of Grammatology*, under the heading "The End of the Book," at the risk of seeing myself accused, quite absurdly, of wishing for the death of the book and pressing for it. What I then called "the end of the book" came at the close of a whole history: a history of the book, of the figure of the book, and even of what was called "the book of nature" (Galileo, Descartes, Hume, Bonnet, Von Schubert, and so on).[7] In speaking of the ongoing "end of the book," I was referring to what was already in the offing, of course, and what we're talking about tonight, but mainly I meant the onto-encyclopedic or neo-Hegelian model of the great total book, the book of absolute knowledge linking its own infinite dispersion to itself, in a circle.

Now what is happening today, what looks like being the very form of the book's to-come, still as the book, is *on the one hand*, beyond the closure of the book, the disruption, the dislocation, the disjunction, the dissemination with no possible gathering, the irreversible dispersion of this total codex (not its disappearance but its marginalization or secondarization, in ways we will have to come back to); but simultaneously, *on the other hand*, a constant reinvestment in the book project, in the book of the world or the world book, in the absolute book (this is why I also described the end of the book as interminable or endless), the new space of writing and reading in electronic writing, traveling at top speed from one spot on the globe to another, and linking together, beyond frontiers and copyrights, not only citizens of the world on the universal network of a potential *universitas*, but also any reader as a writer, potential or virtual or whatever. That revives a desire, the same desire. It re-creates the temptation that is figured by the World Wide Web as the ubiquitous Book finally reconstituted, the book of God, the great book of Nature, or the World Book finally achieved in its onto-theological dream, even though what it does is to repeat the end of that book as to-come.

These are two fantasmatic limits of the book to come, two extreme, final, eschatic figures of the end of the book, the end as death, or the end as *telos* or achievement. We must take seriously these two fantasies; what's more they are what makes writing and reading happen. They remain as irreducible as the two big ideas of the book, of the *book* both as the unit of a material support in the world, and as the unity of a work or unit of discourse (a book in the book). But we should also perhaps wake up to the necessity that goes along with these fantasies.

And I will only point out the necessity of this law, by way of a dry conclusion in four remarks, or four vanishing points that would be worth developing interminably. I utter them or send them telegraphically, to cast them into the discussion like little dots, elliptical dots or throws of the dice.

1. *The playful and the serious.* How can one speak seriously about the book (assuming that one has to be serious, in other words also be governed by the idea of knowledge—circular and pedagogical—that is only one dimension of the book as encyclopedia, the other one being the dimension of play, chance, and literature, which will always raise the question of whether, as a throw of the dice, it includes or lets itself be included by the encyclopedia)? We will only be able to speak seriously about these two fantasies of the book to come if we neutrally give up any kind of eschatological teleology, in other words any kind of evaluation, whether pessimistic or optimistic, reactionary or progressive. So we should on the one hand give up any lamentation, pointless and powerless in any case, that would come along to tell us in the face of the inevitable: "What's befalling us is the death of the book—catastrophe. We must at all costs save the book from this death that threatens us, the death of everything we have held sacred, of everything to which our cultures and our truths and our revelations, and our modes of legitimation, and so on, are indissociably attached." In fact— let's be serious—we know that the book isn't simply going to disappear. For any number of reasons, it is not even certain that in terms of volume its market production is not destined to remain stable, and even to increase, and in a mediatized market that we should also speak about seriously. I would like to come back to this point in the discussion. On the other hand, we should analyze the retention of the model of the book, the *liber*—of the unit and the distribution of discourse, even its pagination on the screen, even the body, the hands and eyes that it continues to orient, the rhythm it prescribes, its relationship to the title, its modes of legitimation, even where the material support has disappeared (the new electronic journals, based in universities across the world, generally reproduce the traditional formats, editorial norms, criteria of evaluation and selection—for better and for worse).

There is, there will therefore be, as always, the coexistence and structural survival of past models at the moment when genesis gives rise to new possibilities. What is more, you can love more than one thing at a time, and not give anything up, as with the unconscious. I'm in love with the book, in my own way and forever (which sometimes leads me, paradoxically, to find that there are too many of them and not at all "not enough"); I love every form of the book and I see no reason to give this love up. But I also love—this is the fate of my generation, of just this one generation— the computer and the TV. And I like writing with a pen just as much, sometimes just as little, as writing with a typewriter—mechanical or electric—or on a computer. A new economy is being put in place. It brings into coexistence, in a mobile way, a multiplicity of models, and of modes of archiving and accumulation. And that's what the history of the book has always been. We must be vigilant in resisting this catastophe-minded pessimism, apart from the fact that it reveals the pointless temptation to oppose the inevitable development of technologies whose advantages, as well, are obvious, not just in terms of efficiency and economy but also ethically and politically. But we must also be wary of a progressivist—and sometimes "romantic"—optimism, ready to endow the new distance technologies of communication with the myth of the infinite book without material support, the myth of universalist transparency, of communication that is immediate, totalizing, and free of controls, beyond all frontiers, in a sort of big democratic village. The optimism of a new *Aufklärung* ready to sacrifice, even burn on its altar, all the old books and their libraries—which would be another form of barbarity. The truth of the book, if I may put it like that, at any rate its *necessity*, resists—and dictates to us (this is also the seriousness of a "must") that we should resist both these fantasies, which are only the flipside of each other.

2. *Another politics of restructuring.* For in what I dare not call the "restructuring in progress" that is neither a death nor a resurrection, we can also trust in the conservative, even fetishistic impulse. Interminably, it will reinvest the book threatened by this "restructuring" of culture and knowledge. This fetishism will sanctify—sanctify once again—the book, the aura of culture or the cult of the book, the body of the book and the body used to the book, the time, the temporality, and the spacing of the book, the habitus of the love of the book that will be revalorized and overvalued exactly according to the possibility of its becoming scarce, not to say commercially secondary or in decline. This fortunately incorrigible fetishism will even protect the signs of post-book technologies threatened by more advanced technologies.

3. *The right to books.* Between the two fantasies I have just mentioned, the turbulence and impasses have, as always, a juridical and ethical-political form. If everything symbolized by the World Wide Web can have a liberating effect (in relation to controls and all forms of policing, and even the censorship exercised by the machines of power—of the nation-state, the economy, the universities, and publishing), it is all too obvious that that only advances by opening up zones without rights, "wild" areas,

areas of "anything goes" (ranging from the most dangerous, politically speaking, to the most insignificant and the most inept, the worst that could come and fill in, paralyze, or break up space). A difficult question in a war for rights and power that was already ongoing at the time of the book's domination, but is obviously taking on new forms and new rhythms. They must be recognized, analyzed, and treated as fairly as possible.

4. Finally, we could speak of a *secondarization of the second* itself, whatever the unprecedented singularity of an ongoing mutation. It is true that this mutation leaves nothing outside itself on earth and beyond earth, in humanity and beyond humanity. This mutation we can call monstrous: as such, at least, and where "it's changing," it has no model and no norm to reproduce. Nevertheless, we know and we can say that what is changing the face of everything on the face of the world in this way is but a little fraction of a fraction of a second in a history which has been transforming the relationship of the living organism to itself and its environment, both progressively and through sudden mutations—the relationship of the face, for instance (since I have just mentioned what is changing the face of everything on the face of the world), the relationship of the head, the eyes, the mouth, and the brain to the rest of the body, to standing up, to the hand, to time and speed, and so on.

It is that much more vertiginous, but we do know it: what we are living through and talking about—at too much length, please forgive me— occupies the time and place of a miniscule comma in an infinite text.

That breathes or lives like the whisper of a tiny and almost invisible punctuation mark in what perhaps does not even make a history.

A history, at the very least, which does not hold fast, a history which cannot be maintained, a history which is no longer held in the hand, now.[8]

It no longer obeys the finger and the eye, as a book would. Might it ever have done so?

The Word Processor

LA QUINZAINE LITTÉRAIRE: We're going to begin with "Heidegger's Hand."[1] You explain how in Heidegger manual work, *Handwerk*, is a noble employment because it is not, "like other professions, organized in relation to public usefulness or making a profit," and that this employment "will also be that of the thinker or the teacher who teaches thinking." In addition, this employment is always "in danger," particularly of being downgraded by the machine. Heidegger is obviously thinking of the typewriter. But what does this machine do in the story, then, this machine that is no longer an obstacle, that makes the text too readable, too easy, too clear for the one who lends an ear to it—since you have also spoken at length of "Heidegger's Ear"?[2]

JACQUES DERRIDA: If only to move away from it, Heidegger's posture or postulation had to be analyzed at the outset. It belongs to a major interpretation of technology that calls forth numerous questions—calls them forth, really, where they are not so easy to hear as we would sometimes like to think . . .

To narrow things down to writing, I wanted to point out in what way Heidegger's reaction was at once intelligible, traditional, and normative. The tradition of these norms is often respectable, and its reserve considerable when it remains vigilant in the face of technological mutations. But it also gives rise, sometimes in its least naive form, to a confident dogmatism, an assurance that we have to interrogate. For instance, Heidegger deplores the fact that even personal letters are now typewritten and that the singular trace of the signatory is no longer recognizable through the shapes of the letters and the movements of the hand. But when we write "by hand" we are not in the time before technology; there is already instrumentality, regular reproduction, mechanical iterability. So it is not legitimate to contrast writing by hand and "mechanical" writing, like a pretechnological craft as opposed to technology. And then on the other side what we call "typed" writing is also "manual."

You would like me to speak about my own experiences. Well, yes, like so many other people I have gone through this history, or I have let it come my way. I began by writing with a pen, and I remained faithful to pens for a long time (faith is the right word here), only transcribing "final versions" on the machine, at the point of separating from them. The machine remains a signal of separation, of severance, the official sign of emancipation and departure for the public sphere. For the texts that mattered to me, the ones I had the slightly religious feeling of "writing," I even banished the ordinary pen. I dipped into the ink a long pen holder whose point was gently curved with a special drawing quill, producing endless drafts and preliminary versions before putting a stop to them on my first little Olivetti, with its international keyboard, that I'd bought abroad. I still have it. My idea must have been that my artisanal writing really would break its way through into that space of resistance, as near as possible to that hand of thought or word evoked by the passage in Heidegger that I later tried to interpret in "Heidegger's Hand." As if that liturgy for a single hand was required, as if that figure of the human body gathered up, bent over, applying, and stretching itself toward an inked point were as necessary to the ritual of a thinking engraving as the white surface of the paper subjectile on the table as support. But I never concealed from myself the fact that, as in any ceremonial, there had to be repetition going on, and already a sort of mechanization. This theater of the prosthesis and the marking very quickly became a theme for me, in all its dimensions, more or less everywhere from "Freud and the Scene of Writing" to *Archive Fever*.[3]

Then, to go on with the story, I wrote more and more "straight onto" the machine: first the mechanical typewriter; then the electric typewriter, in 1979; then finally the computer, around 1986 or 1987. I can't do without it any more now, this little Mac, especially when I'm working at home; I can't even remember or understand how I was able to get on before without it. It's a quite different kind of getting going, a quite different exercise of "getting to work." I don't know whether the electric typewriter or the computer make the text "too readable" and "too clear" for us. The volume, the unfolding of the operation, obeys another organigram, another organology. I don't feel the interposition of the machine as a sort of progress in transparency, univocity, or easiness. Rather, we are participating in a partly new plot. Heidegger points out that the work of thinking is a handiwork, a *Handlung*, an "action," prior to any opposition between practice and theory. Thought, in this sense, would be a *Handlung*, a "maneuver," a "manner," if not a manipulation. But is that a reason for protesting against the machine? Having recourse to the typewriter or computer doesn't bypass the hand. It engages another hand, another "command," so to speak, another induction, another injunction from body to hand and from hand to writing. But it's never at any moment, at least for the time being, a matter of handless writing, writing while keeping your hands in your pockets. Far from it. Handless writing is perhaps what we are doing now as we record our voices. But hands are not only in hands. Basically, the history I have just outlined is not marked by a breaking off of manual gestures or by the event of a hand being cut off; instead it would be another history of the hand, a history still maintained within the hand, a history of a hand-held writing,[4] even if, of course, the hand's destination is being slowly displaced, in a long-term history. Ultimately it's the hand we're talking about, and its relationship with the eye, with the rest of the body, and so on. We would instead have to think about other twists of manual labor, about virtually instant transitions, the time of the mutation, in a flash, by sleight-of-hand. Between the pen-tool and the pencil-tool on the one hand, and machines on the other, the difference is not the hand, because it is maintained and stays relevant, it's also the fingers. With mechanical or electrical writing machines, with word processors, the fingers are still operating; more and more of them are at work. It is true that they go about it in a different way. You do it more with the fingers—and with two hands rather than one. All that goes down, for some time to come, in a history of digitality.

LA QUINZAINE LITTÉRAIRE: In the four-handed book you wrote with Geoffrey Bennington, there is a photograph showing the Bodleian Library miniature that is the subject of *The Post Card*, in which we see Plato planted behind Socrates, and Socrates writing with a quill and a stylet in his hands. In the photographed scene, the person holding the "quill" is you. Perhaps that's about the invention of a new form of dialogue. A dialogue that would be as "serious" as dialogue because it is weighed down with all the heaviness of writing, and would equally be more playful because there's a whole play aspect to the computer, the computer game. Wouldn't this be a sort of advance?

DERRIDA: Can we speak of progress here? Certainly there is a transformation of the scene and, yes, a play aspect. The photograph itself, which wasn't my idea, was a provocation I thought I should agree to. The point was to mime the scene, already a strange one, of an authoritarian Plato standing up, right behind a seated Socrates in the process of writing, "scratching"—relocating the scene in our modern time. The primary reason that we had the idea of this *tableau vivant* is that the long footnote that it was to accompany, namely *Circumfession*, was written on the computer, from the very beginning. Bennington also gave himself the task of setting up what he called, in relation to my work, a database or "Derridabase," according to an IT model, if you like, enabling any reader, without there being any quotations, to find all the propositions and all the places in the corpus of texts, through a sort of ultraformalized index. So Bennington was himself playing with that machine. In *Circumfession* I also gave myself the somewhat random constraint of a software program that, when I got to the end of a paragraph of such and such a length, roughly twenty-five lines, told me: "The paragraph is going to be too long; you should press the Return button." Like an order coming from I know not whom, from the depths of what time or what abyss, this slightly threatening warning would appear on the screen, and I decided to come quietly to the end of this long sequence, after the breathing space of a rhythmic sentence, which did have punctuation, as if rippling with commas, but was uninterrupted, punctuated without a period, if you like—so submitting the fifty-nine long sentences to an arbitrary rule made by a program I hadn't chosen: to a slightly idiotic destiny. We both played with this machine that is the computer; we pretended to obey it even as we were exploiting it. As you know, the computer maintains the hallucination of an interlocutor (anonymous or otherwise), of another "subject" (spontaneous and autonomous, automatic) who can occupy more than one place and play plenty of roles: face to face for one, but also withdrawn; in front of us, for another, but also invisible and faceless behind its screen. Like a hidden god who's half asleep, clever at hiding himself even when right opposite you.

I was very late in coming to this figure of "word processing." I resisted for a long time. I thought I would never manage to submit to the rules of a machine that basically I understand nothing about. I know how to make it work (more or less) but I don't know *how* it works. So I don't know, I know less than ever "who it is" who goes there. Not knowing, in this case, is a distinctive trait, one that does not apply with pens or with typewriters either. With pens and typewriters, you think you know *how* it works, how "it responds." Whereas with computers, even if people know how to use them up to a point, they rarely know, intuitively and without thinking—at any rate, *I* don't know—*how* the internal demon of the apparatus operates. What rules it obeys. This secret with no mystery frequently marks our dependence in relation to many instruments of modern technology. We know how to use them and what they are for, without knowing what goes on with them, in them, on their side; and this might give us plenty to think about with regard to our relationship with technology *today*—to the historical newness of this experience.

To come back to the computer. On the one hand it seems to restore a quasi immediacy of the text, a desubstantialized substance, more fluid, lighter, and so closer to speech, and even to so-called interior speech. This is also a question of speed and rhythm: it goes faster—faster than us; it surpasses us, but at the same time, because of our state of ignorance about what goes on in the night of the box, it surpasses understanding as well: you have the feeling that you are dealing with the soul—will, desire, plan—of a Demiurge-Other, as if already, good or evil genius, an invisible addressee, an omnipresent witness were listening to us in advance, capturing and sending us back the image of our speech *without delay*, face to face—with the image rendered objective and immediately stabilized and translated into the speech of the Other, a speech already appropriated by the other or coming from the other, a speech of the unconscious as well. Truth itself. As though the Other-Unconscious could make use of our speech at the point when it is so close to us, but as though it could just as well interrupt or destroy it. And we maintain a silent awareness of this; we are never safe from accidents, more common with the computer than with the typewriter or the pen. A mere power cut, or a careless or clumsy move, can wipe out hours of work in an instant. That increase in spontaneity, freedom, and fluidity would then be like the bonus to go with precariousness, with a screen display at risk, even calmly distressing; the reward for a sort of alienation. I understand this word neutrally: it would be to do with a "making strange," a mechanical Other-Unconscious sending us back our own speech from a quite different place. Love and hate: this new machine might install another explanation of the body, the eye, and the hand—of the ear too, with the dictation of a foreign body, with the law, with the order of the Other-Unconscious.

LA QUINZAINE LITTÉRAIRE: When a writer writes a text, it goes through a whole series of intermediate stages. There used to be—there still are for many writers—writing by hand, then typing, then the proofs, first and second proofs, then the appearance of the book, and at each point, except at the end, it is possible to make changes, possible to make corrections, possible to come back to it. With "word processing" too it is possible to come back, but this possibility is immediate. It no longer happens in stages.

DERRIDA: It's a different kind of timing, a different rhythm. First of all you correct faster and in a more or less indefinite way. Previously, after a certain number of versions (corrections, erasures, cutting and pasting, Tippex), everything came to a halt—that was enough. Not that you thought the text was perfect, but, after a certain period of metamorphosis, the process was interrupted. With the computer, everything is rapid and so easy; you get to thinking that you can go on revising forever. An interminable revision, an infinite analysis is already on the horizon, as though held in reserve behind the finite analysis of everything that makes a screen. At any rate it can be more intensely prolonged over the same time. During this same time you no longer retain the slightest visible or objective trace of corrections made the day before. Everything—the past and the present—everything can thus be locked, canceled, or encrypted forever. Previously, erasures and added words left a sort of scar on the paper or a visible image in the memory. There was a temporal resistance, a thickness in the duration of the erasure. But now everything negative is drowned, deleted; it evaporates immediately, sometimes from one instant to the next. It's another kind of experience of what is called "immediate" memory and of the transition from memory to archive. Another provocation for "genetic criticism," as it is called, which has developed around drafts, multiple versions, proofs, and the like.

All in all, it's getting a bit too easy. Resistance—because ultimately, there's always resistance—has changed in form. You have the feeling that now this resistance—meaning also the prompts and commands to change, to erase, to correct, to add, or to delete—is programmed or staged by a theater. The text is as if presented to us as a show, with no waiting. You see it *coming up* on the screen in a form that is more objective and anonymous than on a handwritten page, a page which we ourselves *moved down*. So from bottom to top is how things go: this show happens almost above us, we see it seeing us, surveying us like the eye of the Other, or rather, simultaneously, it also happens under the eye of the nameless stranger, immediately calling forth his vigilance and his specter. It sends us back the objectivity of the text much faster, and so changes our experience of time and of the body, the arms and the hands, our embracing of the written thing at a distance. The written thing becomes both closer and more distant. In this there is another distancing or remoteness, *re-mote* here meaning a distancing of the removed, but also a distancing that abolishes the remote. So another distancing, and I assume that it *alters* every sign. That doesn't mean that it perverts or degrades the sign, but it renders *other* our old sorting out, our familiar altercation, our family scene, if I may call it that, when the written thing first appeared. I couldn't specify here in what way this hospitality changes. It occurs each time and differently for each one of us. People often ask me, "Has your writing changed since you have been writing on the computer?" I'm incapable of replying. I don't know what criteria to measure it by. There's certainly a change but I'm not sure that it affects what is written, even if it does modify the way of writing.

LA QUINZAINE LITTÉRAIRE: I've been reading you for a long time, and I don't see a violent change.

DERRIDA: Nor do I. But I'm aware of another dramaturgy, if I can put it like that. When I sit down at the table and switch on my computer, the scenario is different but I don't know if that translates into a change in what is written. It was well before computers that I risked the most refractory texts in relation to the norms of linear writings. It would be easier for me now to do this work of dislocation or typographical invention—of graftings, insertions, cuttings, and pastings—but I'm not very interested in that any more from that point of view and in that form. That was theorized and that was done—then. The path was broken experimentally for these new typographies long ago, and today it has become ordinary. So we must invent other "disorders," ones that are more discreet, less self-congratulatory and exhibitionist, and this time contemporary with the computer. What I was able to try to change in the matter of page formatting I did in the archaic age, if I can call it that, when I was still writing by hand or with the old typewriter. In 1979 I wrote *The Post Card* on an electric typewriter (even though I'm already talking a lot in it about computers and software), but *Glas*—whose unusual page format also appeared as a short treatise on the organ, sketching a history of organology up to the present—was written on a little mechanical Olivetti.

LA QUINZAINE LITTÉRAIRE: We speak about "word processing," *traitement de texte* [literally, "text treatment"]. It's not altogether innocent to speak of "treatment" or "processing."

DERRIDA: The word *traitement* always comes to mind when I think of particular situations. For instance when I teach, since I prepare my seminars on the computer, it is much easier for me, with the help of the "cut and paste" facility, to reorder the seminar at the last minute, in a few seconds, and then at the beginning to read out a section that only came to seem necessary at the end, leaving it as though suspended above the scene; so I move a paragraph or a whole page by adjusting the arguments or articulating them together, economically. All that was possible before, I do know, but the same action was slow, heavy, and sometimes off-putting. The word processor saves us an amazing amount of time; we acquire a freedom that we perhaps wouldn't have acquired without it. But the transformation is economic, not structural. There are all these time-saving devices in the finishing off or polishing stages: playing with italics; separating paragraphs; intervening directly in lexical statistics, if I can call it that, by finding the number of occurrences of a given word. I've recently started using the mechanical spell-check. It's instructive, too: what are the words that are not regarded as normal or acceptable in French usage, and so remain censored, these days by the contemporary dictionary incorporated in the machine, as they would be by some other readership, some other media power for instance?

You said something about the time of proofreading. I do slightly miss the long time, the intervals, and the rhythm that then used to mark the history of a written text, all its comings and goings before publication. It was also the chemistry of a conscious or unconscious process of maturation, the chance of mutations in us, in our desire, in the bodily closeness with our text in the hands of the other. Today, as you know, we send a disk to the publisher at the same time as a manuscript: before all that goes off to the printer's, a new actor checks out the disk and makes copyediting suggestions. The proofing-improving is shared, on disk, with this invisible intermediary, but it is never written on a paper support in an exchange with the printer.

LA QUINZAINE LITTÉRAIRE: You are a teacher; you give lectures. You prepare each lecture on the computer, you write it and then you read it out. So then there is an echo of that lecture but the echo can merge with that of the machine.

DERRIDA: When you are preparing a seminar or a lecture, over a period of weeks, you see a body of letters in page form reappearing in front of you, at once objective, stable, independent, and yet floating, a bit fantasmatic—a body of letters that you no longer bear within you, and at any rate no longer completely within you like the more internal image of those old handwritten drafts. This display in fact returns the murmur of an echoing text that comes from out there, the ultrasound of oneself as another. This is the movement we were talking about a moment ago, this accelerated but suspended, fluid or aerial objectification. And I would point out parenthetically that some of my American colleagues come along to seminars or to lecture theaters with their little laptops. They don't print out; they read out directly, in public, from the screen. I saw it being done as well at the Pompidou Center [in Paris] a few days ago. A friend was giving a talk there on American photography. He had this little Macintosh laptop there where he could see it, like a prompter: he pressed a button to scroll down his text. This assumed a high degree of confidence in this strange whisperer. I'm not yet at that point, but it does happen.

LA QUINZAINE LITTÉRAIRE: We are coming to the complete abolition of the paper support. And even the complete abolition of the interlocutor. There is no longer anything except the text.

DERRIDA: The movement is apparently contradictory: more lucid and vigilant, but also more fantasmatic or dreamlike. The computer installs a new place: there one is more easily projected toward the exterior, toward the spectacle, and toward the aspect of writing that is thereby wrested away from the presumed intimacy of writing, via a trajectory of making alien. Inversely, because of the plastic fluidity of the forms, their continual flux, and their quasi immateriality, one is also increasingly sheltered in a sort of protective haven. No more outside. Or rather, in this new experience of specular reflection, there is more outside and there is no more outside. We see ourselves without seeing ourselves enveloped in the scroll or the sails of this inside/outside, led on by another revolving door of the unconscious, exposed to another coming of the other. And it can be sensed, differently, for the "Web," this WWW or World Wide Web that a network of computers weaves all about us, across the world, but also all about us, *in us*.

Think about the "addiction" of those who travel day and night in this WWW. They can no longer do without these world crossings, these voyages by sail [*à la voile*], or veil [*au voile*], crossing or cutting through them in its turn.

LA QUINZAINE LITTÉRAIRE: With the computer, word processing, and the immediacy of the screen, aren't we caught up in an endless, indefinite text? Whereas the book has the merit of cutting short, at one go.

DERRIDA: Yes, we don't know what tomorrow will be made of,[5] but you feel that the publishing machine, the market for books, printing, and even libraries—in short the ancient world—still all play the role of a cutoff point. The book is both the apparatus and the expiration date that make us have to *cut off* the computer process, put an end to it. This stoppage dictates the end to us, the copy is snatched away from us—"Here, now you must make an end of it"—and there is a date, a limit, a law, a duty, and a debt. It *has* to be transferred to another kind of support. Printing has to happen. For the time being, the book is the moment of this stoppage, the pressure to switch off. The day is coming, will come, when the off-switch or cutoff point—the *interrupteur*—which will never disappear (it is essentially impossible), will no longer be the order of another kind of support, paper, but another audiovisual device, perhaps the CD-ROM. This will be like another arrangement of the cutoff points. The word *interrupteur*—cutoff point—doesn't have a negative meaning in my view. There have to be cutoffs, that's the condition of any form, the very formation of form.

For my own part, I can say that ultimately I accept mutations. And by the same token I accept a certain fetishism of the book that their increasing rarity will be bound to further. *Of Grammatology* named and analyzed the "end of the book," but not at all in celebration of this.[6] I believe in the value of the book, which keeps something irreplaceable, and in the necessity of fighting to secure its respect. Fortunately, or unfortunately—I don't know which to say—we will see what could be called, with a change of emphasis, a new religion of the book. Another bibliophilia will follow in the tracks of the book, everywhere that it will have to yield its place to other kinds of support.

LA QUINZAINE LITTÉRAIRE: Will there be the equivalent of bibliophilia in relation to CD-ROMs or floppy disks?

DERRIDA: Probably. Some particular draft that was prepared or printed on some particular software, or some particular disk that stores a stage of a work in progress—these are the kinds of things that will be fetishized in the future. I already know writers who keep the first versions of an essay or novel or poem on disk. Once these computer archives have been locked (because it will always be easier to use them without leaving any trace), they will have a very different kind of allure. You can feel that is on the way too. Even the computer belonging to the "great writer" or "great thinker" will be fetishized, like Nietzsche's typewriter. No history of technology has wiped out that photograph of Nietzsche's typewriter. On the contrary, it is becoming ever more precious and sublime, protected by a new aura, this time that of the means of "mechanical reproduction"; and that would not necessarily contradict the theory of mechanical reproduction put forward by Benjamin. Some computers will become museum pieces. The fetishizing drive has no limits, by definition; it will never let go.

As for those people who, nowadays, don't themselves use either typewriters or computers, you can count them on the fingers of one hand. I do know some . . .

LA QUINZAINE LITTÉRAIRE: So do I. Our friend Pierre Vidal-Naquet . . .

DERRIDA: Hélène Cixous, Michel Deguy . . . When you give your work to be typed, you reconstitute a sort of "master-secretary" relationship, whether you like it or not. A dictation relationship—one thinks of Goethe, for instance. But there are many of us who do without a secretary. Structurally, the secretary is no more. Those who want to go on marking the authority of their position call on secretaries, even if they also know how to use a computer. I can't imagine a French president, a high official or a minister, typing on their computers. In the old-fashioned way they correct by hand the speech prepared by someone else, and give it back to be made into a "clean" copy. So now, as it happened once upon a time through alphabetic writing, a kind of democratization is happening through the use of the machine (provided you can pay for the thing! the prices don't go down that quickly . . .).

LA QUINZAINE LITTÉRAIRE: You can tell who's the master—the one with no machine on the desk.

DERRIDA: It's the old figure of the master—the political leader, the thinker, the poet. No machine. No direct relationship with the machine. The relationship with the machine is secondary, auxiliary, mediated by the secretary-slave—too often, and it's not accidental, by the *woman* secretary. We should speak about the word processor, power, *and* sexual difference. Power has to be able to be mediated, if not delegated, in order to exist. At any rate—and this is not always different—to appear.

LA QUINZAINE LITTÉRAIRE: It could be said that the text that appears on the screen is a phantom text. There is no longer any matter, any ink. Now there is only light and shadows, whereas the book is a dense, material object.

DERRIDA: The figure of the text "processed" on a computer is like a phantom to the extent that it is less bodily, more "spiritual," more ethereal. There is something like a disincarnation of the text in this. But its spectral silhouette remains, and what's more, for most intellectuals and writers, the program, the "software" of machines, still conforms to the spectral model of the book. Everything that appears on the screen is arranged *with a view* to books: writing, lines, numbered pages, coded indications of forms (italics, bold, etc.), the differences of the traditional shapes and characters. There are some tele-writing machines that don't do this, but "ours" still respect the figure of the book—they serve it and mimic it, they are wedded to it in a way that is quasispiritual, "pneumatic," close to breathing: as if you had only to say the word and it would be printed.

LA QUINZAINE LITTÉRAIRE: This is perhaps taking us a bit far from word processing, even if, in one way, it is an extension of the problematic. The original subject was: "What does the word processor represent for you, a philosopher?" The contribution made by the writing machine, the typewriter, was not all that radical, as you have stressed yourself.

DERRIDA: As to knowing what word processing changes for philosophy, and not only (it hardly matters, in fact) for my work, I'm always wondering what would have happened to Plato, Descartes, Hegel, Nietzsche, and even to Heidegger (who really knew without knowing the computer), if they had encountered this "thing," not only as an available tool but also as a subject for reflection. From Pascal to Descartes to Leibniz to Heidegger, by way of Hegel, philosophers have certainly thought about calculating machines, thinking machines, translating machines, formalization in general, and so on. But how would they have interpreted a culture with the tendency to be dominated, even in daily life, and across the entire universe, by these types of technological devices for writing and archiving? Because everything is involved here—the relationships of thinking to the "image," to language, to ideas, to archiving, to the simulacrum, to representation. How would Plato have had to write what we call the "myth of the cave" so as to take account of these transformations? Would he only have had to change the rhetoric of his teaching, or would he have had to think quite differently about the ontological structure of the relationships between ideas, copies, simulacra, thought and language, and so on?

LA QUINZAINE LITTÉRAIRE: Until quite a recent period, which we could locate at the end of the Middle Ages, the transcription we have, the text, is never the author's, from his hand to the quill. With the signed manuscript there appeared a new configuration that would last for a number of centuries and which we are now coming out of, to return to the point of departure, the separation of the powers of thought and writing.

DERRIDA: There is certainly a sort of parenthesis there, several centuries long. In Greece in the fifth and fourth century B.C.E., in Plato's time, the manuscript was not an object of veneration. The signature did not yet figure; it only started to be fetishized much later on. This is not the end but we are probably moving to another regime of conservation, commemoration, reproduction, and celebration. A great age is coming to an end.

For us, that can be frightening. We have to mourn what has been our fetish. The compensations and the fetishistic substitutes confirm that the destruction is going on (you know, I don't believe there are limits to fetishism, but that's another story, if not another subject). We are frightened and rejoicing witnesses. We have experienced the transition from the pen to the typewriter, then to the electric typewriter, then to the computer, and all this in thirty years, in a single generation, the only one to have made the whole crossing. But the voyage continues . . .

LA QUINZAINE LITTÉRAIRE: Word processing doesn't only raise problems about writing but also, in the shorter or longer term, problems about transmission.

DERRIDA: Yes, serious problems. Because of what we were saying just now, that the text is instantly objectified and transmissible, ready for publication, it is virtually public and "ready for printing" from the moment of its writing. We imagine, or we tend to believe or make people believe, that everything recorded in this way then counts as a publication. What circulates on the internet, for instance, belongs to an automatic space of publication: the public/private distinction is increasingly being wiped out there, with the lawsuits, the allegations of rights and legitimation that proliferate from that, but also the movements toward the appropriation of the *res publica*. Today this is one of the big political issues—it *is* politics. For better and for worse, in a way that was justifiable in some cases, less justifiable in others, the barrier, the "cutoff," the book's stopping point, still protected a process of legitimation. A published book, however bad, remained a book evaluated by supposedly competent authorities: it seemed legitimate, and sometimes sacred, because it had been evaluated, selected, and consecrated. Today, everything can be launched in the public sphere and considered, at least by some people, as publishable, and so having the classic value, the virtually universal and even holy value of a public thing. That can give rise to all sorts of mystifications, and you can already see it, even though I have only very limited experience of what happens on the internet. Say about deconstruction, these international Web sites welcome and juxtapose extremely serious discussions, or ones that are publishable, and then chitchat that is not just dreary but also without any possible future. (It is true, and don't let's ever forget it, that that can also happen at conferences or in journals, academic and otherwise.) There are already learned journals on the internet. They reproduce all the conventional procedures for legitimation and publication; the only thing missing is the paper, so they save on printing and distribution costs. Inversely—and this is true of the media in general—as discussion is more open and anyone can have access to it, there is on the other hand some possibility of critique being encouraged and developed where sometimes those exercising the classical form of evaluation could play a censoring role: the choices of editors or publishing outfits are not always the best ones; there are repressions; things get marginalized or passed over in silence. A new freeing up of the flow can both let through anything at all, and also give air to critical possibilities that used to be limited or inhibited by the old mechanisms of legitimation—which are also, in their own way, word-processing mechanisms.

"But . . . No, but . . . Never . . . , and Yet . . . , as to the Media": Intellectuals. Attempt at Definition by Themselves. Survey.

We ask you to define, briefly, what an intellectual is for you today; what kind you think you are (or should be) yourself; what relationship you consider there to be between the "function" of the intellectual and the work you do in your own discipline; whether your self-justification comes from the authority granted you by this discipline (but in that case would you only intervene in the restricted field permitted by knowledge of your field of study?), or whether this authority authorizes you to have a wider field of intervention. . . . What do you think remains of what used to be defined (and in diverse ways) under the successive heads of responsibility and commitment; what has come to be modified in this by the importance that humanitarianism has acquired in the meantime; above all, what has changed in this as a result of the very considerable importance acquired by the mass media? The question of the media cannot of course be avoided, so what changes do you think this function has undergone over time and what connections have you established with the media?"

1. But in the first place (sorry for beginning like this), how can I not protest? How can I not protest—first, against the format required for responding to this minefield of formidable questions? Two or three pages! And second, against the "survey" form? And against the deadline imposed?

Without being suspicious of your intentions, of course, one can worry about just the fact: at least in its "figure," doesn't this model run the risk of reproducing the constraints within which we often conduct debates? the norms against which we fight (some of us, anyway) so that we can appropriately take on what we try, with such difficulty, to get recognized—namely legitimate demands on "intellectuals"? Had it not been for my friendship for the journal *Lignes* (which will from now on be the principal content and so the act of this response—the greeting I want to give), I wouldn't even have tried to bend myself to these "rules." Perhaps, out of "political" duty, I would even have refused what felt in advance like a concession to the demands of some "media" markets and authorities, the very ones in regard to which you suggest we take a stand. You know—we are so familiar with it—their technique of intimidation and preshaped reply (injunction, seduction, legitimation: if you want to be given a place, and be readable and visible as "intellectuals" on view, intelligible intellectuals, then reply to the questions we have already shaped, come and appear on our pages or our broadcast—we have chosen you). As I often have to do so as to testify in my own way, I would then have stayed silent. And then when one has the opportunity—and this happens so rarely—to appease a good political conscience and save time as well, who could say no?

2. No but now, so as not to yield too much to this "good conscience," I'm going to try to "reply." Within the time limit, and even (I don't much believe in this one) within the space kindly suggested. After all, telegraphic urgency sometimes obliges you to clarify things. By formalizing them at a stroke, you sometimes avoid detours and byways. *First axiom*: supposing (to follow the words of your question, which echo a language assumed to be common and acceptable) that there is something that can be defined *today* with some rigor as the "intellectual," most often of masculine gender; and supposing, secondly, that the said "intellectual" can assign himself or see conferred on him some "function" (another of your words)—well, there is (perhaps, perhaps) someone within me who decides (perhaps) to keep quiet. I say "someone within me" because there are several of us, as you know, and "I" will begin by positively claiming this plurality, close to dizzying heights, especially juridically and politically, which are already turning my head "within me." Can I form a community with myself, and what's more, yet another thing, a *civic* community in a court of innermost justice that doesn't end up being closed in on itself? Being self-identified? Avoiding betraying or perjuring itself? So someone, within me apart from me, gives himself permission not to respond or correspond to this "function" of the "intellectual" or to its usual definition. And thus to this *responsibility*, this responding on one's own behalf by being accountable be-

fore an authority that is already in place. This "someone within me apart from me" retains the infinite presumption of wanting to participate in the very constitution of this authority. He would like to share the responsibility of it and not feel accountable before just any tribunal. Now this "someone" who doesn't "function" or even "work" (or doesn't work, doesn't let himself work, doesn't make himself work except in a non*functional* sense of the word), this "someone" who feels he is both irresponsible with regard to this function and, from another point of view, hyper-responsible, responsible to the point of untenable hyperbole, crushed by a vast responsibility—I would like to make this an insistent point of reference. Why? Because that someone in me takes a share that is perhaps not a negligible one (dare I say the share that interests "me" the most—me? the one I hold to and that has the most hold on me?) in what I write, read, say, think, or teach—and often, not always, *publicly*: all of these being activities where we believe, I'm sure you'll agree, that we recognize what is called an "intellectual." When he thinks, teaches, speaks, reads, or writes, and works too in his own way, this "someone in me apart from me" *endeavors* (there is also an endeavor—a duty and a responsibility) no longer to "*function*": either as an "intellectual" or even (if the word *intellectual* mainly defines a belonging—social, political, or cultural) as the citizen of a community (culture, nation, language, religion, and so on), or even as a "man" (whence my unquenchable interest in "the animal"—a crucial question, to be developed elsewhere, with much more space and time).

For this "someone in me" (undersigned "so-and-so"), these concepts and the prescriptions attached to them will always remain subjects, problems, and even presuppositions that, in their general form or in particular determinations they can be given, are submitted to a questioning, a critique—a "deconstruction," if you like; the necessity of it corresponds to an *unconditional affirmation*.

Thus in a place of *absolute* resistance and remaining.

This affirmation passes through me, it institutes this "someone in me" rather than being actively chosen by me. So it remains for all the others in me, still quite a lot of them, to be *negotiated*. This is sometimes an ugly word; I choose it deliberately. In short, the necessary *transactions* for the inevitable cohabitation do have to be gone through between this someone,[1] who is incapable of coming to terms under any circumstances, and some others, including the "intellectual" that I *also* find I am and whose "functions," burdens, and responsibilities I *also* want to take on, even though they are so difficult in an unstable and turbulent historical space.

What then is the first difficulty? The most general one? The one that determines all the others? The one that in truth comes close to a test of the *impossible*? What it would consist of, it seems to me, is coming to an understanding with someone whose law it is to accept no compromise. This difficulty would return *every time*, day after day, in a way that is *unique and irreplaceable each time*, to discuss terms, to discuss what it is to come to terms, with someone who will never give way, who will always resist any possible compromise, ultimately claiming to be the source and the end—the unity if you like—of all these others.

Kant would have said (but that remains for me, and always will, a place loaded with potential objections) that there is an "I think" that "accompanies all my representations." What is inscribed here beneath this word *penser*, "to think" (a notion that should not be hypostatized, a verb that's no better or worse than any other, as you go from one language to another, for pointing out some essential limits or differences)? That very thing, "thought," which cannot be reduced, for example, either to knowledge or to philosophy or to literature—or to politics. These are all, of course, indispensable skills and capacities for any "status" as an "intellectual." At any rate it is not by chance that I begin by making these distinctions at the moment of signing and saying, "I the undersigned, so-and-so."

3. Never has the task of defining the intellectual rigorously seemed so impossible to me as it does today. So even asking for such a definition would be difficult to justify. Such a "definition" must always have been difficult to guarantee, for generations, throughout the time (not long at all in fact) that people have talked about "intellectuals" in Europe. It remains dependent on *three* conditions, at least, which have always been increasingly precarious:

a. *First*, particular types of skill and knowledge being assumed—in other words *legitimated* (by a dominant and institutional fraction of society). And all these skills and forms of knowledge being linked to an art or a technique of speaking in public, to a *rhetorical* power, in other words to a culture of humanism or the humanities, sometimes an academic discipline (philosophy, literary studies, law, and so on), or the fine-arts institutions (creative writing, above all. And the exemplary figure, in France to begin with, was that of the prose writer: engaged, in the name of universal responsibilities or "the rights of man," in public debate, on questions of law, or to be more precise, questions of *justice*, where the courts, and even the *law* itself, are at fault. "Voltaire-Zola-Sartre": why in France are we always hesitant at the point of going beyond this canonical trinity? As it is unlikely that this is a matter of straightforward decline or resigning from the job, we have to find other causes and with them, I presume, the potential answer to all your questions: these "engaged intellectuals" always speak as lay people. Their commitment is nonreligious. We wouldn't say of a priest or rabbi or mufti who was active and politicized that they were "engaged intellectuals"; Monseigneur Gaillot doesn't look like an "engaged intellectual," the Abbé Pierre even less so.[2] Why does the line of these lay people belong to a big family of writers and lawyers who automatically make a commitment when a case for defense is not guaranteed by the statutory procedures and dominant forces of society, and even of humanity? And so on).

It can seem worrying that this *right* to speech and writing, in the name of *justice*, should be claimed, assigned, reserved, and specialized in this way and initially, however noble the just causes in whose name we stand up to speak. The secondary delights, the "promotion" or "legitimation" that the greed of these "intellectuals" can expect from it are usually, for me, an object of distrust and sometimes even disgust that cannot be overcome.

b. *Second,* a division between the private and the political event, a particular configuration of the places of public speaking (the street, cafés, newspapers, journals, radio, television, what comes with it and what follows it—since the hegemony of one type of TV is on the decline and there is no obvious successor). This division and this configuration are currently undergoing a radical dislocation.

c. *Third,* the assumption of a division of labor between the intellectual and the nonintellectual (the manual worker), dating from the nineteenth century, the very period at which a "role of the intellectual" starts to be recognized under this name. Marx very much reckoned on the existence of this division, in theory, but that doesn't stop us from finding it untenable today, at least in its conceptual rigor, even if it does enable an empirical approach to some massive or mass realities. More than ever, mere technicality, and a fortiori the "high technology" or tele-technology that governs all work, or what is left of it, either nearby or from a distance, makes all workers into "intellectuals," whether or not they are citizens. They should not be denied responsibility and rights, even if they are not recognized as having the old (rhetorical) "skills" (point 1) and routes of access to the media continue to be denied them (point 2).

I deduce from this that now and in the future it would be a betrayal of their "mission" (a new treason of the laity) for a recognized intellectual (points 1 and 2) to write or speak in public, or be an activist in general, without questioning what seems to be a matter of course; without seeking to associate with those who are deprived of this right to speech and writing, or without demanding it for them, whether directly or not. Whence the necessity of writing in different tones—of changing the codes, the rhythms, the theater, and the music.

4. And yet, at a time when an agreed definition of the "intellectual" seems to me more and more debatable, when I am reasserting the necessity for a dissociation between what "I" think, say, write (and so on), and the "culture" that, in such dubious conditions, legitimates and asks for what it calls "intellectuals," I don't think I can give up on the responsibilities, rights, and powers that I am still recognized as having under the title of "intellectual." However limited they are. I even insist on them as a means of fighting the "anti-intellectualism" that is ever more threatening, so as to put that little remaining bit of credit ("authority," to use your word) *into service* (beyond duty and debt; I explain this elsewhere). At the service both of those "without a voice" *and* of that which is approaching and offered for "thinking"—which is always, in a different way, "without a voice" (point 2). Because, for reasons that I would have analyzed if you had given me more space, the "intellectual" (the writer, the artist, the journalist, the philosopher) is the victim, all over the world, of persecutions today that are new and concentrated (think of the plans for an international parliament of writers). Whence the double injunction, the antinomy, the impossible transaction I was speaking about above.

This "impossible" paralyzes me perhaps too often, but I also see in it the figure of a testing out, of a form of endurance that is necessary *as such*, and without which nothing would happen (if there has to be history and if time can be given): no decision, no responsibility, no "engagement," no events, nothing of what would be to come, nothing of what would be to invent, each day, each time, by everyone, without *norm*, with no *horizon* of anticipation—so with no established *criteria*, with no given *rules* for knowledge or determinant judgment, with no assurance, even dialectical, but according to the "dangerous perhaps" that Nietzsche talks about.

By giving the word *intellectual* the necessary twist here, let us say that an intellectual, man or woman, is qualified as such and justifies their assumed intelligence in the one moment of this inventive engagement: in the transaction that suspends the safe horizons and criteria, the existing norms and rules, but also has the ability—intelligently—to analyze, to criticize, to deconstruct them (which is a cultivated skill), yet without ever leaving the space empty, in other words open to the straightforward return of *any* power, investment, language, and so on. So through the invention or proposal of new conceptual, normative, or criteriological figures, according to new singularities.

5. As far as the mass media are concerned, almost all these "engagements" hasten toward the enigmatic place of that name, to which you are right to direct our attention. That is indeed the name of the transformation, even of a rapid and deep-seated revolution, in the *res publica*, in its shifting limits (the front between every kind of force, and the frontiers between the political and its others). I have already gone over the allotted word count, so here again are a few "axioms":

a. That "the intellectual" (see above), despite the media and their subject, tries never to lose sight of the macrodimensional—which is not reducible to what is put out about it in dogmatic ideas of globalization. Examples:

1. The hundreds of millions of illiterate people; the massive scale of malnutrition, rarely taken into account by the media champions of human rights; the hundreds of millions of children who die every year because of water; the 40 to 50 percent of women who are subject to violence, and often life-threatening violence, all the time—and so on. The list would be endless;

2. The way that capitalist powers are concentrated into transnational and cross-state monopolies in the appropriation of the media, multimedia, and productions of the tele-technologies and even the languages that they use.

b. Do not forget that TV, in a state of complete revolution, is on the point of coming into its own, and there are already overlaps with multimedia that are differently powerful and virtually diversifiable. So it makes no sense to be "against" TV, journalists, and the media in general (which can moreover play a "democratic" role that is indispensable, whatever its imperfections). There is even less sense and dignity in condemning the "spectacle" or the "society of the spectacle."[3] Where would we go with no spectacle? Where would society go? And literature, and the rest, and so on? What do they want to impose on us? What do they pretend they want? There is spectacle and spectacle, no doubt about it, markets and markets, and one of them can be a liberation from another; one can also, against the other, free up possibilities of events or inventions worthy of the name. The stereotyped rhetoric against the "society of the spectacle," like the rehashing of set-piece formulas—"Debord"—is becoming a sinister specialism of speakers and journalists. It is often cynically and arrogantly exploited by the worst actors—of patched-up and in fact out-of-date spectacles.

Is it enough to channel-flick, then? Isn't it better to do everything one can to work with the professionals? With those of them who at least have the skills for it, the critical capacity, and the taste? So as to try and introduce the unfamiliar into the contents and techniques of these new media, especially on the internet, the Web, and so on? At any rate everywhere that—here or there, and not without cruelty—an indomitable, uncompromising theater of publications and debates is getting going.[4] To bring alive in it the demands for inventiveness and event (third point)? Maximum diversity and openness? To point out the respect that "intellectuals" may feel in relation to time, rhythm, memory, and the inherited "virtues" of the culture of the book (body and volume of paper, letters, literature, philosophy, knowledge, science and consciousness, a certain amount of time for reading and writing and everything that follows from them)? Is it not urgent to construct new international laws which, as far as possible, will not come along and restore the old powers of legitimation, sanction, and censorship, those that still hold sway in today's media as well as in publishing and universities, and other institutions—public or private, national and international? Will there be "functions of the intellectual," and should there be, in this other political space, in the New International in search of its concept? And perhaps in search of itself *without* concepts? And even beyond knowledge?

There you are—I could imagine some 5 x 5 further points and subpoints to develop, hundreds of other questions to put forward, but the ration has already been exceeded too much—sorry again.

Paper or Me, You Know . . . (New Speculations on a Luxury of the Poor)

LES CAHIERS DE MÉDIOLOGIE: You have written books with various ways into them, with various formats, or folds, as if to elude the surface of the paper and the traditional linearity of writing. You have clearly dreamed of making the page a theatrical scene (for the voice, but also for the body), of hollowing out a depth in it, and also often an abyss. "*L'écriT*, l'écrAn, l'écrIN"—"wriTing, encAsIng, screeNing"—you wrote, in a formulation that has to be read rather than heard.[1] To what extent does paper already function as multimedia? To what extent has it been adequate for you to communicate your thinking?

JACQUES DERRIDA: Seeing all these questions emerging on paper, I have the impression (the *impression*!—what a word, already) that I have never had any other *subject*: basically, paper, paper, paper.[2] It could be demonstrated, with supporting documentation and quotations, "on paper": I have always written, and even spoken, *on* paper: on the subject of paper, an actual paper, and with paper in mind. Support, subject, surface, mark, trace, written mark, inscription, fold—these were also themes that gripped me by a tenacious certainty, which goes back forever but has been more and more justified and confirmed, that the history of this "thing," this thing that can be felt, seen, and touched, and is thus contingent, paper, will have been a brief one. Paper is evidently the limited "subject" of a domain circumscribed in the time and space of a hegemony that marks out a period in the history of a technology and in the history of humanity. The end of this hegemony (its structural if not its quantitative end, its degeneration, its tendency to decline) suddenly speeded up at a date which roughly coincides with that of my "generation": the length of a lifetime.

Another version, in short, of Balzac's *La Peau de chagrin—The Wild Ass's Skin*. The successor to parchment made of skin, paper is *declining*, it is *getting smaller*, it is *shrinking* inexorably at the rate that a man grows old—and everything then becomes a play of expenditure and savings, calculation, speed, political economy, and—as in the novel—of knowledge, power, and will: "to know," "to will [*vouloir*]," and "to have your will [*pouvoir*]."[3]

Ever since I started writing, both the institution and the stability of paper have been constantly exposed to seismic shake-ups. The beasts of relentless writing that we are could not remain either deaf or insensitive to this. Every sign on the paper had to be picked up as an advance sign: it foretold the "loss" of a support: the end of the "subjectile" is nigh. That is also, doubtless, where this body of paper has a bodily hold on us. Because if we hold to paper, and will do for a long time to come, if it gets hold of us bodily, and through every sense, and through every fantasy, this is because its economy has always been more than that of a medium (of a straightforward means of communication, the supposed neutrality of a support)—but also, paradoxically, and your question suggests this, that of a multimedia. It has always been so, already, virtually. Multimedia not, naturally, in the regular and current use of this word, which, strictly speaking, generally presupposes precisely the *supposition* of an electrical support. Paper is no more multimedia "in itself," of course, but—and you are right to stress this—it "already functions," *for us*, virtually, as such. That on its own explains the interest, investment, and economy that it will continue to mobilize for a long time to come. Paper is the support not only for marks but for a complex "operation"—spatial and temporal; visible, tangible, and often sonorous; active but also passive (something other than an "operation," then, the becoming-opus or the archive of operative work).

The word *support* itself could give rise to plenty of questions on the subject of paper. There is no need to trust blindly in all the discourses that reduce paper to the function or *topos* of an inert surface laid out *beneath* some markings, a substratum meant for sustaining them, for ensuring their survival or subsistence. On this commonsense view, paper would be a body-subject or a body-substance, an immobile and impassible surface underlying the traces that may come along and affect it from the outside, superficially, as events, or accidents, or qualities. This discourse is neither true nor false, but it is heavy with all the assumptions that, not accidentally, are sedimented down into the history of the substance or the subject, the support or *hypokeimenon*—but also that of the relationships between the soul and the body.[4] What is happening to paper at present, namely what we perceive at least as a sort of ongoing decline or withdrawal, an ebb or rhythm as yet unforeseeable—that does not only remind us that paper has a history that is brief but complex, a technological or material history, a symbolic history of projections and interpretations, a history tangled up with the invention of the human body and of hominization. It also reveals another necessity: we will not be able to think through or deal with or treat this retreat or withdrawal without general and formalized (and also deconstructive) reflection on what will have been meant—by the *trait* or mark, of course, and retreat (*retrait*), but first of all by *being-beneath*, the submission or subjectedness of subjectivity in general.

To come back now as close as possible to your question: yes, paper can *get to work like a multimedia*, at least when it is for reading or writing—remember there is also wrapping paper, wallpaper, cigarette papers, toilet paper, and so on. Paper for writing on (notepaper, printer or typing paper, headed paper) may lose this intended use or this dignity. Before being, or when it ceases to be, a "backing [*support*] for writing," it lends itself to quite different kinds of use, and there we have two main sources of evaluations. They go against each other but can sometimes be mixed up to fight over the same object. On the one hand there is the condition of a priceless archive, the body of an irreplaceable copy, a letter or painting, an absolutely unique event (whose rarity can give rise to surplus value and speculation). But there is also paper as support or backing for printing, for technical reprinting, and for reproducibility, replacement, prosthesis, and hence also for the industrial commodity, use and exchange value,—and finally for the throwaway object, the abjection of litter.

This inverts a hierarchy that is always unstable: "fine paper" in all its forms can become something thrown out. The virginity of the immaculate, the sacred, the safe, and the indemnified is also what is exposed or delivered to everything and everyone: the undersides and the abasement of prostitution. This "underside" of underlying paper can deteriorate into bumf, better suited to the basket or bin than the fire. Just the word *paper* on its own is sometimes enough, depending on the tone, to connote this kind of deterioration. With "newspaper," already suspect in relation to the quality and survival of what is written on it, we know in advance that it can deteriorate into wrapping paper or toilet paper. (And the press can now exist in two simultaneous forms, on "paper" and online—thus with the suggestion of, indeed exposure to, "interactive" use). A solemn promise, a pact, a signed alliance, a written oath, can all, at the moment of betrayal, become "bits of paper," *chiffons de papier. Chiffons de papier* is all the odder as an expression given that the raw material of paper—which in the West is less than a thousand years old, since it came to us from China and from the Middle East when soldiers returned from the Crusades—was initially chiffon or rags: bits of linen, or cotton, or hemp. To denounce something as a simulacrum or artifact, a deceptive appearance, we will say for instance "paper tiger," or in German "paper dragon." When something is not effective or remains only virtual, we will say—whether to praise or discredit it—that it is "only on paper": "only 'on paper' does this state have available an army of this kind"; "this government has built such and such a number of units of social housing, or has created this number of jobs for young people 'on paper.'" Credit or discredit, legitimation or delegitimation, have long been signified by the body of paper. A guarantee is worth what a signed piece of paper is worth. Devalorization or depreciation, drop in value, the "devaluation" of paper is in proportion to its fragility, to its assumed lower cost, to the straightforwardness of its production, or sending, or reproduction. This is, for instance, the difference between paper money, more subject to devaluation, and the metal piece of gold or silver, or between paper guaranteed by a state or a notary public, stamped paper, and plain paper (a vast series of linked subjects: capital, and so on).

Finally, I was saying, I come back to your question. Paper echoes and resounds, *subjectile* of an inscription from which phonetic aspects are never absent, whatever the system of writing.[5] Beneath the appearance of a surface, it holds in reserve a volume, folds, a labyrinth whose walls return the echoes of the voice or song that it carries itself; for paper also has the range or the ranges of a voice bearer. (We should come back to this question of paper's "range.") Paper is utilized in an experience involving the body, beginning with hands, eyes, voice, ears; so it mobilizes both time and space. Despite or through the richness and multiplicity of these resources, this multimedia has always proclaimed its inadequacy and its finitude.

What—to pick up your words—could be adequate to "communicate" a "thought"? If I place myself within the logic of your question, I must provisionally admit, out of convention, that given a situation of "communicating" a "thought" (which would then exist prior to its "com-

munication") and communicating it by entrusting it to a means, to the me-
diation of a medium, in this instance a trace inscribed on a backing that is
more stable and lasting than the action itself of inscribing—then, and at
that point only, the hypothesis of paper would arise: in history, alongside
or after many other possible backings. So it is true that my experience of
writing, like that of the majority of human beings for just a few centuries,
will have belonged to the era of paper, to this parenthesis which is both
very long and very short, both terminable and interminable. In the experimental works you allude to—*Dissemination*, "Tympan," and *Glas*, but
there's also *The Post Card*, or "Circumfession" (writings "on" or "between"
the card, the page, skin, and computer software), or *Monolingualism of the
Other* (which names and puts into play an "extraordinary tattoo")[6]—I tried
to play with the surface of paper and also to foil it.[7] Through the invention
or reinvention of formatting devices, primarily the breaking or occupation
of the surface, the point was to try to deflect particular typographical
norms, *including even paper*. To twist dominant conventions, the conventions through which you had thought you had to appropriate the historical
economy of this backing by bending it (without bending it: flat, in fact) to
the continuous and irreversible time of a *line*, a vocal line. And a
monorhythmical one. Without depriving myself of the voice recorded
there (which makes paper in fact into a sort of audiovisual multimedium),
I partly—and only partly—and in a sort of continual transaction, exploited the chances that paper offers to visibility, meaning first of all the si-
multaneity, synopsis, and synchrony of what will never belong to the same
time: thus a number of lines or trajectories of speech can inhabit the same
surface, be offered to the eye in a time that is not exactly that of unilinear
utterance, nor even that of reading in a low voice, in a single low voice. By
changing dimension and bending to other conventions or contracts, letters
can thus belong to a number of words. They jump out above their immediate adherence. So they disturb the very idea of a surface that is flat, or
transparent, or translucid, or reflective. To keep to the example you mentioned, the word TAIN overprints its visibility onto *écriT*, *écrAn*, *écrIN*—
"wriTing, encAsing, screeNing."[8] And it can also be heard, not just seen. By
naming the *cr* that repeats and crosses, squeaking, shouting, or cracking
the three words; by opening the hollow without a reflection, the abyss
without *mise en abyme* of a surface that puts a stop to reflection, it thereby
designates that which archives the *written*, the *écrit*, on a page—that
which conserves it or encrypts it or ensures its keeping in an *écrin* or box;

but which also continues, and this is the point I want to insist on, to control the surface of the *screen* (*écran*).

The page remains a screen. That is one of the themes of this text which also takes account of numerology, including computer number-logic and the digitization of writing. It is primarily a figure of paper (of the book or codex), but the page nowadays continues, in many ways, and not only metonymically, to govern a large number of surfaces of inscription, even where the body of paper is no longer there in person, so to speak, thus continuing to haunt the computer screen and all internet navigations in voyages of all kinds. Even when we write on the computer, it is still *with a view* to the final printing on paper, whether or not this takes place. The norms and figures of paper—more than of parchment—are imposed on the screen: lines, "sheets," pages, paragraphs, margins, and so on. On my computer I even have an item called a "Notebook," imitating the one you carry around with you, on which I can jot down notes; on the screen it looks like a box and I can turn its pages; they are both numbered and dog-eared. I also have an item called "Office"—*bureau*—although this word, like *bureaucracy*, belongs to the culture and even the political economy of paper. Let's not talk about the verbs *cut* and *paste* or *delete* that my software also includes. They have lost all concrete and descriptive reference to the technical operations performed, but these infinitives or imperatives also retain the memory of what has disappeared: the paper, the page of the codex. Thus the order of the page, even as a bare survival, will prolong the after-life of paper—far beyond its disappearance or its withdrawal.

I always prefer to say its *withdrawal* [*retrait*], since this word can mark the limit of a structural or even structuring, modeling hegemony, without that implying a death of paper, only a *reduction*. This last word would be fairly appropriate, too. It would redirect the reduction of paper, without end and without death, toward a change of dimension but also toward a qualitative frontier between the duction of production and the duction of reproduction. Contrary to what one would expect, during the same time, that is the time of withdrawal or reduction—well, the production of paper for reproducing, the transformation and consumption of printing paper, can increase in quantity both more widely and faster than ever. The reduction of paper does not make it rarer. For the time being, the opposite is certainly the case.[9] This quantitative increase really involves the paper that could be characterized as "secondary," the sort that has nothing to do with the first inscription (the "first" incision or breaking of a piece of writing) or else only with mechanical printing or the reproduction of writing and image. What must be decreasing proportionally, though, dramatically *withdrawing* and *reducing,* is the quantity of what we might call "primary" paper—the place of reception for an original tracing, for an initial composition or for invention, or writing with a pen, a pencil, or even a typewriter—in other words, paper used for everything we continue to call "first version," "original," "manuscript," or "rough draft."

Withdrawal and reduction: these two words go fairly well together with shrinkage—paper becoming *peau de chagrin.*[10] So before it was a constraint, paper was a virtual multimedia, and it is still the chance of a multiple text and even a sort of symphony, or even a chorus. It will have been this in at least two ways.

First, force of law, just because of the transgression provoked by a constraint (the narrowness of its area, its fragility, hardness, rigidity, passivity or quasi-dead impassiveness, the rigor mortis of what is "without response"—as opposed to the potential interactiveness of the research interlocutor, which a computer or a multimedia internet system now is). And I think that the typographical experiments you were alluding to, particularly the ones in *Glas,* wouldn't have been interesting to me any more; on a computer, and without those constraints of paper—its hardness, its limits, its resistance—I wouldn't have *desired* them.

On the other hand, by carrying us beyond paper, the adventures of technology grant us a sort of future anterior; they liberate our reading for a retrospective exploration of the past resources of paper, for its *previously* multimedia vectors. This mutation is integrative too, with no absolute rupture. It is our "generation's" chance or destiny still to maintain the desire to give nothing up—which, as you know, is the definition of the unconscious. In this the unconscious, or what we still call by that name, is the multimedia itself.

Having said this, while we do have to recognize the "multimedia" resources or possibilities of paper, we should avoid that most tempting but also most serious of mistakes: reducing the technological event, the invention of apparatus that are multimedia in the strict sense of the word—in their external objectality, in the time and space of their electro-mechanicity, in their numerical or digital logic—to being merely a *development* of paper, its virtual or implicit *possibilities.*

LES CAHIERS DE MÉDIOLOGIE: There have been mediological questions running through your oeuvre ever since *Edmund Husserl's "Origin of Geometry,"* in 1962, and of course *Of Grammatology* (1967). This mediology in particular interrogates the book-form of thinking—its typography, its build, its folds. . . . Freud, for instance, you very early on read in relation to the "mystic writing-pad": the *Wunderblock*.[11] You come back to this in *Archive Fever* (1995), where you ask what form Freudian theory would have taken in the era of recording tapes, e-mail, faxes, and the multiplication of screens. Is psychoanalysis—to keep to this conspicuous example—infiltrated right through to its theoretical models by the paper-form of thinking—or, let's say, by the "graphosphere"?

DERRIDA: Definitely, yes. This hypothesis is worth using in a differentiated way—both systematically and prudently. In saying "the paper-form of thinking—or, let's say, by the 'graphosphere,'" you are pointing out a vital distinction. What belongs to the "graphosphere" always implies some kind of surface, and even the materiality of some kind of backing or support; but not all graphemes are necessarily imprinted on paper, or even on a skin, a photographic film, or a piece of parchment. The use of the technological apparatus that was the "mystic writing-pad," as an example for pedagogical or illustrative purposes, raises problems of every kind that I can't come back to here; but Freud's putting paper, literally, to work in this text is still astonishing. He goes with paper, as backing and surface of inscription, as a place where marks are retained; but simultaneously he tries to free himself from it. He would like to break through its limits. He uses paper, but as if he would like to put himself *beyond a paper principle*. The economistic schema that is guiding him at this point could be an inspiration to us for every kind of reflection on the surface-backing in general, and on the surface-backing of paper in particular. Freud does begin, it is true, by speaking of "the pocket-book or sheet of paper." This makes up for the deficiencies of my memory when it keeps my written notations. This "surface" is then compared to a "materialized element of my mnemic apparatus, which I otherwise carry about with me invisible." Again let us stress the scope of this *I carry*. But this finite surface is rapidly saturated; I need (to carry) another virgin sheet to continue and I may then lose interest in the first sheet. If, in order to continue inscribing new impressions without a pause, I write on a board with chalk, I can certainly rub out, write, and rub out again, but without keeping a lasting trace. Double bind of paper, double binding of paper: "Thus an unlimited receptive capacity and a retention of permanent traces seem to be mutually exclusive properties in the apparatus which we use as substitutes for our memory: either the receptive surface must be renewed or the notation must be destroyed."[12] So in practice, Freud claims, the technical model of the *Wunderblock* would make it possible to remove this double constraint and resolve this contradiction—but on condition of making the function of actual paper relative, if I can put it like that, and dividing that function in itself. It is only then that "this small contrivance . . . promises to perform more than the sheet of paper or the slate."[13] For the mystic writing-pad is not a block of paper but a tablet of resin or of dark brown wax. It is only *bordered* by paper. A thin, transparent sheet is affixed to the upper edge of the tablet but it remains loosely placed there, sliding across the lower edge. This sheet is itself double—not reflexive or folded, but double and *divided* into two "layers." (And indeed a reflection on paper ought in the first place to be a reflection on the *sheet* or *leaf* [*feuille*]: on the figure, nature, culture, and history of what some languages, including French and English, call a "leaf," thereby overprinting in the "thing" a huge dictionary of connotations, tropes, or virtual poems. All the leaves in the world, beginning with the ones on trees—which in fact are used to make paper—become, as if this was their promised fate, sisters or cousins of the one on which we are "laying" our signs, before they become the leaves of a newspaper or journal or book. There is the folding of the leaves, the reserve for a vast number of references to Mallarmé and all his "folds"—I ventured this in "The Double Session" [in *Dissemination*]—but there are also all the folds made by the meaning of the word *feuille*. This word *feuille* is itself a semantic *portefeuille* or portfolio. We should also, if we don't forget to later, speak about the semantics of the *portefeuille*, at least in French.)[14] The upper layer, to return to the writing-pad, is made of celluloid, so it is transparent—a sort of film or *pellicule*,[15] an artificial skin; the lower layer is a sheet [*feuille*] of thin, translucid wax. You write without ink, using a pointed pen, and not going through to the wax paper, but only on the sheet of celluloid; hence Freud suggests a return to the tablet of the ancient world. We can't now go back in detail over the implications and limits of what—in memory of Kant—I dubbed the "three analogies of writing." There are other limits that Freud did not think of. But he did have an inkling of more than one. He himself regarded this technology as a mere auxiliary model ("There must come a point at which the analogy between an auxiliary apparatus of this kind and the organ which is its prototype will cease to apply," he says, before pushing it further anyway).[16] I just wanted to flag two or three points in relation to what is important in this connection:

1. In Freud, this "model" is in competition with others (an optical apparatus, for instance, but others too), or complicated by photographic writ-

ing (which presupposes other quasi-paper supports, the camera film and printing paper).

2. Paper is already "reduced" or "withdrawn," "sidelined" in this—at least actual paper, if we can still talk about such a thing. But can we speak here about paper *itself,* about the "thing itself" called "paper"—or only about figures for it? Hasn't "withdrawal" always been the mode of being, the process, the very movement of what we call "paper"? Isn't the essential feature of paper the withdrawal or sidelining of what is rubbed out and withdraws *beneath* what a so-called support is deemed to back, receive, or welcome? Isn't paper always in the process of "disappearing"—dying out— and hasn't it always been? Passed away, don't we mourn it at the very moment when we entrust it with mourning's nostalgic signs and make it disappear beneath ink, tears, and the sweat of this labor, a labor of writing that is always a work of mourning and loss of the body? *What is* paper, itself, strictly speaking? Isn't the history of the question "What is?" always "on the edge," just before or just after a history of paper?

At any rate, with the "mystic writing-pad," paper is neither the dominant element nor the dominant support.

3. What we have here is an apparatus, and already a little machine for two hands. What is printed on paper doesn't proceed directly from a single movement of just one hand; there has to be a manipulation and even a multiple handling, a holding with more than one hand. Division of labor: to each hand its role and its surface, and its period. Freud's last words may recall the medieval copyist (with his pen in one hand and his scraping knife [for erasing] in the other), but also predict the computer (the two hands, the difference between the three stages—the first "floating" inscription; saving; printing out on paper): "If we imagine one hand writing upon the surface of the Mystic Writing-Pad while another periodically raises its covering-sheet from the wax slab, we shall have a concrete representation of the way in which I tried to picture the functioning of the perceptual apparatus of our mind."[17]

That said—I'm not forgetting your question—if we are making a distinction between what you call the "paper form" of knowledge and the "graphosphere," we cannot say that psychoanalysis, *all* psychoanalysis, depends on paper or even the figure of paper in its theoretical models. The scene and the "analytic situation" seem to exclude any form of recording on an external support as a matter of principle (but, since Plato, there remains the vast question of the tracing called metaphorical in the soul, in the psychical apparatus). It is difficult to imagine what institutions, communities, and scientific communication would have been for psychoanalysis in Freud's time and that of his immediate successors, without the paper of publications and especially the tons of handwritten correspondence, or without the time and space governed in this way by the "paper" form or the substance of "paper." But still, the *theoretical* dependence of psychoanalytical knowledge with regard to this medium can be neither certain nor homogeneous. A place and a concept should be reserved for uneven developments (more or less dependence at some one moment than at another; dependence of another type in certain sites of discourse, or sites of the institutional community, or of private, secret, or public life—assuming that they can be rigorously distinguished, which is indeed the problem). The process is still going on. We cannot now go back to the protocols for questions that I put forward in *Archive Fever*, but the very concept of "theoretical model" could appear to be as problematical as that of pedagogical illustration (picture, writing on paper, volume or apparatus made of paper, and so on). There are of course a great many competing models (whether more *technical* ones—optical, as I said, like a photographic apparatus or a microscope; *graphic*, like the writing-pad; or more "natural"—engrams, mnemic or biographical or genetico-graphical traces, with the support being a person's body: going right back to Freud's first writings). These "models" can sometimes, though not always, do without paper, but they *all* belong to what you call the "graphosphere," in the broadest sense that I am always tempted to give it. The prepsychoanalytic traditions invoked by Freud himself (the hieroglyphic code as *Traumbuch* [dream-book], for instance) or those to which he is brought back (a strong Jewish filiation or affiliation, as Yosef Yerushalmi has emphasized),[18] are techniques of decoding. They involve a decoding of graphical marks, with or without paper. Even when Lacan puts linguistic-rhetorical models back to work, in order to displace them, even during the period when he is de-biologizing and, so to speak, "dis-affecting" the Freudian tradition, and even when he makes the notion of full speech his main theme, his dominant figures derive from what you would call the graphosphere.

As for the topological model of the Moebius strip, to what extent is it still a "representation" or a "figure"? Does it irreducibly depend, *as such*, on what we call a body of "paper"? A *feuille* or leaf whose two pages (recto-verso) would develop a surface that was one and the same? For Lacan, as you know, it's a question of a division of the subject "with no distinction of origin," between knowledge and truth. This "internal eight" also marks "the internal exclusion" of the subject "from its object."[19] When Lacan replies in these terms to the question of the "double inscription," we should ask questions about the status and the necessity of these tropes (are they irreducible or not? I wouldn't like to say too hastily):

It [the question of the double inscription] is quite simply in the fact that the inscription does not cut into the same side of the parchment, coming from the truth printing-plate or the knowledge printing-plate.

That these inscriptions are mixed up had simply to be resolved in a topology: a surface where the top and the underneath are such as to be joined everywhere was within reach of the hand.

Yet it is much further away than in an intuitive schema; it is by clasping him round, if I can put it like that, in his being, that this topology can seize hold of the analyst.[20]

Not to speak of the hand, of a "hand's reach," of all those "intuitive schemas" that Lacan does however seem to refuse, the parchment (of skin) is not paper, is not the subject or the subjectile of a printing machine. It's not machine-paper. The two "materials" belong to heterogeneous technological periods and systems of inscription. *Behind* these specific determinations (the support made of skin, or the paper, and other ones too), beyond or before them, might there be a sort of general, even quasi-transcendental structure? A structure both superficial, actually that of a surface, and yet also profound enough and sensitive enough to receive or retain impressions? When we say "paper," for example, are we naming the empirical body that bears this conventional name? Are we already resorting to a rhetorical figure? Or are we by the same token designating this "quasi-transcendental paper," whose function could be guaranteed by any other "body" or "surface," provided that it shared some characteristics with "paper" in the strict sense of the word (corporality, extension in space, the capacity to receive impressions, and so on)?

It is to be feared (but is this a threat? isn't it also a resource?) that these three "uses" of the noun *paper*, the word *paper*, are superimposed or overprinted on each other in the most equivocal way—at every moment. And thus overwritten on each other right from the figuration of the relation between the signifier and signified "paper." To such an extent that in this case the "What is?" question—"What is paper?"—is almost bound to go astray the minute it is raised. And it would be fun to demonstrate—it's what I was suggesting just now—that it is practically the same age as paper, the "What is?" question. Like philosophy and the project of rigorous science, it is barely older or younger than our paper.

As far as the signifier/signified couplet is concerned, you will remember moreover that Saussure, while he vigorously excluded writing from language, still *compared* language itself to a sheet or leaf of paper:

> A language might also be compared to a sheet of paper. Thought is one side of the sheet and sound the reverse side. [Hey! why not the other way around?] Just as it is impossible to take a pair of scissors and cut one side of paper without at the same time cutting the other, so it is impossible in a language to isolate sound from thought, or thought from sound; this could only be done by an abstraction.[21]

What are we to make of this "comparison"? A theoretical model? The paper-form of knowledge? Belonging to the graphosphere? Let's not forget that psychoanalysis claims to interpret fantasies themselves, the projections, cathexes, and desires that are conveyed just as much on typewriters or paper-processing machines as on paper itself. In the virtually infinite field of this overinterpretation, whose models and protocols must themselves be reinterrogated, we are not required to limit ourselves to psychoanalytic hypotheses. But they do point out some ways forward. Between the era of paper and the multimedia technologies of writing that are completely transforming our existence, let us not forget that the *Traumdeutung* [*Interpretation of Dreams*] "compares" all the complicated mechanisms of our dreams—as it does weapons, too—to male genital organs. And in *Inhibitions, Symptoms and Anxiety*, the blank sheet of paper becomes the mother's body, at least when it is being written on with pen and ink: "As soon as writing, which entails making a liquid flow out of a tube on to a piece of white paper, assumes the significance of copulation, or as soon as walking becomes a symbolic substitute for treading upon the body of mother earth, both writing and walking are stopped because they represent the performance of a forbidden sexual act."[22]

We have forgotten to talk about the *color* of paper, the color of ink, and their comparative chromatics: a vast subject. That will be for another time. When it is not associated—like a leaf, moreover, or a silk paper—with a veil or canvas, writing's *blank white*,[23] spacing, gaps, the "blanks which become what is important," always open up onto a *base* of paper. Basically, paper often remains for us the *basis of the basis*, the base figure on the basis of which figures and letters are separated out. The indeterminate "base" of paper, the basis of the basis *en abyme*, when it is also surface, support, and substance (*hypokeimenon*), material substratum, formless matter and force in force (*dynamis*), virtual or dynamic power of virtuality—see how it appeals to an interminable genealogy of these great philosophemes. It even governs an anamnesis (a deconstructive one, if you like) of all the concepts and fantasies that are sedimented together in our experience of letters, writing, and reading.

In a minute, I would like to show that this fundamental or basic chain of the "base" (support, substratum, matter, virtuality, power) cannot possibly be dissociated, in what we call "paper," from the apparently antinomic chain of the act, the formality of "acts," and the force of law, which are all just as constitutive. Let me mention in passing, for the moment, that the philosophical problematic of matter is often inscribed in Greek in a "hyletic" (from the word *hyle*, which also means "wood," "forest," "construction materials"—in other words the raw material from which paper will later be produced). And given what Freud did, as you know, with the semantic or figural series "material"—"Island of 'Madeira,'" "Madeira wood," "*mater*," "matter," "maternity"[24]—here we are back again with *Inhibitions, Symptoms and Anxiety*.

Can we speak here of *abandon, arrest,* or *inhibition* to designate the ongoing *withdrawal* or decline of a certain kind of writing, the decline of steely writing with the point of a pen on a surface of paper, the decline of the hand, or at any rate of a particular and unique way of using the hand? If we were now to associate this withdrawal with a *dénouement* or untying, namely the untying that effectively undoes the symbolic link of this writing to walking, moving along, breaking a path, thereby untying the plotted connections between eyes, hands, and feet, then perhaps we would be dealing with the symptoms of another historical—or historial, or even, as some would say, posthistorical—phase. At any rate another epoch would be hanging in the balance, keeping us in suspense, carrying off another scene, another scenario, keeping us distanced from and raised above paper: according to another model of the prohibited. There would also be a kind of anxiety on the agenda. There is of course the anxiety of the blank page, its virginity of birth or death, of winding-sheet or bed sheet, its ghostly movement or immobility; but there can also be the anxiety to do with a lack of paper. An individual or collective anxiety. I remember the first time I went to the Soviet Union. Intellectuals there were severely deprived of paper—for writing and for publishing. It was one of the serious dimensions of the political question; other media had to make up for the lack.

Another epoch, then; but isn't an *epoche* always the suspension of a prohibition, an organization of withdrawal or retention? This new epoch, this other *reduction*, would also correspond to an original displacement, already, of the body in displacement—to what some might perhaps be quick to call another body, even another unconscious. What is more, the remark of Freud's that I have just quoted is part of a passage on the eroticization of fingers, feet, hands, and legs. While it is tied to the "paper" system (just a few centuries, a second in regard to the history of humanity), this furtive eroticization also belongs to the very long time of some process of hominization. Do tele-sex or internet sex alter anything in this? A program with no base. A program of the baseless.

LES CAHIERS DE MÉDIOLOGIE: You have been concerned with the movement involving African *sans-papiers*, undocumented immigrants in France, and their struggle to get identity papers like everyone else. Without playing on words, this history reminds us of the extent to which identity, the social bond, and the forms of solidarity (interpersonal, media-based, and institutional) go through filters made of paper. Let's now imagine a science-fiction scenario: the disappearance of all the papers, books, newspapers, personal documents . . . on which we literally support our existence. Can we measure the loss, or the possible gain, that would result from this? Shouldn't we be worried about the less obvious but also more efficient effects of electronic identifications and markers?

DERRIDA: The process you describe is not out of science fiction. It's on the way. There's no denying it; the issue seems both serious and boundless. It is true that it's less a matter of a state of things or a *fait accompli* than of an ongoing process and a tendency that can't be challenged, which will involve, for a long time to come, vastly unequal or "uneven developments," as we put it. Not only between different parts of the world, different types of wealth, and different places of technological and economic development, but also within each social space which will have to enable the paper culture and electronic culture to cohabit. So a "balance sheet" of pros and cons is risky. Because the process is speeding up and becoming investment-based. In addition, its effects are essentially equivocal; they never fail to produce a logic of *compensation*. We always soften the traumatic irruption of novelty. But more than ever, it is a case of "loser wins." The potential "gain" is only too obvious.

The "de-paperization" of the support,[25] if I can put it like that, is to begin with the economic rationality of a profit: a simplification and acceleration of all the procedures involved; a saving of time and space, and thus the facilitation of storage, archiving, communication, and debates beyond social and national frontiers; a hyperactive circulation of ideas, images, and voices; democratization, homogenization, and universalization; immediate or transparent "globalization"—and so, it is thought, more sharing out of rights, signs, knowledge, and so on. But by the same token, just as many catastrophes: inflation and deregulation in the commerce of signs; invisible hegemonies and appropriations, whether of languages or places. It is not in itself a novelty or a mutation that the modes of appropriation are becoming spectral, are "dematerializing" (a very deceptive word, meaning that in truth they are moving from one kind of matter to another and actually becoming all the more material, in the sense that they are gaining in potential *dynamis*); that they are virtualizing or "fantasmatizing"; that they are undergoing a process of abstraction; it could be shown that they have always done this, even in a culture of paper. What is new is the change of tempo and, once again, a *technical* stage in the externalization, the objectal incorporation of this possibility. This virtualizing spectralization must now resign itself to the loss of schemata whose sedimentation seemed natural and vital to us—that's how old it is—at the level of our individual or cultural memories. Once they have been identified with the form and material of "paper," these incorporated schemata are also privileged ghost-members, supplements of structuring prostheses. For a number of centuries they have supported, propped up, and so really constructed or instituted the experience of identifying with oneself ("I who can sign or recognize my name on a surface or a paper support"; "The paper is mine"; "Paper is a self or ego"; "Paper is me"). Paper often became the place of the self's appropriation of itself, then of becoming a subject in law. As a result, in losing this tangible body of paper, we have the feeling that we are losing that which protected that subjectivity itself, because it stabilized the personal law in a minimum of real law. Indeed a sort of primary narcissism: "Paper is me"; "Paper *or* me" (*vel*).[26] Marking out both public and private space, the citizenship of the subject of law ideally assumed a self-identification with the means of autograph whose substantive schema remained a body of paper. The tendency of all the "progressive" changes of the current trend is to replace this support for the signature, the name, and in general autodeictic enunciation ("me, I who . . . "; "I, the undersigned, authenticated by my presence, in the presence of the present paper"). In substituting for this the electronic support of a numerical code, there is no doubt that these forms of "progress" are secreting a more or less muffled anxiety. An anxiety that may here and there accompany an animistic and "omnipotent" jubilation in the power of manipulation; but an anxiety that is both motivated and justified. Motivated by the always imminent loss of the paper ghost-members that we have learned to trust, it is also justified before the powers of concentration and manipulation, the powers of information expropriation (electronic mailings almost instantly available to every international police force—insurance, bank accounts, health records; infinitely faster and uncheckable filing of personal data; espionage, interception, parasiting, theft, falsification, simulacra, and simulation).

These new powers delete or blur the frontiers in unprecedented conditions, and at an unprecedented pace (once again, it is the extent and the pace of the "objectalization" that form the qualitative or modal novelty, since the structural "possibility" has always been there). These new threats on the frontiers (that also get called threats on freedom) are *phenomenal;* they border on phenomenality itself, tending to phenomenalize, to render perceptible, visible, or audible; to expose everything on the outside. They do not only affect the limit between the public and the private—between the political or cultural life of citizens and their innermost secrets, and indeed secrets in general; they touch on actual frontiers—on frontiers in the narrow sense of the word: between the national and the global, and even between the earth and the extraterrestrial, the world and the universe—since satellites are part of this "paperless" setup.

Nowadays, although the authentication and identification of selves and others increasingly escapes the culture of paper—although the presentation of selves and others increasingly does without traditional documents—a certain legitimating authority of paper still remains intact, at least in the majority of legal systems and in international law, in its dominant form today and as it will be for some time to come. In spite of the seismic shake-ups that this law will soon have to undergo, on this point and on others, the ultimate juridical resource still remains the signature done with the person's "own hand" on an irreplaceable paper support. Photocopies, facsimiles (faxes), or mechanical reproductions have no authenticating value, except in the case of signatures whose reproduction is authorized by convention—banknotes or checks—on the basis of a prototype that is itself authentifiable by a classic procedure, namely the assumed possibility of attestation, by oneself and by the other person, of the manual signature, certified "on paper," of a signatory deemed responsible and present to his or her own signature, capable of confirming aloud: "Here I am, this is my body, see this signature on this paper—it's me, it's mine, it's me so-and-so, I sign before you, I present myself here; this paper that remains represents me."

Since we are speaking of legitimation, the publication of the book remains, for good or bad reasons, a powerful resource for recognition and credit. For some time to come, biblioculture will be in competition with plenty of other forms of publication outside the received norms of authorization, authentication, control, accreditation, selection, sanction—in fact thousands and thousands of forms of censorship.[27] Euphemistically, we can say: a new legal age is imminent. In reality we are being precipitated toward it, at a rate which as yet cannot be calculated. But in this revolution there are only stages of transition. Economies of compensation always succeed in dulling the pain of mourning—and melancholia. For instance, at the very moment when the number of electronic journals on the Web is rapidly increasing, traditional procedures of legitimation and the old protective norms are being reaffirmed, in the academy and elsewhere—the norms that are still tied to a culture of paper: presentation, formatting, the visibility of editorial boards and selection committees who have gained their experience in the world of the classic library. Above all, people exert themselves to obtain the final consecration: the publication and sale of electronic journals, at the end of the day, on quality paper. For a certain time to come, a time that is difficult to measure, paper will continue to hold a sacred power. It has the force of law, it gives accreditation, it incorporates, it even embodies the soul of the law, its letter and its spirit. It seems to be indissociable from the Ministry of Justice, so to speak, from the rituals of legalization and legitimation, from the archive of charters and constitutions for what we call, in the double sense of the word, *acts*. Indeterminate matter but already virtuality, *dynamis* as potentiality but also as power, power incorporated in a natural matter but force of law, in-formal matter for information but already form and act, act as action but also as archive—there you have the assumed tensions or contradictions that have to be thought under the name of "paper." We are coming back to this in a moment in relation to undocumented persons, the "paperless"—I haven't forgotten your question.

Now if the earthquake that is happening sometimes leads to "losing one's head" or loss of "sense," that is not because it would be merely vertiginous, threatening the loss of propriety, proximity, familiarity, singularity ("This paper is me," and the like), stability, solidity, the very place of *habitus* and *habilitation*—accreditation. It would in fact be possible to think that the paper that is threatened with disappearance guaranteed all that, as close as could be to the body, to the eyes and hands. But no, this loss of place, these processes of prosthetic delocalization, expropriation, and becoming fragile or precarious, were already going on. They were known to be started, represented, and figured by paper itself.

What is it then that makes some people "lose their heads"—all of us, in fact—head and hands, a certain way of using head, eyes, mouth, and hands, tied to paper or a certain habit (*habitus, hexis*) in relation to them? It is not a *threat*, a mere threat, the imminence of *an* injury, *a* lesion, *a* trauma; no, it is the fold or *duplicity* of a threat that is divided, multiplied, *contradictory*, twisted, or perverse—for this threat inhabits even the promise. For reasons I would like to remind you of, it is possible only to desire both to keep and to lose paper—a paper that is both protective and destined to be withdrawn. What we have there is a kind of logic of self-immunization, whose results I have attempted elsewhere to deploy, generalize, or formalize, particularly in "Faith and Knowledge."[28] Paper protects by exposing, alienating, and first of all by threatening withdrawal, which it is always in one way in the process of. Protection is itself a threat, an aggression differing from itself, which then twists and tortures us in a spiraling movement. For the "same" threat introduces a sort of twisting that makes head and hands spin; it causes vertigo in the conversion of a contrariety, an internal and external contradiction, on the limit—between the outside and the inside: paper is *both, at the same time*, more solid *and* more fragile than the electronic support, closer *and* more distant, more *and* less appropriable, more *and* less reliable, more *and* less destructible, protective *and* destructive, more *and* less manipulable, more *and* less protected in its capacity for being reproduced; it guarantees a protection that is both smaller *and* greater of the personal or the appropriable, of what can be handled. It is more and less suitable for accreditation. That confirms for us that everywhere and always, appropriation has followed the trajectory of a reappropriation, in other words endurance, detour, crossing, risks—in a word the experience of a self-immunizing expropriation that has had to be trusted.

Since this structure of *ex-appropriation* appears to be irreducible and timeless; since it is not tied to "paper" any more than to electronic media, the seismic feeling depends on a *new* figure of ex-appropriation, one as yet unidentifiable, not sufficiently familiar, and inadequately mastered: on a new economy, which is also to say a new law and a new politics of prostheses or supplements at the origin. This is why our fright and our vertigo are both justified or irrepressible—and pointless, in fact ridiculous. For the reasons described above, this threat does certainly put us in a twist—it tortures us—but it is also funny, even side-splitting; it threatens nothing and no one. Serious as it is, the war sets only fantasies—in other words, specters—against each other. Paper will have been one of them, for several centuries. A compromise formation between two resistances: writing with ink (on skin, wood, or paper) is more fluid, and thus "easier," than on stone tablets, but less ethereal or liquid, less wavering in its characters, and also less labile, than electronic writing. Which offers, from another point of view, capacities for resistance, reproduction, circulation, multiplication, and thus survival that are ruled out for paper culture. But as you may know, it is possible to write directly with a quill pen, without ink, projecting from a table, on a computer screen. You thus reconstitute a simulacrum of paper, a paper paper, in an electronic element.

It is no longer even possible to speak of a determinate "context" for this historical shake-up—which is more and something else than a "crisis of paper." What it puts in question is in fact the possibility of outlining a *historical* context, a space-time. So it is a question here of a certain interpretation of the concept of history. If we now fold ourselves back into "our countries," toward the relatively and provisionally stabilized context of the "current" phase of the "political" life of nation-states, the war against "undocumented" or "paperless" people testifies to this incorporation of the force of law, as noted above, in paper, in "acts" of legalization, legitimation, accreditation, and regularization linked to the holding of "papers": power accredited to deliver "papers," power and rights linked to holding certificates on official paper on one's person, close up to oneself.[29] "Paper is me"; "Paper or me"; "Paper: my home." At any rate, whether they are expelled or made legal, it is made clear to the "paperless" that we don't want any illegal immigrants or "paperless" people in our country. And when we fight on behalf of "paperless" people, when we support them today in their struggle, we *still* demand that they be issued with papers. We have to remain within this logic. What else could we do? We are not—*at least in this context*, I stress—calling for the disqualification of identity papers or of the link between documentation and legality. As with bank address details and as with names, "home" presupposes "papers." The "paperless" person is an outlaw, a nonsubject legally, a noncitizen or the citizen of a foreign country refused the right conferred, *on paper*, by a temporary or permanent visa, a rubber stamp. The literal reference to the word *papers*, in the sense of legal justification, certainly depends on the language and usages of particular national cultures (in France and Germany, for instance). But when in the United States for example, the word *undocumented* is used to designate analogous cases, or *undesirables*, with similar problems involved, it is the same axioms that carry authority: the law is guaranteed by the holding of a "paper" or document, an identity card (ID), by the bearing or carrying [*port*] of a driving permit or a *passport* that you keep on your person, that can be shown and that guarantees the "self," the juridical personality of "here I am." We shouldn't be dealing with these problems, or even approaching them, without asking questions about what is happening today with international law, with the subject of "human rights and the citizen's rights," with the future or decline of nation-states. The earthquake touches nothing less than the essence of politics and its link with the culture of paper. The history of politics is a history of paper, if not a paper history—of what will have preceded and followed the institution of politics, bordering the "margin" of paper. But here too, there are processes of technological transition at work: the recording of marks of identification and signatures is computerized. Computerized but, as we were saying, via the inherited norms of "paper" that continue to haunt electronic media. It is computerized for citizens and their citizen status (consider what happens at passport controls), but it can also be computerized for the physical-genetic identification of any individual in general (digitalized photography and genetic imprints). In this, we are all, already, "paperless" people.

LES CAHIERS DE MÉDIOLOGIE: Recently, you did a book of interviews with Bernard Stiegler in which you reflect on television. Without taking up once again the usual denunciation of its crimes, you are manifestly attentive to some things that are promised and performed by the audiovisual, since TV is both behind and ahead of the book. Elsewhere, you have often insisted on the importance of computers and word processing. At present these screens are clearly distinct from one another, but they will become compatible, and we frequently go between them in our search for information. Being yourself an indefatigable paper worker, do you think of yourself as someone nostalgic for this support, or do you envisage for instance using e-mail for certain types of letters, debates, or publications? Couldn't it be said that archives taken from oral contributions and "published" on the internet for example (cf. Gilles Deleuze's seminars recently made available on the Web) bring about the emergence of a new "written-oral" status?

DERRIDA: Definitely, and this "new status" gets displaced from one technological possibility to another; for several years now it's been transforming so quickly, been so far from static, this status, that for me, as for any number of people, it becomes an experience, a test, or a debate that is going on every minute. This destabilization of the status of "written-oral" has not just always been an organizing theme for me, but first of all—and these things are indissociable—the very element of my work. "Indefatigable [*acharné*] paper worker," you say. Yes and no. At any rate, I'd take this word *acharnement* literally, in the code of the hunt, the animal, and the huntsman.[30] In this work *on paper*, there is a sort of wager of the body or flesh—and of the bait, that taste of flesh that a huntsman gives the dog or birds of prey (simulacrum, fantasy, trap for taking hold of consciousness: to be preyed on by paper). But if we think about it, this "status" was already unstable under the most unchallenged rule of paper, and paper alone—which can also be regarded as a screen. For anyone who speaks or writes, and especially if they are "meant" for or "specialized" in this, whether professionally or in another capacity, in the sometimes undecidable limit between private space and public space (this is one of the subjects of *The Post Card*)—well, the passage from oral to written is *the* place for the experience, exposure, risk, problems, and invention of what's always a *lack of fit*.[31] We don't need the "audiovisual performances" of TV and word processors to have experience of this vertiginous metamorphosis, the instability of the situation or "status" itself, and thus to feel some nostalgia, among other feelings of noncoincidence or lack of adaptation. Nostalgia is always in there. Exile was already there in paper; there was "word processing" in writing with a quill or a pencil. I'm not saying this to run away from your question or neutralize it. Nostalgia, another nostalgia, a "grief" or *chagrin* for paper itself?[32] Yes, of course, and I could offer numerous signs of this. The pathos of paper already obeys a law of the genre; it is just as coded—but why not yield to it?[33] It is an inconsolable nostalgia for the book (about which, however, I wrote, more than thirty years ago, and in a book, that it had been coming toward its "end" for a long time).[34] It is nostalgia for paper before the reproducible "impression," for paper once virginal, both sensitive and impassive, both friendly and resistant, both very much on its own and coupled to our bodies, not only with every mechanical impression, but before any impression not reproducible by my hand. It is nostalgia for the proffered page on which a virtually inimitable handwriting creates a path for itself with the pen—a pen which, not so long ago, I still used to dip in ink at the end of a pen holder; a nostalgia for the color or weight, the thickness and the resistance of a sheet—its folds, the back of its recto-verso, the *fantasies* of contact, of caress, of intimacy, proximity, resistance, or promise: the infinite desire of the copyist, the cult of calligraphy, an ambiguous love for the scarcity of writing, a fascination for the word incorporated in paper. These are certainly *fantasies*. The word condenses all together image, spectrality, and simulacrum—and the weight of desire, the libidinal investment of affect, the motions of an appropriation extended toward that which remains inappropriable, called forth by the inappropriable itself, the desperate attempt to turn affection into auto-affection. These fantasies and affects *are* effectiveness itself; they constitute the (virtual or actual) activation of my commitment to paper, which never guarantees more than a *quasi* perception of this type. It expropriates it from us in advance. It has already ruled out everything that these fantasies seem to give back to us, and render perceptible for us—the tangible, the visible, intimacy, immediacy. Nostalgia is probably inevitable—and it's a nostalgia that I like, and that also makes me write: you work *on nostalgia*, you work at it and it can make you work. With regard to what comes after paper, it doesn't necessarily mean rejection or paralysis. As for the *biblion* (writing paper, exercise book, pads, jotter, book), this "nostalgia" is thus not only derived from some kind of sentimental reaction. It is justified by the memory of all the "virtues" rooted in the culture of paper or the discipline of books. These virtues or requirements are well known, even often celebrated in a backward-looking tone and with backward-looking connotations; but this should not prevent us from reaffirming them. I am one of those who would like to work for the life and survival of books—for their development, distribution, and sharing, as well. The inequalities we were talking about a little while ago also separate the rich and the poor, and one of the indicators of this is "our" relationship to the production, consumption, and "waste" of paper. There is a correlation or a disproportion there that we should continue to think about. And among the benefits of a hypothetical decline of paper, secondary or not, paradoxical or not, we should count the "ecological" benefit (for instance fewer trees sacrificed to becoming paper) and the "economic" or techno-economic-political benefit: even deprived of paper and all the machinery that goes with it, individuals or social groups might nonetheless gain access by computer, television, and the internet to a whole global network of information, communications, education, and debate. Although they are still expensive, these machines sometimes get through more easily; they are more easily appropriated than books. And they get hold of the actual "market" (purchasing, sales, advertising), which they are also part of, much more quickly—there's a massive discrepancy—than they get hold of the world of "scientific" communication and, a fortiori, from a great distance, the world of "arts and letters," which are more resistant in their link to national languages. And therefore, so often, to the tradition of paper.

Writing, literature, even philosophy—as we think we know them—would they survive beyond paper? Survive beyond a world dominated by paper? Survive the time of paper? Survive "these 'paperies,' as Françoise called the pages of my writing"—books of notes, jotting pads, bits stuck on, large numbers of photographs?[35] If it seems impossible to deal with these inexhaustible questions, that is not only because we are short of time and space—in more ways than one. At any rate they would stay that way, impossible to deal with, as *theoretical* questions, on a horizon of knowledge—on a *horizon*, quite simply. The response will come from decisions and events, from what the writing of a future that cannot be anticipated will make of it, from what it will do *for* literature and *for* philosophy, from what it will do *to them*.

And then nostalgia, even "action" on behalf of book culture does not oblige anyone to confine themselves to it. Like many people, I make the best of my nostalgia, and without giving anything up, I try, more or less successfully, to accommodate my "economy" to all the paperless media. I use a computer, of course, but I don't do e-mail, and I don't "surf" the internet, even though it is something I use as a theoretical topic, in teaching or elsewhere. A matter of abstention, abstinence—but also of self-protection. One of the difficulties is that nowadays any public discourse (and sometimes any private action, any "phenomenon") can be "globalized" in the hour after it happens, without it being possible to exercise any rights of control. This is sometimes terrifying (and once again, new not so much in its possibility as in its power, the speed and the scope, the objective technicality of its phenomenality), and sometimes it's funny. It is always leading to new responsibilities, another critical culture of the archive—in short, another "history."

But why should one sacrifice one possibility at the point of inventing another one? To say farewell to paper, today, would be rather like deciding one fine day to stop speaking because you had learned to write. Or to stop looking in the rearview mirror because the road is in front of us. We drive with both hands and both feet, looking both in front and behind, speeding up at some points and slowing down at others. Presumably it is not possible *at the same time*, in one single, indivisible instant, to look behind *and* in front; but if you drive well you dart in the blink of an eye from the windshield to the mirror. Otherwise, you're blind or you have an accident. You see what I'm getting at: the end of paper isn't going to happen in a hurry.

Two more points, to finish, on my "paper spleen."

First, when I dream of an absolute memory—well, when I sigh after the keeping of everything, really (it's my very respiration)—my imagination continues to project this archive *on paper*. Not on a screen, even though that might also occur to me, but on a strip of paper. A multimedia band, with phrases, letters, sound, and images: it's everything, and it would keep an impression of everything. A unique specimen from which copies would be taken. Without me even having to lift my little finger. I wouldn't write, but everything would get written down, by itself, right on the strip.[36] With no work: the end of the "indefatigable worker." But what I would thereby *leave* to write *itself* would not be a book, a codex, but rather a strip of paper. It would roll itself up, on itself, an electrogram of everything that had happened (to me)—bodies, ideas, images, words, songs, thoughts, tears. Others. The world forever, in the faithful and polyrhythmic recording of itself and all its speeds. Everything all the same without delay, and *on paper*—that is why I am telling you. On paperless paper. Paper is in the world that is not a book.

Because on the other hand, I also suffer, to the point of suffocation, from *too much paper*, and this is another spleen. Another ecological sigh. How can we save the world *from* paper? And its own body? So I *also* dream of living paperless—and sometimes that sounds to my ears like a definition of "real life," of the living part of life. The walls of the house grow thicker, not with wallpaper but with shelving. Soon we won't be able to put our feet on the ground: paper on paper. Cluttering; the environment becoming litter, the home becoming a stationery store. I'm no longer talking about the paper on which, alas, too little of my illegible writing is written with a pen; but the kind that just now we were calling "secondary": printed paper, paper for mechanical reproduction, the kind that remains, paper *taken from* an original. Inversion of the curve. I consume this kind of paper and accumulate a lot more of it than I did before computers and other so-called "paperless" machines. Let's not count the books. So paper expels me—outside my home. It chases me off. This time, it's an *aut aut*: paper *or* me.[37]

Another dilemma about hospitality to "paperless" people: who is the host or guest or hostage of the other?

6

The Principle of Hospitality

LE MONDE: Throughout your latest book, *Of Hospitality*,[1] you contrast the unconditional "law of unlimited hospitality" with "the laws of hospitality," the rights and duties that are always conditioned and conditional. What do you mean by this?

JACQUES DERRIDA: It's between these two figures of hospitality that responsibilities and decisions have to be taken in practice. A formidable ordeal—while these two hospitalities are not contradictory, they remain heterogeneous even as, perplexingly, they share the same name. Not all ethics of hospitality are the same, of course, but there is no culture or form of social connection without a principle of hospitality. This ordains, even making it desirable, a welcome without reservations or calculation, an unlimited display of hospitality to the new arrival. But a cultural or linguistic community, a family or a nation, cannot fail at the very least to suspend if not to betray this principle of absolute hospitality: so as to protect a "home," presumably, by guaranteeing property and "one's own" against the unrestricted arrival of the other; but also so as to try to make the reception real, determined, and concrete—to put it into practice. Hence the "conditions" that transform gift into contract, openness into legal pact; hence rights and duties, frontiers, passports and ports; hence laws about an immigration of which we say that we have to "control the flow."

It is true that the issues involved in "immigration" do not strictly coincide with those of hospitality, which reach beyond the civic or political arena. In the book you are referring to, I analyze what is not, however, a straightforward opposition between the "unconditional" and the "conditional." The two meanings of hospitality remain irreducible to one another, but it is the pure and hyperbolical hospitality in whose name we should always invent the best dispositions, the least bad conditions, the most just legislation, so as to make it as effective as possible. This is necessary to avoid the perverse effects of an unlimited hospitality whose risks I have tried to define. Calculate the risks, yes, but don't shut the door on what cannot be calculated, meaning the future and the foreigner—that's the double law of hospitality. It defines the unstable place of strategy and decision. Of perfectibility and progress. It is a place that is being sought today, in the debates about immigration for instance.

We often forget that it is in the name of unconditional hospitality, the kind that makes meaningful any reception of foreigners, that we should try to determine the *best* conditions, namely particular legal limits, and especially any particular implementation of the laws. This is always forgotten, by definition, when it comes to xenophobia: but it can also be forgotten in the name of a certain interpretation of "pragmatism" and "realism." When, for instance, we think we should give electoral pledges to forces of exclusion or occlusion. These tactics, with their shady principles, could well lose more than their soul: they could lose the calculated benefit.

LE MONDE: In the same book, you raise this question: "Does hospitality consist in interrogating the new arrival?" in the first place by asking their name, "or does hospitality begin with the unquestioning welcome?"[2] Is the second of these attitudes more in keeping with the principle of "unlimited hospitality" that you are talking about?

DERRIDA: Here again, the decision is taken from within what looks like an absurdity, like the impossible (an antinomy, a tension, between two laws that are equally imperative but not opposed). Pure hospitality consists in welcoming the new arrival before imposing conditions on them, before knowing and asking for anything at all, be it a name or an identity "paper." But it also assumes that you address them, individually, and thus that you call them something, and grant them a proper name: "What are you called, you?" Hospitality consists in doing everything possible to address the other, to grant or ask them their name, while avoiding this question becoming a "condition," a police inquisition, a registration of information, or a straightforward frontier control. A difference both subtle and fundamental, a question that arises on the threshold of "home," and on the threshold between two inflections. An art and a poetics, but an entire politics depends on it, an entire ethics is decided by it.

LE MONDE: You say, in the same text, "The foreigner is first of all foreign to the legal language in which the duty of hospitality is formulated, the right to asylum with its limits, norms, policing, and so on. He has to ask for hospitality in a language which by definition is not his own."[3] Could it be otherwise?

DERRIDA: Yes, because this is perhaps the first violence to which foreigners are subjected: to have to assert their rights in a language they don't speak. It is almost impossible to suspend this violence; at any rate it is an interminable task. It is another reason to work urgently to transform things. A vast and formidable duty to translate is imposed here that is not only pedagogical, "linguistic," domestic, and national (educating foreigners in the national language and culture—in the tradition of state or republican law, for instance). That requires a transformation of law—of the languages of law. Progress is being made in this area, however vaguely and painfully. It involves history and the most fundamental values of international law.

LE MONDE: You mention the Vichy government's abolition of the Crémieux decree of 1870, which granted French citizenship to Algerian Jews. When you were young, you experienced this strange situation of having no nationality. How do you see that period now, in retrospect?

DERRIDA: Too much to say on that, too. Rather than what I do recall, from the depths of my memory, here is just what I would like to recall, today. Now, retrospectively, the Algeria of that period looks like an experimental laboratory, where a historian can scientifically and objectively isolate what was a purely French responsibility for the persecution of the Jews. This is the responsibility we asked President Mitterrand to recognize, as President Chirac, fortunately, has subsequently done. Because there was never a single German in Algeria. Everything stemmed from the French, and only the French, applying the two statutes on the Jews. In the civil service, in schools and universities, in the expropriation of property, they were sometimes applied more brutally than in France itself. Item to be added to the files of the ongoing trials and apologies.

LE MONDE: Some years ago now, Michel Rocard said, "France cannot take in all the wretched poverty of the world." What does this statement suggest to you? What do you think of the way that Lionel Jospin's government is currently working toward a partial granting of official status to illegal immigrants?

DERRIDA: I seem to remember that Michel Rocard withdrew that unfortunate phrase. Because *either* it's a truism (who ever did think that France, or any other country, has ever been able to "take in all the wretched poverty of the world"? Who has ever asked for that? *Or* its rhetoric is that of a joke meant to produce restrictive effects and to justify cutbacks, protectionism, and reactionary attitudes ("after all, since we can't take in all the wretched poverty, don't let anyone ever reproach us for not doing enough, or even for not doing it at all any more"). This is presumably the effect—the economic, economistic, and confused effect—that some people sought to exploit, and that Michel Rocard, like so many others, came to regret. As to the current politics of immigration, if we must speak so rapidly: those who have lobbied on behalf of asylum seekers (and who put them up when necessary, as I now do too) are anxious about it—those who had been full of hope because of certain promises. There are at least two things to regret:

First, that the Pasqua-Debré laws haven't been abolished altogether, rather than modified. Apart from the fact that they carried a symbolic value (which is not nothing), once again it comes to the same thing: *either* the essential is kept, and it is wrong to claim the opposite; *or* they are essentially changed, and it is wrong to try to please or appease a right-wing or far-right electoral opposition just by giving them the label "Pasqua-Debré." The far right, at any rate, will benefit from this climb-down and won't allow itself to yield. What we need here is political courage, and a change of direction, and promises kept, and education of the public. (For instance, people need to be reminded that the quota of immigrants has not increased for decades—nor is it threateningly high, in fact quite the opposite.)

Second, within the limits officially in force, the procedures for legalizing people's situations that are promised appear both slow and minimalist, taking place in an atmosphere that is depressed, tense, and frustrating. Hence the anxiety of those who, without ever asking for a straightforward opening up of the frontiers, have argued for another kind of politics, with figures and statistics to support this (based on methods tried out by experts and relevant associations, who have been working in the field for years). And they have done this "responsibly," not "irresponsibly," as I believe one minister had the nerve to say—one of the sort who nowadays (and it's always a bad sign) make carefully controlled little slips. The decisive limit, from which a politics is judged, comes somewhere between "pragmatism" and even "realism" (both indispensable for an effective strategy), and their dubious double, opportunism.

"Sokal and Bricmont Aren't Serious"

Le Monde asks for my comments on Alan Sokal and Jean Bricmont's book *Impostures intellectuelles,* although they consider that I am much less badly treated in it than some other French thinkers. Here is my response:

This is all rather sad, don't you think? For poor Sokal, to begin with. His name remains linked to a hoax—"the Sokal hoax," as they say in the United States—and not to scientific work. Sad too because the chance of serious reflection seems to have been ruined, at least in a broad public forum that deserves better.

It would have been interesting to make a scrupulous study of the so-called scientific "metaphors"—their role, their status, their effects in the discourses that are under attack. Not only in the case of "the French"! and not only in the case of *these* French writers! That would have required that a certain number of difficult discourses be read seriously, in terms of their theoretical effects and strategies. That was not done.

As to my modest "case," since you make a point of mentioning that I was "much less badly treated" than some others, this is even more ridiculous, not to say weird. In the United States, at the beginning of the imposture, after Sokal had sent his hoax article to *Social Text*, I was initially one of the favorite targets, particularly in the newspapers (there's a lot I could say about this). Because they had to do their utmost, at any cost, on the spot, to discredit what is considered the exorbitant and cumbersome "credit" of a foreign professor. And the *entire* operation was based on the few words of an off-the-cuff response in a conference that took place more than thirty years ago (in 1966!), and in which I was picking up the terms of a question that had been asked by Jean Hyppolite.[1] Nothing else, absolutely nothing! And what is more, my response was not easy to attack.

Plenty of scientists pointed this out to the practical joker in publications that are available in the United States, and Sokal and Bricmont seem to recognize this now in the French version of their book—though what contortions this involves. If this brief remark had been open to question, something I would willingly have agreed to consider, that would still have had to be demonstrated and its consequences for my lecture discussed. This was not done.

I am always sparing and prudent in the use of scientific references, and I have written about this issue on more than one occasion. Explicitly. The numerous places where I do speak, and speak precisely, about the undecidable, for instance, or even about Gödel's theorem, have not been referenced or visited by the censors. There is every reason to think that they have not read what they should have read to measure the extent of these difficulties. Presumably they couldn't. At any rate they haven't done it.

One of the falsifications that most shocked me consists in their saying now that they have never had anything against me (cf. *Libération*, October 19, 1997: "Fleury and Limet accuse us of unjustly attacking Derrida. But no such attack exists"). Now they are hastily classifying me on the list of authors they spared ("Famous thinkers like Althusser, Barthes, Derrida, and Foucault are mainly absent from our book"). This article in *Libération* is a translation of an article in the *Times Literary Supplement*, where my name, and only mine, was opportunely omitted from the same list. In fact this is the sole difference between the two versions. So in France, Sokal and Bricmont added my name to the list of honorable philosophers at the last minute, as a response to embarrassing objections. Context and tactics *obligent*! More opportunism! These people aren't serious.

As for the "relativism" they are supposed to be worried about—well, even if this word has a rigorous philosophical meaning, there's not a trace of it in my writing. Nor of a critique of Reason and the Enlightenment. Quite the contrary. But what I do take more seriously is the wider context—the American context and the political context—that we can't begin to approach here, given the limits of space: and also the theoretical issues that have been so badly dealt with.

These debates have a complex history: libraries full of epistemological works! Before setting up a contrast between the *savants*, the experts, and the others, they divide up the field of science itself. And the field of philosophical thought. Sometimes, for fun, I also take seriously the symptoms of a campaign, or even of a hunt, in which badly trained horsemen sometimes have trouble identifying the prey. And initially the field.

What interest is involved for those who launched this operation in a particular academic world and, often very close to that, in publishing or the press? For instance, a news weekly printed two images of me (a photo and a caricature) to illustrate a whole "dossier" in which my name did not appear once! Is that serious? Is it decent? In whose interest was it to go for a quick practical joke rather than taking part in the work which, sadly, it replaced? This work has been going on for a long time and will continue elsewhere and differently, I hope, and with dignity: at the level of the issues involved.

As If It Were Possible, "Within Such Limits"

Despite the lateness of what is beginning here, we can be quite sure that it won't be a question of some kind of last word. It's crucial for readers not to expect it, the last word. It's out of the question, practically impossible, that on my side I should dare to claim it. One should even—and this is another point in the contract—*not* claim it or expect it.

Perhaps, the Im-possible (Aphoristic 1)

I already don't know how the declaration I have just risked making in very ordinary language may be read. As a sign of modesty or a posturing presumptuousness? "Does he mean, humbly, perhaps affecting shyness, that he will not be capable of proposing, as a response, anything certain and definitive—not the least 'last word'?"—that's what one reader might wonder. "Is he arrogant enough to suggest that he still has so many replies in reserve, after what would basically be, instead of a last word, just a foreword?" someone else would add. "But then, how are we to interpret the possibility of these two interpretations of the last word?" a third person might whisper. Then the fourth would come in sententiously with: "Have you read Austin on 'the crux of the Last Word,' speaking about ordinary language, in 'A Plea for Excuses'? Or Blanchot three times on 'The Last Word,' 'The Very Last Word,' 'The Last Word,' in fact on a certain *Il y a* which will resemble that of Levinas and is quite impossible to translate without remainder into irreducible ordinary language?[1] Especially not as 'there is' and '*Es gibt*'?"

Will I again dare to add my voice to this concert of hypotheses and virtual quotations? Perhaps I should orient things otherwise. For example toward an irreducible modality of the *perhaps*. It would make every instance of the *last word* tremble. Didn't I attempt elsewhere to analyze both the possibility and the necessity of this *perhaps*?[2] Its promise and its fateful necessity, its implication in every experience, at the approach of *this* that comes, of the one (the other) that comes from the to-come and gives rise to what is called an event? This experience of the "perhaps" would be that of *both* the possible *and* the impossible, of the possible *as* impossible. If all that arises is what is already possible, and so capable of being anticipated and expected, that is not an event. The event is possible only coming from the impossible. It arises *like* the coming of the impossible, at the point where a *perhaps* deprives us of all certainty and leaves the future to the future. This *perhaps* is necessarily allied to a *yes*: yes, yes to whoever or whatever comes about. This *yes* is common to both the affirmation and the response; it would come even before any question. A *peut-être* like the English *perhaps* ("It may happen," one would be saying), rather than with the lightness of the German *vielleicht*, and rather than the appeal to being or the ontological insinuation, the *to be or not to be* of a *maybe*—it is this, perhaps, displayed like the *yes* to the event, in other words to the experience of what happens and of *who* then arrives, which far from breaking off the question, gives it room to breathe.

Is there a way of not ever abandoning the question, the urgency of it or its interminable necessity—yet without making the question, still less the reply, into a "last word"? That is what grips me, in heart and thought, but perhaps what I have just said is no longer either a question or a reply. Perhaps something quite different—we will have to come to that. *Perhaps* keeps the question alive, it guarantees, perhaps, its survival, its living-on. What then is the meaning of a *perhaps*, at the disarticulated joining of the possible and the impossible? of the possible *as* im-possible?

Of Ordinary Language: Excuses (Aphoristic 2)

With all the essays that concern us here, I have taken too long, as their authors know, to respond. Can this be forgiven?

Well, I apologize. Sincerely. But not without again promising to reply. I thereby promise to *do* something called "replying" and to *do* it, as a reply should always be done, it is thought, i.e., by *speaking*. Not in joining gestures and speech, as we say in ordinary language, but by *doing* something *with words*, in J. L. Austin's formulation.

Why at this point name the man well known for inventing what is now a familiar distinction? That pair of concepts (performative and constative) may be fairly recent in origin, but it has become canonical. Despite its author's amused insistence on dealing only with "ordinary language," it has changed plenty of things in the less ordinary language of philosophy and theory in the twentieth century. First paradox: what that involved was a distinction in whose purity Austin often said he didn't himself believe.[3] He even declared, in the course of what seems to me an irrefutable argument about ordinary language, and in fact about excuses and apologies, my own subject here: "Certainly, then, ordinary language is *not* the last word [a phrase he had written a little before that, not without irony, but as a quotation from ordinary language, with capital letters: "Then, for the Last Word"]; in principle it can everywhere be supplemented and improved upon and superseded. Only remember, it [ordinary language] *is* the *first* word."[4]

At this point, where he is alluding to the "first *word*," Austin added a footnote. You can see in it the singularity and effectiveness of his philosophical style: "And forget, for once and for a while, that other curious question 'Is it true?' May we?" I did for a moment think of suggesting a sort of interpretation or close reading of "A Plea for Excuses," as a kind of excuse and to serve as a reply to all the magnificent texts I have been given to read here.

I won't do it. But "for once and for a while"—how prudent! What a trick! How wise! *For a while* means "for the moment," a fairly short time, sometimes "quite a long time," or even "for a very long time," perhaps for ever, but not necessarily once and for all. For how long, then? Perhaps the time it takes for a lecture or an article, for instance an article on excuses or apologies. "A Plea for Excuses." Without apologizing and without offering any excuses, at least without doing this explicitly but yet not failing to excuse *himself* for it, Austin begins his article by announcing ironically that he is not going to treat the subject. He is not going to reply to the question, and what he is going to say will not correspond to the subject announced. *Excuses.* He will perhaps *reply* to readers and audience, since he is addressing them, but perhaps without replying to the question, or their questions, or their expectations. First sentence: "The subject of this paper, Excuses, is one not to be treated, but only to be introduced, within such limits."[5]

So he excuses himself for not treating excuses seriously, and for thus remaining in ignorance or leaving others that way on the subject of what apologizing or making excuses means. And this happens at the point when (a performative contradiction?) he begins by himself apologizing—or rather by pretending to, by making an excuse for not treating the subject of excuses.

Does he treat it? Perhaps. It is for the reader to judge, for the addressee to decide. It is like a postcard whose virtual addressee has to decide whether or not he is going to receive it, and whether it is really to him that it is addressed. The signature is left to the initiative, responsibility, and discretion of the other. To work. The signature, if there is one, will take place at the point of arrival at the destination, and not at the origin. (As to the hypothesis that Austin of all people would have let himself be caught out in a "performative contradiction," when we couldn't even have formulated the suspicion without him, then we beg leave to smile at this along with Austin's ghost. As if it were possible to overcome all "performative contradictions"! And as if it were possible to rule out the possibility of someone like Austin playing a little with fire!)

Would a great philosopher from the main tradition have dared to do that? Can we imagine Kant or Hegel confessing that they are not going to treat the stated subject? Can we for instance see them making their excuses for not doing right by excuses, by the subject or stated title "A Plea for Excuses," "within such limits"?

"A Plea for Excuses" could always (perhaps) have just been the title naming the one singular gesture, that particular day, on the part of Austin, or the scene, in a word, that he makes, and no one else, when he asks to be excused for not treating the subject. A title is always a name. Here the reference of this name is what Austin does (he asks to be excused), and not what he treats, since he is making excuses for not treating it. Perhaps he will only have introduced the subject by giving an example, his own, here and now: namely that he apologizes for not treating the subject. But as soon as he introduces it, he knows what he should be talking about, and so he begins to treat it, even while he is saying he is incapable of doing it "within such limits."

I would really like to take him as a model, meaning as an example, or a pretext—or an excuse. Remember Rousseau, who, in relation to the famous episode of the stolen ribbon, admits in his *Confessions* (book 2): "I had simply used as an excuse the first object that presented itself to me."[6]

Replying—Some Analogies (Aphoristic 3)

And in any case if one were to reply to the other without flinching; if one replied exactly, fully, and adequately; if one perfectly adjusted the reply to the question, demand, or expectation—would one still be replying? Would anything be occurring? Would an event happen? Or just the completion of a program, an operation that can be calculated? To be worthy of the name, shouldn't any *reply* have the *surprise* of some newness bursting in? And thus of an anachronous maladjustment? In short, should it not reply "to one side of the question"? *Just* that, and *just* to one side of the question? Not just anywhere, anyhow, any old thing, but *just* that and *just* to one side of the question—at the very moment when, however, it does everything to address the other, really, the other's expectations, in conditions that are defined by consensus (contract, rules, norms, concepts, language, codes, and so on), and does this with absolute straightforwardness? How can there be surprises within straightforwardness? These two conditions of replying appear to be incompatible, but it seems to me that they are each as incontestable as the other one. This is perhaps the impasse in which I find myself, paralyzed. This is the aporia in which I have placed myself. In truth I do find I am placed there even before installing myself there myself.

If I could treat my subject, myself, and reply to all these virtual questions, I would perhaps let myself be tempted, at great risk, to *retranslate* all the problematics so powerfully elaborated in the essays preceding me.[7] I would be tempted to *reformulate* them into the great question of ordinary language. Let me give just two examples, looking toward the fine studies by John Sallis and Karel Thein, which help us, in different ways but in both cases with force and necessity, to rethink our philosophical memory where it is indebted to Greek idiom: Within a so-called natural language, so one that cannot be totally formalized, where is the frontier between ordinary usage and philosophical usage? How do we make that distinction in relation for instance to words used in everyday life in Greece, but also in Plato's writings, such as *pharmakon* (poison and/or remedy, sometimes undecidably); or *chora*, meaning ordinary place, locality, village, and the like, as opposed to the unique *chora* of Plato's *Timaeus*, which, despite many appearances to the contrary, no longer has any connection, even *by analogy*, with the other one? (This question of analogy awaits us, at the point where Thein in fact names the "limits of analogy"; I will have to come back to it as it will probably govern everything I say; it will supply me with the most general form of my address to the authors of the articles collected here [in the special issue].

In a word—which won't be the last one: How—using what kind of economy, or transaction—can one treat the subject of analogy? Of the analogy (1) between analogical relations and analogy; (2) between heterological relations, *between* the maintaining *and* the breaking of analogy? Is the first analogy possible or impossible, legitimate or wrong? How can it be explained that the relationship (*logos*) of analogy is called by one of the terms of the relation of proportionality, for instance between *logos* and soul, *pharmakon* and body? This is a question impressively developed by Thein. It will run through this whole discussion, more or less visibly. An analogous question seems to demand consideration, on the subject of the different uses of the word *chora*, in ordinary life and in philosophical discourse, but also in philosophical contexts (such as the *Republic* and the *Timaeus*) that are both common *and* heterogeneous. These contexts seem to have mutual relationships involving both articulable analogy *and* irreducible dissociation—we could say aphoristic or diaphoristic. They remain radically untranslatable into each other, at least if we care about the stability of what we are calling here a discursive context. Especially in those passages discovered and rigorously analyzed by Sallis, when the word *chora* seems to have a different meaning from the one it has in the *Timaeus* (unconnected to the Good and the *epekeina tes ousias* [beyond being]) and so designates the place of the sun itself, "where the good and the *chora* are brought into a very remarkable proximity."

And here already, caught in the ordinary words of a number of natural languages, is the syntax of a first question, a first problem. It is the a priori supplementary question to a complement. A complement for a word of the language that is a verb: *reply*, yes, one should, here, now. Yes, one could try it, be tempted to try it, by all means, but reply *to whom? Before whom?* Answer *for what?* And answer *what?* As far as *replying* goes, both the grammar of the verb and the pragmatics of the act, we have to do justice to *four complements and four syntaxes.*

1. First reply perhaps possible on the subject of replying, then, and first of all with regard to the *two first complements* (*to whom? before whom?*): to reply *to* whoever, and *before* whoever has at least *read*—this is the first condition—*read* and, of course, understood, analyzed, even written the texts that precede mine—meaning a number of previous works that they treat themselves, for instance (forgive the brevity) those of the great and

canonical tradition, from Plato and Aristotle to Kant, Hegel, Husserl, or Heidegger, and so on, in their relation to science, but also the texts that are their descendants today, more or less legitimately and in a minor mode, including mine, presumably; we are all here bound by the contract offered us by the editor of the *Revue internationale de philosophie*. All readers are assumed to accept such a contract, as are those whose names appear on the contents page.

2. Second reply perhaps possible on the subject of replying, the one I think I have to choose at any rate, but this time with regard to the *two last complements (on behalf of what and what?)*: not to reply *on behalf of* what I have written (can I answer for it, respond on its behalf, responsibly? don't they speak about it more lucidly than me?)—but perhaps to reply (and here is *what*) by saying a few words, "within such limits," about the questions, difficulties, aporias, and impasses (I don't dare say "problems" any longer) in the midst of which I am presently struggling and will doubtless go on being troubled for a long time to come.

I will borrow (I say this to ask forgiveness or offer excuses) one of the economic formulas for this trouble from the course of seminars I am giving right now on forgiveness, excuses, and perjury. Here it is, quite stark and apparently quite simple: *one only forgives the unforgivable*. In forgiving only what is already forgivable, one forgives nothing. As a result, forgiveness is only *possible, as such*, where, in the face of the unforgivable, it seems *impossible*.

As I try to show elsewhere more concretely, less formally but with more logical sequence, that requires us to think the *possible* (the *possibility* of forgiveness, but also of the gift, of hospitality—and by definition the list is not exhaustive; it is that of all the *unconditionals*) *as the impossible*. If the possible *"is"* the im-possible *here*; if, as I have often ventured to say on different themes but therefore in a relatively formalizable way, the "condition of possibility" is a "condition of impossibility," then how should the thought of the possible be re-thought, the thought that comes to us from the heart of our tradition (Aristotle, Leibniz, Kant, Bergson, and so on: Heidegger too, whose use of the words *mögen* and *Vermögen*, especially in the "Letter on 'Humanism,'" would be worth a separate treatment here; and so on)?[8]

How should we understand the word *possible*? How should we read what affects it with negation around the verb *to be*, such that the three words of this proposition, "the possible *'is'* the impossible," are no longer associated merely by a play on words, an amusing paradox or dialectical facility? But how should we understand that they end up, seriously and necessarily, weakening the propositionality itself of a proposition of the type *S is P* ("the possible 'is' the im-possible")? And is that a *question* or a *problem*? And what is the complicity between this thinking of the *im-possible possible* and the importance of the *perhaps* that I drew attention to earlier?

I have already seemed to count on the distinction between *who* and *what*, to shake it up a bit (reply to *whom*? before *whom*? but also answer for *what*? and answer *what*?), so let me be clear that in my present work, above all in my teaching (for instance for the past few years on the subject of the gift, the secret, witnessing, hospitality, forgiveness, the excuse, the oath, or perjury), I try to reach a place *from* which this distinction between *who* and *what* comes to appear and become determined, in other words a place "anterior" to this distinction, a place more "old" or more "young" than it, a place also that both enjoins determination but also enables the terribly reversible translation of *who* into *what*.

Why call that a *place*, a placement, a spacing, an interval, a sort of *chora*?

Rules for the Impossible (Aphoristic 4)

Starting up at top speed, as it were. Let me apologize again and begin in another way.

To reply, if that is the right word. Michel Meyer generously offered to let me or asked me to. I was imprudent enough to promise it and so to risk perjury. After reading all these strong, lucid, and generous texts several times, with admiration, still my lateness will only have been that of an anxious and nervous run, slower and slower and faster and faster. Slower and faster at the same time—get that. There was the rush of a hastening by which, as we say, I was heading straight for failure. I was giving in to a disaster that I could see coming more and more clearly, without being able to do anything about it. Obviously, I didn't want the silence of simply not replying to be liable to interpretation—wrongly, of course—as arrogance or ingratitude. But just as obviously, given a time limit and a page length also reduced in proportion, "within such limits" (Austin), I couldn't claim to reply to so many texts differing in their approach, in their style, in the corpus of texts they were dealing with, and in the problematics they developed—to so many modes of address that were all so demanding in the force and exactness of their questions, the richness of their propositions, and the depth of the concerns for which they take responsibility. There would thus be not only the insufficient sufficiency of a rapid or brief reply, but added to it a sort of philosophical lack of responsibility.

I am sure I won't escape either one of these. At least I will perhaps have begun by admitting the failure and the wrong—and by apologizing. If only to give a little more support to the proposition I was putting forward just now, on the very subject of forgiveness. Once the *possibility* of forgiveness, if there is such a thing, consists in a certain *im-possibility*, should we infer from that that it is therefore necessary to *do the impossible*? And to do it with words, only with words? Is it necessary to do the impossible for a pardon as such to arise?

Perhaps, but that cannot be set up as a law, a norm, a rule, or a duty. There should be no "it is necessary" or "you must" for a pardon. This "must" always remain disinterested and unforeseeable. Giving or forgiving is never done "according to a duty" (*pflichtmässig*), not even "out of duty" (*eigentlich aus Pflicht*), to use Kant's excellent distinction. One forgives, if one does forgive, beyond any categorical imperative, beyond debt and duty. And yet *one should* forgive. What indeed is implied by infinite forgiveness, "hyperbolical" and thus unconditional forgiveness, of which the "commandment" seems, in terms of its heritage, to come to us from the tradition of Abraham, passed on in different ways by St. Paul and the Koran? Does it imply, as its condition (thus the condition of unconditionality) that the pardon be asked for and the wrongdoing admitted, as Jankélevitch so emphatically tells us?[9] But then it would no longer be unconditional. Conditioned once again, it would no longer be pure forgiveness, it would become impossible again, differently impossible. Or else might it only be unconditional, and thus possible *as unconditional*, by forgiving the unforgivable (so by becoming possible *as* impossible)? Can it only be what it must be, unconditional, by not even requiring that admission or that repentance, that exchange, that identification, that economic horizon of reconciliation, redemption, and salvation?

I would be tempted to think so, both *in* and *against* this powerful tradition. What does "inheriting" from a tradition mean in these conditions, when one thinks from within it and thinks in its name, for sure, but *against it in its name*, against the very thing it will have thought it had to save in order to survive by losing itself? Again the possibility of the impossible: inheritance would only be possible at the point where it becomes the im-possible. This is one of the possible definitions of deconstruction—as inheritance. I did propose this once: deconstruction might perhaps be "the experience of the impossible."[10]

I must now, without further delay, without giving more space and time to introducing so many subjects that I won't be dealing with, present and justify, as far as I can, the rule I believed I had to choose in order to limit the gravity of this long failing. I couldn't, "within such limits," give a detailed reply to each one of the texts you have just read; they would need an article per page, at least. But I can't group my replies together by general themes, and nor do I want to; that risks obliterating the signed originality of each of the texts that it has been my privilege to read. Finally, in none of these pieces have I found anything to object to or even to prompt a plea in defense of my past work (another way of saying that they are not only courteous and generous but in my view impeccable in their readings and the discussions they thus open up). So in the end I resigned myself to proposing myself—in other words to proposing a more or less disjunctive series of *quasi* propositions, following a number of rules. Concerning my current work and the difficulties it remains for me to come through, these *quasi* propositions would resound or reason "to one side"; they would correspond to the anxieties, concerns, and questions of those who do me the honor here of being interested in what I have written, with a slight displacement of their harmony. Which amounts to saying that, being limited to the obligatory small number of pages, these *quasi* propositions, as we already see, will remain, at least to begin with, *aphoristic*. But does one ever do without all discontinuity in making an argument? It is true that there are leaps and leaps. One can defend a few hiatuses: some are worth more than others.

On the other hand these aphoristic *quasi* propositions are and will remain *oblique* in their relationship to the texts with which I shall endeavor, always, nevertheless, to bring them into harmony. Doing all I can to give a *just to one side* reply. But that does not mean that I will yield to some kind of *oratio obliqua* or that I will try to sidestep the issues. Even where it appears impossible, and exactly there, a *straightforwardness*, as I was saying above, remains obligatory. Inflexibly. If I have been multiplying the detours and the contortions since a moment ago, including the place where I humbly ask for forgiveness and commiseration, it is because I am, I am placed, I have placed myself, in an untenable position, faced with an impossible task. Forgiveness and pity: mercy.

Yes to Hospitality (Aphoristic 5)

Thus the *problems* of replying and delay have just introduced themselves. Do I still have the right, after reading Michel Meyer, to give them that name, to call them "problems"? And just now I spoke imprudently of "propositions." To specify "*quasi* propositions," as I have done, is certainly to demonstrate an attentiveness to the problem of propositionality that is exactly what Meyer stresses.[11]

But this *quasi*, just on its own, doesn't do a lot to move things forward. Another concept must be necessary.

I have never found a concept that was grasped in a word. Should that be surprising? Has there ever been a concept that was really nameable? I mean nameable with a single name or a single word? The concept always demands sentences, discourses, work, and process: in a word, text. For instance, the word *chora* definitely doesn't designate the same concept in the *Timaeus* and the *Republic* (516b, a passage cited by Sallis). One could say that it is only a homonym, almost another word. The consequences of this necessity (of what at any rate I take as an experience that cannot be denied), seem to me fearful but ineluctable. I sometimes feel I have never done anything, ever, other than to try to be coherent in this regard. Perhaps what I have wanted is quite simply to take note of this necessity and bear witness to it.

But it is definitely not by chance that the modality of *quasi* (or the logical-rhetorical fiction of *as if*) has so often imposed itself on me to make a word into a phrase, and first of all, especially—it has often been noted and commented on—around the word *transcendental.* A question of problematic context and strategies, presumably: one must *in this place* relentlessly reaffirm questions of the transcendental type; and *in that place*, almost simultaneously, also ask questions about the history and the limits of what is called "transcendental."

But in the first place it was necessary to take account of the essential possibility of an *as if* affecting any language and all experience with *possible* fictionality, the fantasmatic, or spectrality. This word *transcendental* is not one example among others. The category of the "quasi-transcendental" has played a role that is deliberately equivocal but also determinant in many of my essays. Rodolphe Gasché oriented a powerful interpretation toward it.[12] Of course, the use I had to reconcile myself to making of *quasi* or the "ultra-transcendental" is still, and was already, a way of saving, even while betraying it, the philosophical inheritance, namely the demand for the condition of possibility (the a priori, the originary, or ground, all different forms of the same radical demand and of any philosophical "question"). It was also to be engaged, without dissimulating the difficulty, in the task of thinking again about what is meant by the "possible," and the "impossible," and to do it around the so-called condition of possibility, often demonstrated as being a "condition of impossibility." What is thus said of the condition of possibility also goes, by analogy, for the "ground," the "origin," the "root" of "radicality," and so on.

Even before I started to name them so as to admit my wrongdoing, the related *problems* of reply and delay had been treated by at least three of my colleagues. First Michel Meyer, who goes back to the drawing board with the question of the question and thus the question of the reply, of what he calls "answerhood," equated with "propositionality"—"answerhood, i.e., propositionality"—but also of "problematical difference" as "differance . . . when we leave propositionalism"; and differance is also a sort of originary delay. Then Daniel Giovannangeli, who draws attention to everything that is governed by belatedness or *Nachträglichkeit* at the point where that "anachrony," "the anachrony of time itself . . . borders and overflows philosophy."[13] Lastly, by John Sallis, for whom the question or the reply of returning to the things themselves, philosophy *itself,* assumes, as "the very opening in question," the opening of an interval that delays (behind) imminence itself: "to intend to begin, to be about to begin, is also to delay, to defer the very beginning that one is about to make"—which, as you will have been thinking for some time, I am still doing here, not proud of it.

Reply and delay, then: a reply, at least in the good sense of the word, is always second and secondary. It is behind on the question or the demand, at any rate on the expectation. And yet everything begins with a reply. If I had to use an elliptical paradox to summarize the thinking that has always run through everything I say or write,[14] I would speak of an *originary reply:* "yes," everywhere that that indispensable acquiescence is implicated (which is to say everywhere that one speaks to and addresses the other, to deny, to discuss, to object, and so on), is first of all a reply. To say "yes" is to respond. But nothing precedes its delay—and therefore its anachrony.

Coming *after* them, after the texts and the authors we have just read, without judging it possible or necessary to do anything other than listen to them, and to ask that others read and reread them, I will only describe the movement I feel caught up in with this. Although I never restrict it to the propositional form (in the necessity of which I also believe, of course), I have never thought I had to give up questioning (or that anyone could or should be able to)—give up any form of question, a certain "primacy of questioning" (Michel Meyer), or that which ties the question to the problem, to *problematization*. Is there ever a question pure of any problem, in other words on the one hand pure of any elaboration, any syntax, any articulable differentiality; but also, on the other hand, pure of any self-protection? For problematization is certainly the only *consistent* organization of a question, its grammar and semantics, but also a first *apotropaic* measure to protect oneself against the starkest question, both the most inflexible and the barest, the question of the other when it *puts me in question* at the moment it is addressed to me. I have tried elsewhere to take into account this *shield* of the *problema*. The *problema* also designates "the substitute, the deputy, the prosthesis, whatever or whomever one *puts forward* to protect oneself while concealing oneself, whatever or whoever comes in the place or the name of the other."[15]

Problematization is already an articulated organization of the response. That is true everywhere, particularly in the history of philosophical or scientific configurations. Whatever name you call them by, however you interpret them (paradigm, *episteme*, *themata*, and so on), these historical configurations that act as a basis for questions are already possibilities of response. They preorganize and render possible the event, the apparent invention, the emergence and elaboration of questions, their problematization, and the reappropriation that makes them for a moment determinable and treatable.

In the inevitability of the question, it seems to me, there is not only an essence of philosophy but an unconditional right and duty, the joint ground of philosophy as science and law. Since this unconditionality is pointed out where it seems to be a matter of course, I must also make the following clear: although I have constantly used everything I have written as a *question of the question*,[16] *this same necessity* is not reducible to the question. A double necessity, double law of the inevitable and the imperative injunction ("It is necessary"), it exceeds the question at the very moment of reaffirming its necessity. In confirming so often that everything begins not with the question but with the response, with a "yes, yes,"[17] that is in origin a response to the other, it is not a matter of again "putting into question," as the phrase goes, this unconditionality, but rather of thinking both its possibility and its impossibility, the one *like* the other.

Almost thirty-five years ago, I was already getting anxious (should I say that I was wondering—*questioning myself* on the subject?) about "unanswerable questions":

> By right of birth, and for one time at least, these are problems put to philosophy as problems philosophy cannot resolve.
>
> It may even be that these questions are not *philosophical*, are not *philosophy's* questions. Nevertheless, these should be the only questions today capable of founding the community, within the world, of those who are still called philosophers; and called such in remembrance, at the very least, of the fact that these questions must be examined unrelentingly. . . . A community of the question, therefore, within that fragile moment when the question is not yet determined enough for the hypocrisy of an answer to have already *invited* itself beneath the mask of the question, and not yet determined enough for its voice to have been already and fraudulently articulated within the very syntax of the question. . . . A community of the question about the possibility of the question. This is very little—almost nothing—but within it, today, is sheltered and encapsulated an unbreachable dignity and duty of *decision*. An unbreachable responsibility. Why unbreachable? Because *the impossible has already occurred* . . . there is a history of the question. . . . The question has already begun. . . . A founded dwelling, a realized tradition of the question remaining a question . . . the correspondence of the question with itself.[18]

Please forgive too this long quotation of an ancient text. Shall I say that I apologize for it, again? Beyond the weakness I could be accused of, I first wanted to acknowledge a trajectory that at least intersects with—and has done for such a long time—many of the "problematological" motifs elaborated by Michel Meyer, especially when he writes, "Problematicity is historicity." But I was surprised myself (can I admit this without seeming too naive or stupidly reassured about what might only be immobility and monotony?) by the insistence or the constancy of the matter and by the continuity of the displacement, and I wanted above all to situate the new motifs that, with no rupture (because they have been of continual concern to me in my seminars over the past few years) have not yet been approached, here, in this collection of texts. I had declared that rather than *respond* to all the essays in the volume, I wished to *correspond* with them, by instead laying out some difficulties in my ongoing work. The words italicized in the quotation just given are primarily indications of this, and trails for me to follow. They point toward the themes and problems that are besieging me today: another way of thinking the limit of philosophy in relation to questions like *hospitality* (*invitation* / *visitation*, and a whole chain of associated motifs: the *promise, witnessing,* the *gift, forgiveness,* and so on), but also tested against an im-possible that would not be negative. This kind of testing implies another way of thinking the event, the "taking place": only the im-possible takes place; and the deployment of a potentiality or possibility that is already there will never make an event or an invention.

What is true for the event is true for the decision, and thus for responsibility: a decision that I *can* take, the decision *in my power* and that manifests the taking of action or the deployment of what is *already possible* for me, the actualization of my possibility, a decision that is dependent only on me—would that still be a decision?

Whence the paradox without paradox to which I am trying to submit: a responsible decision must be that im-possible possibility of a "passive" decision, a decision by the other in me that does not exonerate me from any freedom or any responsibility.

Necessity of Impossibility (Aphoristic 6)

There are many passages of an aporetical type, where I have elaborated on "the singular modality of this 'impossible.'" Particularly in relation to the *gift,* in *Given Time*:

One can think, desire, and say only the impossible, according to the measureless measure [*mesure sans mesure*] of the impossible. If one wants to recapture the proper element of thinking, naming, desiring, it is perhaps according to the measureless measure of this limit that it is possible, possible as relation *without* relation to the impossible. One *can* desire, name, think in the proper sense of these words, if there is one, *only* to the *immeasuring* extent [*que dans la mesure démesurante*] that one desires, names, thinks still or already, that one still lets announce itself what nevertheless cannot *make itself (a) present* [*un don qui ne peut pas se faire présent*].[19]

The figure of "given time" had been named, long before, and italicized.[20] This came after a passage elaborating on the "possibility of the impossible," which was stated then like another name for time: "But it has already been remarked that this impossibility, when barely formulated, contradicts itself, is experienced as the possibility of the impossible. . . . Time is a name for this impossible possibility."[21] Later, the concept of invention would obey the same "logic":

Invention is always possible, it is the invention of the possible. . . . Thus it is that invention would be in conformity with its concept, with the dominant feature of the word and concept "invention," only insofar as, paradoxically, invention invents nothing, when in invention the other does not come, and when nothing comes to the other or from the other. For the other is not the possible. So it would be necessary to say that the only possible invention would be the invention of the impossible. But an invention of the impossible is impossible, the other would say. Indeed. But it is the only possible invention: an invention has to declare itself to be the invention of that which did not appear to be possible; otherwise, it only makes explicit a program of possibilities within the economy of the same.[22]

In the intervening period, *The Post Card* entails the same necessity destined for destination, for the very concept of destination. Once a letter *can not arrive* at its destination, it is impossible for it to arrive *fully*, or *simply*, at a single destination.[23] Always, im-possibility—the possible as impossible—is linked to an irreducible divisibility that affects the very essence of the possible. Whence the insistence on the divisibility of the letter and its destination:

The divisibility of the letter—this is why we have insisted on this key or theoretical safety lock of the Seminar: the atomystique of the letter—is what chances and sets off course, without guarantee of return, the remaining [*restance*] of anything whatsoever: a letter does *not always* arrive at its destination, and from the moment that this possibility belongs to its structure one can say that it never truly arrives, that when it does arrive its capacity not to arrive torments it with an internal drifting.[24]

Why this allusion to a *torment*? It names a suffering or a passion, an affect that is both sad and joyful, the instability of an anxiety belonging to any possibilization. This would submit to being haunted by the specter of its impossibility, by mourning itself: the mourning of itself borne in itself, but which also gives it its life or its survival, its very possibility. For this *im*-possibility opens its possibility, it leaves a trace, both a chance and a threat, *in* what it makes possible. The torment would sign this scar, the trace of this trace. But in *The Post Card* that is also said in relation to the "impossible decision," apparently impossible, in as much as it only returns to the other.[25] (This motif was extensively explicated in *Politics of Friendship*.)[26] It recurs again in connection with Freud and the concept of *Bemächtigung* [mastery]—of the limit or paradoxes of the possible as power.[27]

It is no accident that this discourse on conditions of possibility, at the very point where its claim is obsessed by the impossibility of overcoming its own performativity, should extend to all the places where some performative force occurs, or brings something about (the event, invention, the gift, forgiveness, hospitality, friendship, the promise, the experience of death—possibility of the impossible, impossibility of the possible, experience in general, etc. *Et cetera*, for the contagion has no limit; it ultimately involves all concepts, and probably the concept of the concept).

Promising to give replies straightforwardly, thus *just beside* the question: the possible-impossible. Pointing out that on the untenable line of this possible-impossible is written everything I have written under the heading of *destinerrance*, and this was always at the crossroads between many of the paths outlined and reinterpreted by the texts gathered here. The risk of misunderstanding, the wandering of a reply beside the question—that's what must always remain possible in this straightforwardness exercise. Otherwise there would be no straightforwardness, no ethics of discussion. But what I am putting forward here is not the outline of some "ethical turn," as it has been described, any more than the previous allusions to responsibility, hospitality, the gift, forgiveness, witnessing, etc. I am simply trying to pursue with some consistency a thinking that has been engaged around the same aporias for a long time. The question of ethics, law, or politics hasn't arisen unexpectedly, as when you come off a bend. And the way it is treated is not always reassuring for "morale"—and perhaps because it asks too much of it.

The *possibility* of this evil (misunderstanding, failure of comprehension, making a mistake) is in its way a chance. It gives time. So what is needed [*il faut*] is the "it's needed [*il faut*]" of the wrongdoing and that the adequation should remain *impossible*. But there is nothing negative, ontologically, in this "what's needed is some wrongdoing." What's needed, if you prefer, is that *in*adequation should remain *always possible* in order that interpretation in general, and the reply, be *possible* in its turn. Here is an example of this law linking the possible and the impossible. For a faultless interpretation, a totally adequate self-comprehension, would not only mark the end of a history exhausted by its very transparency. By ruling out the future, they would make everything *impossible*, both the event and the coming of the other, coming to the other—and therefore replying, the very *yes* of the reply, the *yes as* reply. This can only be adjusted in an exceptional way: and again we have no prior and objective criterion for being assured of that, to assure ourselves that the exception is really happening *as* an exception.

Perhaps the haunting of the exception could indicate the path, if not the way out. I say "haunting" advisedly, for it is spectral structure that makes the law here, of both the possible and the impossible—of their strange entanglement. The exception is always obligatory. This is, perhaps, to do with that stubbornness of *perhaps*, in its modality that is ungraspable but also irreducible to any other, fragile and yet indestructible. *Quasi* or *as if, perhaps, spectrality* of the *phantasma* (which also means the revenant): these are the elements of another way of thinking of the virtual, of a virtuality that is no longer ordered according to traditional thought (*dynamis, potentia, possibilitas*).

When the impossible *makes itself* possible, the event takes place (possibility *of* the impossible). That, indisputably, is the paradoxical form of the event: if an event is only possible, in the classic sense of this word, if it fits in with conditions of possibility, if it only makes explicit, unveils, reveals, or accomplishes that which was already possible, then it is no longer an event. For an event to take place, for it to be possible, it has to be, as event, as invention, the coming of the impossible. That's a meager statement of the obvious, an obviousness that is nothing less than obvious. This is what has always guided me, between the possible and the impossible. This is what has so often prompted me to speak of a *condition of impossibility*.

The issue is thus nothing less than the powerful concept of the *possible* that runs through Western thought, from Aristotle to Kant and Husserl (then differently to Heidegger), with all its meanings, virtual or potential: being-in-potential, in fact; *dynamis*, virtuality (in its classic and modern forms, pretechnological and technological), but also power, capacity, everything that renders skilled, or able, or that formally enables, and so on. The choice of this thematic does of course hold a strategic value, but it also carries with it a movement for going further, beyond any calculable stratagem. It carries what is called deconstruction toward a question that causes trembling, tormenting it from the inside, the most powerful and the most precarious axiomatic—powerless in its very power—of dominant thinking about the possible in philosophy—a philosophy that is thus a slave to the power of its very dominance.

But how is it possible, it will then be asked, that what renders possible renders impossible the very thing that it renders possible, and introduces; but as its chance, a chance that is not negative, a principle of ruin in the very thing that it is promising or promoting?

The *im-* of the im-possible is surely radical, implacable, undeniable. But it is not only negative or simply dialectical: it *introduces* into the possible, it is *its usher today*: it gets it to come, it gets it to move according to an anachronic temporality or an unbelievable filiation—which moreover is also the origin of faith. For it exceeds knowledge, it conditions the address to the other, it puts any theorem in the space and time of a witnessing ("I am speaking to you, believe me"). To put it another way, and this is the introduction to an aporia that has no examples, an aporia of logic rather than a logical aporia: here we have an impasse of the undecidable, by which a decision cannot not get through.

All responsibility has to go by way of this aporia, which, far from paralyzing, sets in motion a new thinking of the possible. It guarantees it its rhythm and respiration: diastole, systole, and syncope, beating of the *im*-possible possible, of the impossible as condition of the possible. From the very heart of the im-possible, one would thus hear the impulse or pulse of a "deconstruction."

The condition of possibility would then give a chance to the possible, but by depriving it of its purity. The law of this spectral contamination, the impure law of this impurity—that is what has to be continually reelaborated. For example: the possibility of failure is not only set down as a prior risk in the condition of the possibility of success of a performative (a promise must *be able not* to be kept; in order to be a freely given promise, and even in order to succeed, it must threaten not to be kept or to become a threat:[28] whence the originary inscription of guilt, confession, excuse, and forgiveness in the promise). It must continue to mark the event, even when it succeeds, as the trace of an impossibility, sometimes its memory and always its haunting. This im-possibility is thus not simply the opposite of the possible. It seems only to be opposed but it also supports possibility: it passes through it and leaves in it the trace of its taking away.

An event would not be worthy of its name, it would not make anything happen, if all it did was to deploy, explicate, or actualize what was already possible: which is to say, in short, if it came back down to unfolding a program or applying a general rule to a case. For there to be event, it has to be possible, of course, but also there has to be an interruption that is exceptional, absolutely singular, in the regime of possibility; it must not be reducible to explication, unfolding, or the putting into action of a possibility. The event, if there is such a thing, is not the actualization of a possibility, a straightforward putting into action, a realization, an effectuation, the teleological accomplishment of a capacity, the process of a dynamic dependent on "conditions of possibility." The event has nothing to do with history, if what we understand by history is teleological process. It must in a certain way break off that type of history. These are the premises which led me to speak, particularly in *Specters of Marx*, of messianicity without messianism. Thus *it must be* that the event is also introduced as impossible or that its possibility be threatened.

But then why this "it must be [*il faut*]," it will be asked? What is the status of this necessity, of this law that, all things considered, is apparently contradictory and doubly obligatory? What is this "double bind" on the basis of which it "would be necessary [*il faut*]" again to rethink the possible as *im*-possible?

It is perhaps a necessity that also escapes from the habitual regime of necessity (*ananke, Notwendigkiet*)—from necessity as natural law or as law of freedom. For it is not possible to think the possibility of the impossible *otherwise* without rethinking necessity. We have just been recalling the area of my analyses that concerned the event or the performative, and I have also attempted these analyses, in an analogous way, and particularly over the past fifteen years, in relation to destination, witnessing, invention, the gift, forgiveness, and also that which links hospitality to the im-possible promise, to the pervertibility of the performative in general—and above all, in relation to death, to the aporicity of the aporia in general.

It is not so much that this pervertibility is transcendental as that it affects the classic mode of reflection on the transcendental, on the transcendental "condition of possibility," in all its forms: medieval onto-theology, criticism, or phenomenology.[29] It does not delegitimate transcendental questioning, it de-limits it and interrogates its original historicity. For nothing can discredit the right to the transcendental or ontological question. This is the only force that resists empiricism and relativism. Despite appearances to which philosophers in a hurry often rush, nothing is less empiricist or relativist than a certain attention to the multiplicity of contexts and the discursive strategies they govern; than a certain insistence on the fact that a context is always open and nonsaturable; or than taking into account the *perhaps* and the *quasi* in thinking about the event; and so on.

Transaction and Event (Aphoristic 7)

In this insistent displacement of strategy and nonstrategy (meaning a vulnerable exposure to that which happens), there is a sort of *transaction*. You negotiate, you transact *with* and *on* the limit of philosophy as such. This limit takes the double form of a differential logic of analogy: *on the one hand* the *quasi*, the *as if* of a differance that maintains delay, relay, postponement, or deadline in the economy of the same; and *on the other hand* rupture, the event of the im-possible, differance as *diaphora*, the aphoristic experience of the absolutely heterogeneous. On the one hand the concatenation of syllogistic sequences, and on the other, but "at the same time," the seriality of aphoristic sequences.

Karel Thein is thus right to take his rich analysis of analogy in "Plato's Pharmacy" [in *Dissemination*] as far as the point where, with the authority of decision, the question bears on what he calls "the conditions and limits of analogy as such." The interpretation of the *chora* that I attempt has the effect of disturbing the regime of analogy. As John Sallis stresses so well (in the dialogue we have been pursuing for years, and which has been so important to me, around this text of Plato, in which we can really feel the power of implosion that it keeps in reserve), it is also a matter of that which, in the definition of the Good and of *epekeina tes ousias* as beyond being, would remain in a sort of ana-onto-logy. It's about another excess. The "other time" stressed by Sallis is also what carries all the proofs I was mentioning earlier (the im-possible, passive decision, the "perhaps," the event as absolute breaking off of the possible, and so on). All Sallis's questions certainly seem to me legitimate ones, as do the replies he brings to them ("Can there be, then, a metaphorizing of the *khora*? If not, then how is one to read the passage on the *khora* of the sun . . . ? How is the *khora* itself—if there be a *khora* itself—to be beheld? What is the difference marked by the 'as' [on the assumption that *chora* [or *khora*] would be apprehended 'as in a dream']?").

But these legitimate responses come under the law of the philosophical, dominated by the necessities of ana-onto-logy (which are those of ontology but also of phenomenology, in other words of the appearance as such of the *as such*, the *as*. The rupture that concerns me in the reading of *chora*, as I felt I had to venture it, is that *chora* becomes the name of what never lets itself be metaphorized, even though *chora* can and cannot not give rise to a great many analogical figures. It doesn't seem possible to me that the *chora* of the sun in the *Republic* can be a metaphorical value of the *chora* in the *Timaeus*. Nor the inverse either. Although in both cases the word clearly designates a "placement" or "locality," there is no possible analogy or commensurability between these two places, I think. The word "place" itself has such a different semantic value in the two cases that what we are dealing with, I think, and was suggesting before, is instead a relationship of homonymy and not of figurality or synonymy. It was this conviction which led me, wrongly or rightly, to treat *chora* in the *Timaeus* as a *quasi*-proper name. If *chora* is removed from all metaphor, that does not mean it remains inaccessible in its own ownness, in its ipseity, in the itself of what it is. Rather, earlier, because what there is there is not *chora itself.* There is no *chora* itself (as John Sallis rightly suspects when he specifies "if there be a *khora* itself"). That seems very perturbing, I grant. This uniqueness without ownness or proper identity puts in crisis, for instance, here and not necessarily elsewhere, any distinction between figure and nonfigure, and thus that distinction between "literal reading" and "figural reading" that Michel Meyer is probably correct to separate out, in other cases, as two "steps." What we have here in the singular case of *khora* (but also of its analogues, which however remain absolutely singular and different) is a name with no referent, without a referent that is a thing or a being or even a phenomenon appearing *as such.* This possibility thus disorganizes the whole regime of the philosophical (ontological or transcendental) type of question, without yielding to a prephilosophical empiricism . . . It is only introduced under the figure of the im-possible which is no longer a figure and which I have tried to show never appears as such.[30] It disorientates the "as such," taking away its status as a phenomeno-ontological criterion. I try to explain myself on the necessity of this singular nomination, on its contingency too, and on what we are inheriting there, namely a noun in natural language in its ordinary usage (*chora*), a noun that is both replaceable and irreplaceable. To be replaceable in its very irreplaceability is what happens to any singularity, to any proper noun, even and especially when what it "properly" names does not have a relationship of indivisible propriety with itself, with some self that would properly be that which it is *as such*, with some intact ipseity. Prosthesis of the proper name that comes to mean, to call by its name (without any ontic referent, without anything that appears as such, with no corresponding object or existent, without a meaning either in the world or outside the world) some "thing" that is not a thing and that has no analogical relationship with anything. This nomination is an event (both impossible and decisive, which we can decide whether or not to inherit). But isn't every inaugural nomination an event? Is not the giving of the name the performative par excellence? But also that which *happens* to the *named*, to the *nameable*, beyond all performative mastery, beyond all power?

Savoir-Penser: Inheriting "The Critical Mission of Philosophy" (Aphoristic 8)

Without being any kind of "program," what then does differance "say" or "do"?[31] (Differance "is" not either a word or a concept, I was saying back then in an obvious denial,[32] but one whose traces remain in some way, to the point of making the denial of denial legitimate as well as ineffective, as if many of us sensed in advance that this unsustainable denial must positively mean "something," even in its inconsistency, that might perhaps still be worth taking seriously.) The singularity of what was being introduced as "differance" in this way was this: at the same time, but without the ease of dialectics, it took in both the same and the other, both the economy of analogy—the same just deferred, relayed, put back—*and* the rupture of all analogy, absolute heterology. Now it would be possible, in this present context, to treat again this question of differance as a question of *inheritance*. Inheritance would here consist in remaining faithful to that which one receives (and *chora* is also that *which* receives, the enigma of what "receptacle," *endechomenon*, can mean and do, where *chora* says nothing and does nothing), while also breaking with any figure of that which is received. One must always break off out of fidelity—and in the name of an inheritance that is necessarily contradictory in its injunctions. For instance, with regard to the gift, forgiveness, hospitality, and so on, in the name of the Old Testament inheritance, which commands a certain hyperbolical unconditionality on my part here, I would be ready to break with all the economic and conditional reappropriations which are always compromising that inheritance. But that rupture itself will still have to handle the transactions and define the necessary conditions, in history, law, politics, economics (and economy here is economy in the narrow sense, but also the economy between different fields), to make this inheritance of hyperbole as effective as possible. Coming out of this necessity which is paradoxical but broadly capable of formalization, out of this (*still* economic) rupture with the economy, this heterogeneity that breaks off analogy (by *still* lending itself to analogy to be understood)—this is how I would be tempted to interpret all the contributions which here so lucidly, and against all the prejudices, elaborate on the commitment of deconstruction, at any rate in the way that I try to practice and interpret it, with regard to science, technology, and Enlightenment reason. I am thinking in particular of the demonstrations offered by Christopher Johnson, Christopher Norris, and Arkady Plotnitsky.

For a long time now it has been possible to follow Norris's most original, determined, and acute work in countering numerous misunderstandings and a host of prejudices that are both tenacious and crudely polemical (the "relativism" or "skepticism" or "nihilism" or "irrationalism" of deconstruction, or its being "anti-Enlightenment," "prisoner of verbal language and rhetoric," "ignorant of the distinction between logic and rhetoric, philosophy and literature," and so on). It is no accident that Norris so often, and again in the text here, makes the case for a reexamination of the status of *analogy* in my work, and for a reworking of the problem of concept and metaphor. There is a strategy often privileged in all his writings which I find particularly judicious. It occurs here too, with an argument moving on through "White Mythology" in its relationship to Nietzsche, but also via Canguilhem, and Bachelard—and "The Supplement of Copula." And I find particularly effective the resituation of the demonstrative handles he proposes with regard to Anglo-American developments which his work has been helping me to read and understand (Davidson, for example) for a long time now. I am not shocked, even though it makes me smile, to see myself defined by Norris, in a deliberately provocative and ironic way, as a "transcendental realist." I said earlier why I did not think I had to abandon the transcendental motif. And the deconstruction of logocentrism and linguisticism and economism (the "own" and home, the *oikos* of the same), etc., as well as the affirmation of the impossible, have always come forward *in the name of the real*, of the irreducible reality of the real—not the real as an attribute of the *thing* (*res*), objective, present, sense-able or intelligible, but the real as a coming or event of the other, where it resists all reappropriation, even ana-onto-phenomenological appropriation. The real is this not negative im-possible, this im-possible coming or invention of the event, the thinking of which is not an onto-phenomenology. What this is about is a thinking of the event (singularity of the other, in its coming that cannot be anticipated, *hic et nunc*) that resists being reappropriated by an ontology or a phenomenology of presence as such. I attempt to dissociate the concept of event and the value of presence. It is not easy but I try to demonstrate this necessity, like that of thinking the event without being. In this sense, nothing is more "realist" than deconstruction. It is what or who comes along [*arrive*]. And that is not a matter of necessity in the face of the *fait accompli*: neither empiricism nor relativism. Is it being empiricist or relativist to take serious account of what comes along, as well as of differences of every kind, starting with the difference of contexts?

I don't wish to reduce the richness and the different directions of his analysis to this one thing, but I do find it equally interesting that Christopher Johnson, *also* following this thread of the analogy without analogy, should begin by setting apart the word *metaphor*. He writes: "The metaphor of writing, as it is articulated with the genetic and the biological in Derrida's texts, is not simply metaphor." After proposing "a more discriminating vocabulary," here the word *isomorphism*, he reorients the very premise of this choice (and he does this I think with great lucidity and assurance) toward another logic or another structure, that of "metaphorical catastrophe" that changes the whole scene and makes necessary a reconsideration of the structure of a semantic inversion or a conceptual classification. For instance: "not only is the term a germ, but the germ is, in the most general sense, a term." (It might perhaps be fruitful to cross this analysis with that of Karel Thein around "strong" or "weak" "germs" and the *sperma athanaton*.) This important analysis finds its privileged horizon in the so-called life sciences, biology and cybernetics (but without yielding to vitalism, as Johnson is right to stress); and we should certainly take account of this. But is that only Johnson's choice (not that it has prevented him from opening up a rich and varied field of questioning)? Or rather, taking on board what he says at the end of the piece about the "open" system and its limit, about the necessity of including your own discourse as an example of the system described (and "more than an example," he adds: I would have wanted to ask him to help me think through this "more than an example")—can what he demonstrates be extended then to other sciences, sciences that would no longer be life sciences? Can it, for instance, be extended in the direction indicated by the article here and by so many other persuasive writings by Arkady Plotnitsky concerning the relationships between deconstruction and the physical or mathematical sciences? (This impressive reflection on the folds, positions, points, and counterpoints of a particular "Hegelian" inheritance of deconstruction does show Plotnitsky's insistence on what he has long considered a "conceptual" proximity between quantum mechanics—especially as interpreted by Niels Bohr—and a certain theoretical strategy, a certain relationship to the calculated risk in deconstructive practice. The motif of "strategy" moreover receives a degree of attention that I consider justified and crucial.)[33]

I also wonder, without at all wanting to make this an objection, how to determine the "outside" of science that Johnson refers to, and what name to give to what he calls a "*position* outside *of science*." He recognizes the intention, rightly attributed to me, of moving beyond a certain frontier of scientific discourse, "by taking the notion of the open system to its logical limit, including his own discourse as an example, and more than an example, of the system he describes." Is this still a philosophical gesture, as Johnson seems to think it is—"the critical mission of philosophy"? Or is it a move that also goes beyond the closure of philosophy, so that philosophical discourse is in this respect on the same side as scientific discourse? I confess I have no simple, stable answer to this question. And that is also a result of the somehow invaginated structure of this limit, this form of frontier that, if I can put it like this, includes the outside in the inside without integrating it. Plotnitsky articulates well the paradoxes of the limit in this connection. Sometimes, I think I have to determine certain limits to scientific discourse in the name of classical philosophical requirements (transcendental, phenomenological, ontological). More often, it is in the name of something I call, for the sake of convenience, "thought" [*la pensée*] (as distinct from either knowledge, philosophy, or faith) that I seek this position of exteriority. But this word *thought* isn't wholly satisfactory to me, for several reasons. First, it recalls a Heideggerian move (*Das Denken* is neither philosophy nor science nor poetry nor faith) which does interest me very much, and the need for which I can quite see, but which I don't completely subscribe to, especially when it supports declarations of the type "Science does not think." Second, I'm not unreservedly happy either with the traditional semantics of the word *pensée*—with its figural aspect or etymological values (weight, examination, etc.). Lastly, I have been trying for a long time, and not in so simple a way as some overhasty readers have thought, to justify the statement that says, "In a certain sense, *thought* means nothing. . . . This thought has no weight. It is, in the play of the system, that very thing which never has weight."[34] Yes—"in a certain sense," at least.

As one can tell in advance, this is not only a matter of labels, titles, or terminology. When Johnson needs to use three words—thought, philosophy, and science—to situate the most obscure frontier difficulty, he is good at pointing out the awkward efforts I try to make both to mark *and to pass beyond* these frontiers.[35] To pass them in the sense in which *passer*, "pass," means to exceed or surpass, to pass over to the other side—to exceed the limit by confirming it, by taking it into account; but also the sense in which *pass* means not to let oneself be stopped at a frontier, not take a frontier as a frontier, as an uncrossable opposition between two heterogeneous domains. This double "logic" of the limit—that's what I would have liked to try to formalize here via the "replies" I have been sketching out, from one aphoristic sequence to another. Thus I think that the orders of thought and philosophy, while they cannot be reduced to the order of scientific knowledge, are nonetheless not simply external to it. Both because they receive the essential from it, and because, from the other side of the limit, they can have effects on the inside of the field of science (elsewhere I have also tried to connect the order of "faith" to this, too).[36] Scientific progress or scientific inventions also respond to questions of a philosophical "type." This is why I will never say, "Science does not think." I cannot but be most grateful to Johnson, Norris, and Plotnitsky, not only for having understood, argued, and elaborated on this, but for having done this each time in a new way. Like all the writers in this collection, they have taken on board the necessity of this and explored it far beyond the point I could ever claim to have reached myself.

9

My Sunday "Humanities"

The movement of the heart in politics: at the moment of saying yes, almost without hesitation, and sending my best wishes to the new *L'Humanité*, I hold back my sighs.

What does it mean, *l'humanité*, in the back of my memory? An amazing word—what a history. And this offshoot of an unbelievable title, ever since Jaurès. For me, it's almost as if *L'Humanité* were ageless.

Awesome phrase, isn't it? This title has been there ever since newspapers have existed for me. Nothing else like it. If I had the time and the space to do it, I could go on endlessly commenting on a memorable and provocative sentence, the one which, in speaking of a future and not of a past, gives us the most to think about and do. In *Notre but* [Our Aim], written to present the new paper in 1904, Jaurès said this: "Humanity does not exist at all yet or it barely exists" ["*L'humanité n'existe point encore ou elle existe à peine*"].

Magnificent! Unbearable! Daring like that must awaken murderous drives in some people, and not only in Jaurès's murderers, even in those who murdered him again after his death.[1] They could not bear to see what they *think they know* hesitantly questioned—what they take as given and bandy about all the time on the subject of man, and of humanism. You can hear in this their heavy common sense: "You cannot say that"—say that "humanity does not exist at all yet or it barely exists"—"without already having a certain idea of man, and believing in it. The adequation of the thing to the concept may be yet to come, but not this idea of man."

Well it's true. Jaurès does not leave the content of humanity totally indeterminate. He says the "realization" of humanity is what "all socialists are working toward": "reason," "democracy," "common ownership of the means of production," "humanity reflecting its superior unity in the diversity of friendly and free nations."

Of course, of course. But at this level of abstraction (it's *abstraction* I'm going to talk about, good and bad abstraction), it is impossible not, simultaneously, to admit that what you think you have is not yet at your disposal in a sufficiently determined, sufficiently determining, or sufficiently decidable way: you are not yet in a position to determine the very figure of humanity which nonetheless you are announcing and promising yourself here. Otherwise it would not be a real promise; man would be already there, already given. Thus in all rigor you don't know what you think you know you want to say, in the name of humanity; you don't know what it is you are promising at the moment of the most serious of promises . . .

So Jaurès promises a humanity of which he seems unable to state the essential—unless, like Nietzsche had done it, in fact, not long before, in *The Genealogy of Morals*, it is that man is a promising animal, or to be more precise an animal capable of promising (*das versprechen darf*). A minimal definition: it means very little, unless some revolution comes along and invents both the promise and fidelity to the promise. Tell me, isn't that the revolution—ethics and politics, responsibility, decision?

Humanity? I often quote—at the risk of repeating myself—a statement of Austin's. He says more or less this: a "word" means nothing; only sentences mean something. Well what I'd like to do is to make a bouquet to send my good wishes to *L'Huma* (the newspaper of tomorrow, the one that also, despite its great age, and like "humanity," doesn't exist yet or barely exists)—a bouquet that will get people to say "that does it! [*c'est le bouquet*]," a garland gathering together a few typical or unusual sentences that would still mean something around the word *humanity*. As if, to give a pledge of political friendship (the "from-the-heart movement"), I was spending my Sunday morning doing the homework of a student who had decided to study "humanities." Or as if for once I was replying to the classic question from the caricature journalist: "So for you, Jacques Derrida, humanity today is what? What does *humanity* mean?" (A reply ordered in *ten points* [that are not commandments], and ten sheets of paper.)[2]

The replies, then:

1. *L'Humanité* is the title of a major *French* newspaper. (Let's keep in

reserve, here, tons of possible commentary, dangerous and fueled by history, on this epithet: French enough? Too French? Why so French? At what moment in France's history? Give us dates! Which France? In which Europe? Is it possible to imagine a more "French" paper, but with a more universal title? And so on.) *L'Humanité* is also the proper name (even though it's the commonest one in the world) for the newspaper that has gone through the greatest number of historical experiences in the twentieth century, but without abandoning what it is called. No other paper has real militants, and who are disinterested, and thus strangers to any concern for making money, if not to the market altogether. (Jaurès, at any rate, also promised this: "The paper's independence is total. The capital investments . . . have been underwritten with no attached conditions at all. . . . To sustain a large newspaper without it being at the mercy of any business group is a difficult problem, but not an insoluble one.") It was during the worst period of Stalinism, a time of great suspicion for me, that I started meeting and getting to know these people selling *L'Humanité dimanche* [Sunday *L'Humanité*] on the street and door-to-door. They worked with a devotion, with a form of conviction, that will always give the lie to those confusions of analogy which, on the supposed grounds that they do belong to the same configuration and the same historical possibility, draw parallels between the totalitarian corruption of communism and the other European totalitarianisms. My respect for this militantism has not altered—a militantism I know I am incapable of myself, alas, in this case, for hundreds of reasons and with a bad conscience that there is no need to display here today.

2. *L'Humanité* is the name of the only French newspaper for which all men and women on the left agree to write a guest article at one time or another, however irreconcilably radical their disagreement, at one moment or another, with the dominant line of the [French] Communist Party, though they know *L'Huma* is its newspaper. That means at least two things, which it is important to remember today, more than ever:

a. There has always been a certain space of play between a kind of center or centralism of the politics of the Communist Party (throughout its history) and the cultural politics (plural or less monolithic practices) of some communists. This sort of play has always been the place and the chance of a transformation of political dogmatism.

b. Another space of play, another space of liberty: All the noncommunist parties on the left, and still today, pursue a politics that leaves a margin of dissatisfaction that is more or less well articulated among all those who, even if they think they have good reasons for not belonging to the Communist Party, maintain the wish to signal this discontent by writing in *L'Huma* rather than anywhere else. (The impasse over immigration and the undocumented, or national education, today fastens onto two of many possible examples of this margin for dissatisfaction, but they are highly symbolic ones.) Together with *Libération* (but in comparison, this is a very young paper), *L'Humanité* often represents the dream space, and a left margin for people who don't all the time believe in the arguments for "realism" or "pragmatism" on the part of social democrats, both French and European.

3. Humanity (still the "promise"), the humanity of mankind, is still a very new concept for philosophers who aren't sleepwalking. The old question about what is specifically human needs to be entirely reworked. Not only in relation to the life sciences, not only in relation to what is called by that general, homogeneous, and confused word, "the *animal,*" but also in relation to all the traits that metaphysics restricted to humans, of which *not one* is resistant to analysis (by definition this list is indefinite; I won't enter into it here for lack of space: the journalist in me is starting to get impatient).

4. Humanity is obviously the humanity of both men *and* women. Still, one opens one's eyes wide at the learned authority of those, male or female, who, in 1998, discovered America—by which I mean phallogocentric hegemony.[3] There they were claiming the patent, the paternity or maternity, of the discovery, explaining why your daughter doesn't speak. Well of course, if there were a referendum today, I would vote *against* those who are *against* what we call in France parity (what a word!). Which is another way of saying, unfortunately, that I am not overconvinced by the discourses—of those who attacked this concept, of course, but no more by those who produced and supported it in what was one of the most underhand possible Paris debates, with cheap shots, poisonous unspoken statements, unanalyzed resentment, and knives drawn (and as to who started it, we won't be finding that out in the near future).

As a result, faced with an alternative so badly expressed and so badly thought out, I would prefer, for my part, not to have to choose ("I would prefer not to," as Melville's Bartleby would say). So it remains true that if I was forced (which is basically the situation now, unfortunately) to vote according to a binary choice between two possibilities of which neither one is satisfactory to me, I couldn't then do anything other than calculate what was not so bad or the lesser evil: so go for parity. A purely French lesser evil, in truth, not to say a Parisian one, and so unamenable to universalization (so much is said, and so lightly, of universality on both sides) that plenty of other European democracies have managed to reach or come near to the result that was sought without a constitutional modification of this type: through a real political struggle, through effective mobilization, through the votes of men and women citizens. The trap of the constitutional debate signifies that no one trusts in their own political forces. As if the parties on the left and the president of the Republic had to stand with their backs to the wall and dose themselves with a constitutional medicine for an evil that they go on liking and that they cannot or will not cure themselves of.

But once one has voted, as I would, for the lesser evil, once one has taken account of France (or the French male) being so far behind, and thus of the urgency of fighting this effectively; once one has seen the specifically political powerlessness of the parties to transform the situation (so this includes the powerlessness of the parties of the present majority, which would have had no need to look for a strange constitutional provision if they had wanted—with that energetic "will" people talk about, which would indeed have been, and will remain, indispensable—to utilize the political and legal means that were already at their disposal)—well, one still maintains the right, without necessarily suspecting anyone's conscious good intentions, to discern symmetrical and equally reactive symptoms, signs of political "demobilization," *on both sides*: on the part of those who attack and also of those, men and women, who support this thing for which such a cringe-making and equivocal word has been found, the word *parity*—as if *equality* wasn't good enough. Besides, why limit this so-called parity to elections?

So there is a shared misrecognition of what *good* abstraction, abstract universalism, must signify and guarantee in the constitution of the juridical or civic subject. In one case, arguing from republican principles and indivisible sovereignty, it is believed necessary to ignore or subordinate sexual differences (in the plural). The old phallocentric strategy is thereby reproduced and upheld, and we know the result of that, at least the French result—big, if I may say so, like the nose in the middle of a face.

On the other side, sexual difference (in the singular) is being reintroduced into civic responsibility and the subject of law. It is determined as the decisive trait in a division, even an opposition, that is calculable, in other words automatized and homogenizing (whereas an elementary version of deconstruction long ago showed that difference as an oppositional duality tends to homogenize, in other words to continue to play the game of phallocentrism and to delete all sexual differences—and this silent will to delete remains, I think, what the two discourses of raging resentment that are at war in Paris have as their common signature). Thus a constitutional status is given to the measurable competition between two sexes. This fails to recognize the progress that, through *good* abstraction, was made by the inclusion of human subjects of *any sex* (even if there were more than one or two in each person, and even if people sometimes changed sex without authorization and without surgery or hormone treatment) in a Constitution which, furthermore, and let's not forget it, stipulates equality and nondiscrimination. There is thus reason to fear that this rush to constitutionalism (which may also—it's so vague—remain a dead letter, an alibi or virtual fetish) may for some considerable time produce what are called perverse effects. Everywhere: (1) *both* in media rhetoric, unless the "deconstruction" that is referred to so readily, and began so long ago, in this connection, is not conducted with more rigor or finesse, more prudence and effectiveness; (2) *and* in people's unconscious minds as long as the real political work has not been done, and that will take time; (3) *and* above all, in elections, in the concrete determination of electoral law, that moment of truth, at least if it gets enacted. To be continued, then.

At any rate, it's not going to be possible right away to dispense with a deconstruction that is ongoing now and finally worthy of the name. Nor to isolate a "French" solution; it will surely be necessary—it already is—to rework the old concept of *indivisible sovereignty*, whether in relation to the nation-state or the political subject.

The concept of inalienable sovereignty can certainly still maintain a degree of value, here and there, and some good "effects." But even where, for the time being—and this is a huge problem—it remains *linked* to the dominant concepts of democracy or the republic, this archaic link is neither natural, nor essential, nor eternal. "Sovereignty" remains a theological inheritance that has not really been secularized. Today (and how can we pretend not to see this and fail to recognize its most serious consequences), it is subject to a worldwide shake-up in which humanity is in search of itself. At any rate, it is there, in this concept of sovereignty (either indivisible or "partially" divided) that phallogocentric theology has always built its nest. Apropos: how should parity be treated in the most crucial cases, where the indivisible sovereignty of the state is embodied in a single person, a single electoral mandate—which would par excellence, but not only, mean the presidency of the Republic? Alternation, couple, marriage, Pacs?[4] And why should parties be the ultimate instances (with or without a law of proportional representation) in the deciding of candidacies to stand for actual elections to office? The concept of sovereignty plays a role in this debate that is still determinant. It has been obvious for a long time in relation to an insistent immobility and to phallogocentric patriarchy, but now it is also being sketched out on the other side, in some kinds of discourse, in the somnambulant form of a fantasy of maternal sovereignty: the woman determined, in her essence, as mother—and who could choose to be that herself, naturally, all on her own. With a little note of heterosexual normalization here and there, which is confusing. Always the same symmetry, the same mirror logic, the same fantasy. For as regards humanity at least, sovereignty has only ever run on fantasy, whether we are talking about the nation-state, its leader, the king or the people, the man or the woman, or the father or the mother. It has never had any other theme or motive, this thing called sovereignty, than that old fantasy that sets it going. An omnipotent fantasy, of course, because it is a fantasy of omnipotence. For those who prefer more refined or scholarly languages, the word *sovereignty* has only ever translated the performative violence that institutes in law a fiction or a simulacrum. Who wants to create belief in sovereignty, and in whom? In the sovereignty of anything or anyone, the Nation-State, the People, the King, the Queen, the Father, or the Mother? For example.

5. Humanity remains a problematic concept, certainly. Although "humanity does not exist at all yet or it barely exists" (Jaurès), it must be possible to declare without contradiction (or by learning the most responsible way to take on board that contradiction) that the concept of "human rights" has always been and will always be in the process of being determined. Thus both as concept and as reality it is still, for the most part, to come. The same is true for the even more obscure concept of "crime against humanity" (1945, Nuremburg trials, etc.).

These are instances of irreversible progress that change the world, and represent what Kant would call the sign that the progress of humanity is *possible.* So they have to be reaffirmed, and all the practical consequences must be drawn from them—improvements in international law, international courts of law, tasks that are so difficult but so necessary, and so on. But this must be done without however ceasing to meditate on the relative indeterminacy of the concept of man that is involved here, and without ceasing to deconstruct the stupidities and the dogmatic ideas that circulate on this subject. On the contrary, it is because these concepts are not natural, because they mark advances that are irreversible but only relative, that their rigor needs to be questioned and sharpened.

6. Humanity is also what I have called the horizon of a "new international."[5] It reaches beyond that Europe that all the competing discourses still present within the rhetoric of *sovereignty*: "loss of sovereignty" fears "Pasqua" for instance; "gain in sovereignty," rather (in the competition with the United States) replies, for instance, "Strauss-Kahn": the same language, basically—always the theo-logic of sovereignty.[6] The "new international" reaches even beyond cosmopolitanism—which still, via citizenship, assumes sovereignty of the nation-state type—even beyond the schema of fraternity.[7] As regards the Europe that is currently in the process of formation, a criticism of the market that is conventional, magical, and incantatory, a straightforward denunciation of European monetary union, seems pretty inadequate. Sometimes it sounds childish and animistic. No denial will be weighty enough: there exists and there will exist the market, the euro, the banks, and capital. Another kind of left-wing expertise is therefore necessary, and new skills. They are still rare; you don't hear them often in politicians' rhetoric.

7. Humanity, whether in relation to the new bio-genetic technologies, or to multimedia virtualization, or to the new public space, will be a new "spectral" beyond of the opposition of life and death, and presence and absence. And of the opposition of private and public, and state or civil society and family.

8. Plural humanity is also the issue for the old and young humanities subjects, which are under threat more than ever before in secondary education, research, and the universities. The humanities (language and the book; works of philosophy, literature, and the arts, etc.) remain the last place where the principle of free speech or free thought can still *be presented* as such. The same is true of the principle of a "question of man," freed from old presuppositions; it is true of new Enlightenments, of a *forever irredentist resistance* to the powers of economic, media, and political appropriation, to dogmatism of every kind.[8]

9. Humanity is the theme of critical but not reactive reflection on what is called globalization.[9] Globalization does resemble humanization, but beneath this word and this rhetoric it often hides the strategies of new forms of capitalist imperialism. Questions such as: "What is the world?" "What is the philosophical, theological, and political history of this concept of *world*?" "Why do we sometimes say *mondialisation* and at other times *globalisation*, and so on?" "In what language do we name and do this thing?" "Why is this globalization also the universal theater of confession,

repentance, etc.?" These questions outline a number of tasks for a decon-struction that would be more than a critique.

10. The humanity of the "humanitarian" calls for tasks of the same order. It is certainly a good thing that the sovereignty of the nation-states is outflanked by humanitarian initiatives (NGOs), but we have to con-tinue to be vigilant in the face of hegemonic phenomena that can still, un-der the aegis of the humanitarian, set up all kinds of scrutiny exercises (po-litical, governmental, and capitalist—and at either international or national level).

11. Sunday humanity. If my Sunday was endless, I would like in the same "spirit" to examine the great question of "work." "Shared ownership of the means of work," said Jaurès, once again. Between two supposed "ends of work," for tomorrow's humanity: first, the biblical and doloristic one of Augustine's *City of God* (liberty finally sovereign; the day of the Lord; sabbatical and dominical rest that knows no more evening; the end without end of work and of the expiatory sentence); and second, that of Je-remy Rifkin, who, in his book *The End of Work*, points out some virtually indisputable givens about the possible effects of the fourth technological revolution—but unfortunately without changing the language.[10] Let's not forget that as early as in the Christian Middle Ages there were people de-manding a reduction in working hours, while there were others who com-plained because they had no work.[11]

I'll stop—the interviewer is getting impatient. In the end, I'd rather proceed differently, take the time of my Humanities, not write like this and especially not bring things to a halt like this. What would have been best: neither to hold on to the last word nor to leave it to algebra or the telegram style. So, like Bartleby, I would prefer not to. One last word, how-ever—not mine, but that of the narrator, a lawyer—and these words, this last sigh, were also the last words of the book, Melville's *Bartleby the Scrivener*: "Ah, Bartleby! Ah, humanity!"

Sunday, February 22, 1999

10

For José Rainha: What I Believe and Believe I Know

On December 13, José Rainha, leader of the Landless Workers' Movement (MST) in Brazil,[1] has to appear before the tribunal of Vitoria (in the state of Espirito Sanro), to appeal a judgment condemning him to twenty-six and a half years of imprisonment with no remission, for murders. The circumstances of the first trial, like those of the trial in preparation, give rise to the worst fears (see *L'Humanité*, November 19, 1999). In order to prevent another mockery of justice, the support that is "demonstrated" for José Rainha can play an essential role.

What happened subsequently seems to have shown that this support was not ineffective.[2]

A few years ago—will I have the nerve to mention it here? (well I will, then)—I had the nerve to write a personal letter to President Cardoso. I thanked him at that time for having done what was necessary one Sunday, by phone, at the request of one of my Brazilian colleagues, so that a visa could be immediately delivered to me, at Santiago in Chile, where I was held up, enabling me to come to São Paulo the next day to give my lecture as advertised. I didn't know that, contrary to what everyone thought, French citizens required a visa to enter Brazil, for obscure convoluted reasons of diplomacy. This was a minor incident, of course. I'm embarrassed to mention it. At any rate it demonstrates that the perversions of little juridical-administrative machines can be foiled immediately, even from within a state, by a just decision.

Change of scale. Today, still without a visa or any special authorization, if I had the nerve (well I do, then) to write an open and public letter this time to President Cardoso, I would tell him what I believe and believe I know. I am dating my letter. It is the opening day of a summit on world trade. What will happen in it is fairly uncertain but I believe I know that it is already mobilizing, on the spot, as its inauguration, a large number of men, women, and nongovernmental organizations, all of them worried about what is in store for them under the name and the often confused, mystifying, and prechecked concept of "globalization."

I believe I am picking up there a signal whose echoes will continue to spread and increase. I believe that it is here that the large issues of tomorrow are to be found, if not the new "front" (since it will not only involve a war between states or even a war with recognizable features).

Now I believe I also know that the Landless Movement today represents one of those extremely revealing examples: a struggle against all the effects of submitting to the imperatives of the so-called ongoing globalization, and to the current logic of the IMF, probably one of the most powerful operators in this. Among the effects of this submission, I believe I know that in Brazil repressive measures, failures of justice, and failures to keep promises, and the like, are on the increase.

I believe I know that people are getting more and more worried about this: in Brazil itself, to begin with, of course (where I believe I have the right to believe on this point from many comparable testimonies, including that of the Episcopal Conference), and also far from Brazil. Like José Saramago, I believe that if there is any positive, irreversible, and undeniable effect of this globalization, it is minimally the legal rights shared by all the citizens of the world, and even, beyond the citizenship of nation-states, beyond the "sovereignty" so often invoked, the recognized right of anyone to be concerned and to have a voice in relation to any case of injustice.[3] For a long time I have believed it necessary to distinguish, as Saramago did in these pages a few days ago, between justice and law. But I also believe that for this very reason law has a history, and that justice must be incorporated into a transformation of juridical power. Therein lies the ethical and political responsibility of those who are mandated to "decide." That is where we judge their sensitivity to justice.

Now I think I also know, on the strength of so many testimonies, that in a political situation that is profoundly marked by the constraints of the global market, or at least by a particular interpretation and implementation of that "market," a terrifying injustice is in the process of taking place: the condemnation of José Rainha, one of the best-known representatives of the Landless Movement.

I believe I know that the trial and judgment against which he is appealing were falsified by many irregularities. At the same time the perpetrators of terrible repressive measures have been absolved, and you yourself, Mr. President, have apparently denounced this as an "injustice." Yet I believe I know that a court decided to take no account of the fact that on June 5, 1989, José Rainha was thousands of miles from the scene of the crime of which he is accused; for the past year he had no longer even lived in that country. I believe I know that many witnesses have confirmed this, including an army officer. I believe I know that the weapon used in the crime was not the one that the prosecution was claiming in its argument.

At any rate, and here *I no longer believe I know—I believe I can say* this in all certainty: this trial is also a political trial. Beyond the fate of one man, it will be interpreted throughout the world as a symbol of far-reaching importance. In relation to Brazil and also in relation to what is happening in the world of "globalization." People will seek to discern from this the chances for justice when statesmen calculate the strategies for which they have to be accountable and weigh up the political responsibilities that they have to take: within a large state but also, undeniably, in full view of the world.

That is what I believe and what I believe I would say to President Cardoso if I had the nerve (well I do, then) to address him with such familiarity—as I would the academic and the French colleague (which he also was) whose coming to power raised so many bright hopes.

11

"What Does It Mean to Be a French Philosopher Today?"

FRANZ-OLIVIER GIESBERT: What does it mean to be a French philosopher today?

JACQUES DERRIDA: Would you ask a scientist that question? In principle, a philosopher should be without a passport, even undocumented [*sans-papiers*]; he should never be asked for his visa. He should not represent a nationality, or even a national language. To want to be a philosopher, in principle and in relation to the most long-standing tradition, is to want to belong to a universal community. Not only cosmopolitan, but universal: beyond citizenship, beyond the state, and thus beyond even the cosmo*political.*

But at the same time, philosophy is always registered in idioms, starting with Greek. A philosopher's first obligation is perhaps not to refuse this trial, the most difficult trial possible: that of confronting the urgency of those universal questions (globalization, as we say, is just one of several), while insisting on signing in their own language, and even on creating *their own* language within their own language. This singular language, this idiomatic language, does not have to be pure, or even national.

Philosophers must take account of this history of their filiation. A "French" philosopher of the twentieth century is marked, whether he likes it or not, by the very distinctive formation he received in secondary school—there are not many countries that teach philosophy in secondary school—and at university, then afterward in a philosophical, literary, and political milieu that has no equivalent. Among other reasons, the "success" abroad of some philosophers of my generation stems from the fact of their remaining, each in their own way, very "French." In the 1960s there was a quite unique "French" configuration of philosophy (and lots of other disciplines—psychoanalysis, the human sciences, literature), and we are its actors or at any rate its heirs. The importance of what happened then has yet to be given its full weight and remains to be analyzed, beyond the phenomena of rejection or fashion that it continues to provoke.

For my part, I jealously watch over the singular idiomaticity of what I write. This is why some people consider my texts to be too "literary" and philosophically impure—starting with those whose concept of the universal is a bit simplistic and who think that philosophy has to be written in a sort of one-size-fits-all esperanto. It is true that idiom is resistant to translation. But it doesn't necessarily discourage it—in fact it often provokes it. It fosters reading and thinking and it also offers resistance to passive or lazy reading. I am lucky enough to be translated more or less everywhere—and not only in the United States, as some people would like to imagine or seek to make out. (*Laughter*)

GIESBERT: You are also rather hermetic. That's what is most often held against you.

DERRIDA: Hermetic? Definitely not. People who say that have obviously not tried to read other philosophers, such as the "classics." They're much more difficult. You have to work around thought and language. I do everything I can, as a duty initially, to be intelligible and widely accessible. But at the same time without betraying what in fact isn't simple in the things themselves. Everyone must do the same, mustn't they?—experts, doctors, journalists, politicians.

To come back to language. I am both very French (some would say too French) and not very French at all—for the reasons I have given and because fidelity to language presupposes that you treat it in a certain way. Out of love for the language, you sometimes have to do violence to a kind of dormant francophony.

GIESBERT: Your work has been translated into around forty languages. But you are still somewhat misunderstood in France. How do you deal with that?

DERRIDA: Just fine. But don't let's exaggerate. It is true that my work seems not to belong with a certain type of public notoriety. And often elicits rejection and hatred on the part of a certain academic or media family—sometimes crudely declared, sometimes more of an undertone. But

I'm far from being the only person in this situation. For some considerable time, these phenomena of rejection and misunderstanding have been the objects of analyses and critical evaluations which, by definition, are not visible or readable in the space occupied by academic or media authorities. Often it would be the last thing to cross the minds of the academics and journalists I mean, the functionaries of nonreading, that they too are analyzed and assessed dispassionately in places that, by definition, are not referred to in "their" public space.

GIESBERT: If your philosophy is the object of a sort of cult in the United States, isn't that because that is *the* country of deconstruction, par excellence?

DERRIDA: Forgive me for putting it like this to you, but this reference to the United States has become a cliché in relation to me, and I always wonder what it is that motivates this keenness to pack me off to the United States or confine me there. (I have said a lot about this elsewhere, for instance in *La Contre-allée*.)[1] This "deconstruction" interests people in places quite some way from the United States, and in many countries, European and non-European, it is often better received and understood, and not attacked so much. Nowhere more than in the United States does deconstruction give rise to "war."

Cult? No. Leaving aside a few quirks of fashion (which in fact have been going on for over thirty years, and likewise not only in the United States), the main thing there is is work, often original and influenced by traditions other than the "French." Apart from translation, some remarkable transplantations can be observed, active graftings onto different domains such as architecture, law, and the visual arts. And let's not act as if quirks of fashion were unknown in France. I don't believe there is a "country of deconstruction." And you should also recognize that in today's world the United States is not just one country among others. I have tried elsewhere to explain my views of the complicated relationship of the United States to deconstructions. Nor is there one "deconstruction," and what this word designates is not a doctrine or a speculative theory. Going far beyond the academy or "culture," it's the law of a sort of process that affects everything—the ideological, the political, the juridical, the economic, even the military; and so forth. On occasions when I have to be quick, like now, I often define deconstructions by saying, "It's what comes along [*arrive*: happens]," but also, "It is the possibility of the impossible."

GIESBERT: You have said that deconstruction consists in "undoing, de-sedimenting, decomposing, deconstituting sediments, assumptions, and institutions." You want to break everything up?

DERRIDA: No. If I now say that deconstruction "breaks nothing," you can see what I'm exposing it to. No, as you have just said yourself, it's not about destroying anything: only, and out of fidelity, trying to think how it came about, how something that is not natural is made: a culture, an institution, or a tradition. And then trying to analyze it through an act of memory but also to take account of everything that cannot be decomposed into simple elements or theoretical atoms (which is something that an *analysis* in the strict sense of the word can't do).

And then you must also do the history of analysis itself and the notion of critique—and even of deconstructions. Because there is also a tradition of deconstruction, from Luther to Heidegger (Luther was already speaking of *Destruktion* to refer to a sort of critique of institutional theology in the name of the original authenticity of the evangelical message). The "deconstruction" I attempt is not that deconstruction, it's definitely more "political" too, differently political; but it would take too many words to explain this. And some people might judge what I said to be hermetic, as you were saying.

GIESBERT: Can it not be said that your interest in politics is recent?

DERRIDA: That would be unfair, to say the least. It would be not to read, or to rely on appearances, from the titles of the most recent books, such as *Specters of Marx* (1993), *Politics of Friendship* (1994), or *Of Hospitality* (1997). It could be shown that that all began much earlier. But I had first of all to prepare the premises of a political discourse in harmony with the demands of a deconstruction, and avoid the prevailing codes and criteria that it's thought necessary to rely on for deciding whether or not a language is political. These shared codes often have a depoliticizing effect, which I try to avoid.

GIESBERT: Deconstruction is resistance?

DERRIDA: Yes—not yielding to the occupying power, or to any kind of hegemony. I have always dreamed of resistance—I mean the French Resistance. Going back to my childhood, and being too young to do it—to do some Resistance—I dreamed of it, I identified with the heroes of all the Resistance films: secrecy, bombs on the rails, capturing German officers, and so on. But deconstruction is not only an act of resistance; it also derives from an act of faith. It says "yes" to justice, for instance, which is not law.

GIESBERT: What do you mean?

DERRIDA: Law is deconstructed in the name of justice. Take for example "civil disobedience," in the United States or France. It's about objecting to a particular positive and national legality in the name of a superior law (such as the universality of the rights of man), or in the name of a justice that is not yet inscribed in law. The rights of man themselves have a history; they are always being enriched, and thus being de-limited. At any given time juridical limits can always be contested in the name of a justice yet to come. That does not come down to a plea for anarchy against institutions, or for a wild nature against the state. When you oppose a restrictive policy on "the undocumented [*les sans-papiers*]," for example, it's not a matter of demanding that the state open its frontiers to any new arrival and practice an unconditional hospitality that would risk causing perverse results (even though it conforms to the idea of pure hospitality, in other words hospitality itself). The state is simply being asked to change the law, and especially the way the law is implemented, without yielding to fantasies of security or to demagogy or vote seeking.

GIESBERT: What is your explanation for the return to religion that is occurring in so many parts of the world, but not in Europe?

DERRIDA: In Europe too! Is it a return? Church attendance aren't the only way of measuring religion. What gets called for short a "return," and is not confined to Islam, far from it, is marked above all by the appearance of "fundamentalisms" or "integration movements" that are aggressively "political." They seek either to contest the authority of the political or the state or else quite simply to subject democracy to theocracy. The thing needs to be analyzed in many dimensions. For instance, it would be difficult to explain the force of these movements if the concepts of the "political," the state, and sovereignty especially, weren't themselves concepts that are theological in origin. And hardly secularized at all. On the other hand, contrary to what is often thought, these "fundamentalisms" fit very well with the advances in technology and science. Iran is just one example. So it is a matter of actively opposing the modern technologies that result in delocalization, uprooting, and deterritorialization—and, simultaneously, of reappropriating them.

The so-called return of religion tries to go back to the literality of idiom, the proximity of home, the nation, the earth, blood, filiation, and so on. In order to spirit away the threat, you therefore incorporate it in yourself, by appropriating technology, telecommunications, internet access, the effects of globalization, and so on. A process of self-immunization. It destroys the organism that it thereby seeks to protect, and that is why, in the end, I do not believe in the future of these "fundamentalisms" as such, at any rate not in their political expression. But what is interesting to observe is this sometimes refined marriage of rationalism, even scientism, and obscurantism. But in the same way as I make a distinction between justice and law, I think you have to distinguish between faith and religion . . .

GIESBERT: The philosophy you put forward is a philosophy of freedom, hospitality, and cosmopolitanism. How do you react to the rise of new nationalisms?

DERRIDA: Oh! I am not putting forward any philosophy! Deconstruction is not a philosophy. As for freedom [*liberté*], let's leave that for another interview. I'm "for" it, obviously, but if we had the time and the space I would try to explain why it is that I use this word very soberly and actually quite rarely.

Those "new nationalisms" make an infernal couple with "globalization"—which is also a concept just as problematic as that of nationalism. I like cosmopolitanism, of course, and I think it should be cultivated, well beyond its Stoic or Christian traditions (the Christian tradition is really that of St. Paul), just as international law should be cultivated and improved. But where this notion still refers decisively to the state and to citizenship, even citizenship of the world, the world state, I wonder whether we should not go even further than cosmopolitanism—although without being against the state, since there are many situations where the state is still the best resource. Political decision making or responsibility thus consists in determining in which situations to be on the side of the state and in which against it.

GIESBERT: Are you a *mondialiste*, an internationalist?[2]

DERRIDA: We get asked to swallow a lot of things with that word *mondialisation* [globalization]. Of course, it's well known, there are many phenomena of homogenization, market unification, the permeability of frontiers, the speed and power of transnational communication, and so forth. But never in the history of humanity have there been so many victims of inequality and repression (economic, neocolonial, and other forms). Today the wealth of a few hundred families exceeds that of many overpopulated countries.

GIESBERT: Come on, the world has always lived under the sign of inequality!

DERRIDA: Well from that point of view globalization would be offering nothing new and it would be a lie to say that it changes the world order and human relationships. It's that notion of "world" [*monde*] and its history that I'm interested in, particularly its religious history. The world is neither the earth nor the universe nor the cosmos. Why do the English, the Americans, and the Germans speak of globalization and not (as the French do) *mondialisation*?

GIESBERT: How would you define nationalism?

DERRIDA: We have to separate off its modern form, where it is given its literal meaning by being linked to the recent but also short-term forms of the nation-state. Because of this essential fragility, this "crisis" of the nation-state, nationalism is a tightening up—reactive and, beneath its aggressive exterior, afraid. It is not content with recommending love of the nation (which is normal and legitimate and anyway impossible to suppress), but it inspires hegemonic plans and would like to subject everything to the national imperative or, as they say, and given that nationalism is still linked with the nation-state, to sovereignty.

GIESBERT: And your definition of sovereignty?

DERRIDA: That is what I was talking about just now in connection with the theological and political legacy. The word means omnipotence, self-determination of the will, unlimited and unconditional power. In absolute monarchies, the omnipotence of the sovereign, the incarnation of the nation, is divine right. Then this sovereignty was transferred to the people (but still a "sacred" sovereignty, Rousseau said in the *Social Contract*). This democratization or republican popularization did not erase theological filiation, I think. What is happening today in the world through all these contestations (themselves more or less problematical) of the sovereignty of nation-states (the Gulf War, Kosovo, Timor, and others) requires us to reconsider—to "deconstruct," if you will, and thus to reinterpret this legacy.

GIESBERT: Is it an idea which has a future?

DERRIDA: Yes and no. It will survive for a long time but divided, changing its shape and place. Even if it retains theological and Western roots, it remains indissociably linked, everywhere, to the values of freedom and self-determination. It is thus difficult, and even dangerous, to be too straightforwardly hostile to sovereignty. That is where a prudent and differentiated deconstruction must be differentiated from destructive criticism.

GIESBERT: What do you think of the growing demands for identity today?

DERRIDA: Who could be against "identity"? But like nationalism or separatism, pro-identity politics encourage a misrecognition of the universality of rights and the cultivation of exclusive differences, transforming difference into opposition. I have tried to show the way this opposition also tends, paradoxically, to erase differences. But it is also true that in situations of oppression or exclusion, "identity" movements or strategies can be legitimate, I think. Up to a certain point and in very limited conditions.

GIESBERT: How is philosophizing possible in the age of communications and the internet, when everyone thinks they know everything about everything?

DERRIDA: The internet has to be accepted. Besides, there is no way and no chance of doing anything else. Communication between philosophers is beginning to adapt to it. Even in teaching. Which destabilizes or marginalizes the classic institutions and modes of communication, sometimes dangerously. You find very good and very bad things on these new Web sites. It's a threat—with an "anything goes" bonus. But it is also a chance. That sometimes makes it possible to have instant discussions involving Tokyo and Paris, Helsinki and Sarajevo, and importantly without having to go via processes or systems of legitimation that are slow, heavy, discriminatory, and censoring. What worries me more than the technology itself in these exchanges is the increasing dominance of one language, and thus of one culture, the Anglo-American.

GIESBERT: It's a time of dialogue, exchange, and synergy. Isn't this why it is not possible to be a serious philosopher nowadays without doing psychoanalysis, history, literature, and linguistics all together?

DERRIDA: Is being connected or wired up enough to make you a good philosopher? Someone can think things essential for our time without having any taste for these knowledges and technologies or even any real competence around them. Heidegger never, I would imagine, took a plane or drove a car, and so on. He was a very bad typist and obviously he never used a computer. But you don't have to agree with what he says about technology to recognize, as I'm tempted to do, that he said some strong things, offering more to thinking about technology than many experts, technicians, and technologists. Having said that, it is better for philosophers to be theoretically and technically competent in the areas you have mentioned. Those we call the philosophers of the great tradition—Plato, Descartes, Leibniz, and Kant—had encyclopedic minds and lived closely with science. That is not true of the majority of French philosophers.

GIESBERT: You are very literary yourself.

DERRIDA: Am I "literary"? If that were the case, I would try to explain myself. But nothing can justify the limits of my scientific knowledge, which I admit with both regret and humility. In France, and especially in the twentieth century, the model of the writer-philosopher (Sartre, for my generation!) has been completely dominant. With some very negative results, but also an appeal to philosophy that it should go and look outside, beyond the official university disciplines (in the direction of politics, literature, painting, architecture, or the human sciences . . .).

GIESBERT: You are very famous abroad; can you tell us the state of French philosophy in the rest of the world?

DERRIDA: Without being chauvinistic: everyone can see that the philosophers who are most present—certainly the most influential, and at any rate the most taught and the most translated in the world today—are French thinkers of Levinas's or Lacan's generation, then that of Althusser, Foucault, Deleuze, Lyotard, and so on. In philosophy, or at the border between philosophy and a good number of other "domains," something singular and unprecedented happened in France, and only in France, over the course of the past forty years.

Why only in France? That would need a lengthy analysis and I won't try to do it off the cuff here. This is not a personal evaluation; I'm just reporting what is recognized as being the case more or less everywhere. And better abroad than in France.

Not Utopia, the Im-possible

THOMAS ASSHEUER: M. Derrida, you have always been engaged as a philosopher in current debates, such as the arguments around the New Right or in the Parlement international des écrivains [International Parliament of Writers].[1] Following the [1997] elections in Great Britain and France, can it be said that the political climate has changed? Can intellectuals take heart [*courage*] again after those years when they seemed to be paralyzed by cynicism or a posthistory stance?

JACQUES DERRIDA: Had "intellectuals" lost "heart"? There is no justification for saying so. In the past few decades, and at an unprecedented rate, they have had to take account of far-reaching transformations of the public sphere. The conditions for having a voice in the media or through distance technologies have been completely shaken up, exposed to endless deflections and reappropriations—political or economic. In fact every "responsible" citizen has needed a lot of courage to analyze these developments and try to act, while avoiding these traps.

All the more so when some of them sought to exploit these new media potentials for purposes of personal promotion; when they did it to fight for just causes, showing solidarity was often as difficult as ruling it out. Intellectuals have been more present and active than your question assumes, in every field of public life, in Europe and elsewhere, in places where political or government authorities were often paralyzed by outdated frameworks. Besides, if courage is a virtue, and also a virtue for intellectuals, still it's not the most specific quality that it would be appropriate to demand of an intellectual qua intellectual. An incompetent and irresponsible intellectual can have the courage to do the worst.

No more do I believe either that all "intellectuals" have been, as you suggest, "paralyzed by cynicism or a posthistory stance." It is very difficult for me to reply in just a few words to this question. We would have to agree on what you understood by "cynicism" or "posthistory," but also, if I had the time and space for it, to challenge the hasty assimilations that often circulate in this connection.

So I prefer, for the sake of economy, to confess my unease at the start of this interview, once and for all, without coming back to it again. This is all about the conditions made by the media and the public domain for intellectuals to speak. If for instance I say I refuse to get into a debate on this point ("cynicism," "posthistory," "the status of the intellectual," and so on) in four or five sentences, as has been suggested, will I be accused of taking refuge in silence or elitism? Will it be complacent, condescending, or unjournalistic to refer to published texts where I try to deal with these questions? In fact I think this would be the most "responsible" response. It could illustrate the historical difficulty I have just alluded to. What changes, and what needs to be changed, are the conditions of public speech. And with that the figure of the intellectual in the public domain.

To go more directly and simply now to what is at the center of your question—yes, the elections in Great Britain and France are a "good sign," the less bad sign. I say this with a great deal of prudence and moderation. Besides, in spite of one or two surface analogies upon which it is in some people's interest to insist, the last British "round" has a quite different historical meaning, a quite different "function" than the regular French alternation. The declared aims of the two new elected majorities (the Labour Party and the socialists) are also more different and perhaps incompatible than is often said. The same goes for the anxieties and hopes that they inspire. It is true that they can make it possible to hope for a more vigilant political and social resistance to the economism and monetarism that are coming to dominate the new spirit of Europe. But the "pragmatic" "realism" that both governments claim risks reproducing the very thing that they were claiming to break with. In relation to a certain concept of what is confusingly called globalization, to the supposed adaptation to the "market," to the politics of frontiers and immigration, and to plenty of other sensitive questions, I see lots of nuanced adjustments and changes of rhetoric (and this is not nothing), but no break with the immediate past. I confess that I still, today, find it extremely difficult to make my own judgment about the implementation of the French government's electoral promises, about the strategy of the supposedly "realistic" choices (the partial and at least nominal preservation of the "Pasqua-Debré" laws on immigration, the symbolic preservation of the names "Pasqua-Debré" meant to reassure voters on the right and even the far right, although they are claiming to change the content of the law; the closure of the Vilvorde factories, for instance—and so on). But it is true that the space will perhaps be a bit more (careful!) open for another kind of political discussion and for it to be expressed in public. The "style" does change a bit, it's true; the "politicians" in power certainly show themselves to be more open to questions of culture, research, and teaching—they say they are more aware of these issues. Let's wait and see . . .

ASSHEUER: Should we, as Richard Rorty for instance does, criticize the left for being too concerned with questions of cultural identity and for having forgotten the questions of social justice? How do you situate your own reflections on justice within these two trends when the question of whether they are related or not is currently dominating some debates within political philosophy?

DERRIDA: Here too it would be important to make precise distinctions. I don't believe that the entire "left" in general has been more concerned with cultural identity than with social justice. But if some who say they are on the left had been, they would have deserved Rorty's criticisms. On this point, and to that extent, I would agree with him.

For two serious risks would have been neglected. First, legitimate as it is under certain conditions and within certain limits, the claiming of cultural identity (and I place under this head all the many forms of "separatism") can sometimes feed right-wing "ideologies"—nationalist, fundamentalist, and even racist. Second, this claiming of identity can have the effect of reducing the importance of other struggles and seriously neglecting them—social and even civic forms of solidarity, and universal causes (meaning causes that are transnational and not just cosmopolitan, because the cosmopolitan still presupposes the categories of the state and the citizen, even if the citizen is a world citizen—we will come back to this). But why should it be necessary to choose between these two concerns (cultural identity and social justice)? They are two forms of concern for justice, two responses to forms of oppression and violence between unequals. It is doubtless very difficult to keep them both on the go and at the same rhythm, but you can fight on both fronts at once, the cultural and the social, if I can put it like that, and you have to. The task of an intellectual is to say so, to make available discourses and elaborate strategies that resist any simplistic choice between the two. In both cases, effective responsibility for an engagement ought to consist in doing everything to transform the existing state of law in both fields, between the two, from one to the other, the cultural and the social; and of inventing new laws, even if they always remain inadequate for what I call justice (which is not the same thing as law, even if it has to guide the history and progress of law).

ASSHEUER: In your book *The Other Heading*, you conceive of Europe as a political project.[2] Can we and should we continue to conceive of it this way after the long, hard discussions around the euro? Should we not rather say that Europe is in the process of becoming an enterprise defined only by monetary criteria, a sort of enterprise of coordination for the exchange of commodities?

DERRIDA: This is in fact the risk I have just been alluding to (economism, monetarism, "performative" adaptation to competitiveness on the world market, often on the basis of brief, supposedly scientific analyses). I think that what we need to do is indeed to set against that a resolutely political project. That's what is at stake in many of the sources of tension between the different European governments, and in each one of them, but also between the social forces that dominate Europe.

I will add a few clarifications, because you want us to speak about "intellectuals": the necessary resistance to economism or monetarism cannot take the form of damning incantations, or magical protestations, on a basis of incompetence, against an entity called the euro or wicked manipulative bankers. Even if we should not believe just anyone and anything on this subject, we should not either ignore the constraints of the laws of the market; they do exist, they are complex, and they require analyses of a kind that are not accomplished by the institutional "experts" themselves. Perhaps a different political logic should be set against the current liberal dogmas, but also a different socio-economic logic, one that is informed and convincing. The euro is perhaps not an "evil" in itself. There can be another kind of social and political implementation of the "transfer to the euro." Each European nation-state has its own calculations to make and its own responsibilities in this regard. Germany's and France's are especially serious, as you know. Lastly, even if, as you can certainly see, my sympathies go toward a political resistance (the resistance of a certain political Europe) to a Europe that would be no more than just the manager of its economy, nonetheless I am not wholly satisfied either by the concept of the "political" that underpins this discourse. It transfers onto Europe, and the frontiers of Europe, a tradition of the political, of the nation-state, and I would have plenty of questions and reservations about this. It's in what I have written on the subject.

ASSHEUER: You have yourself demonstrated very well, in *Specters of Marx*, that Francis Fukuyama's thesis of the end of history was refuted from the moment of its propagation, and even before. Liberal societies, which he praises, cannot resolve their social problems. What is more, "globalization" creates serious social problems in the world. Once again, then, the most important question is that of justice. Looking particularly at the global situation, what might be the contribution of philosophy? In *Specters of Marx* you speak of the "New International." Could you specify some ideas and political projects linked to this New International?

DERRIDA: I am thinking of a worldwide solidarity, often silent, but ever more effective. It is no longer defined like the organization of the socialist internationals (but I keep the old term *International* to recall something of the spirit of revolution and justice that was meant to unite the workers and the oppressed across national boundaries). It is not recognized in states or international organizations dominated by particular state powers. It is closer to nongovernmental organizations, to some projects called "humanitarian"; but it also goes beyond them and calls for a profound change in international law and its implementation.

Today this International has the figure of suffering and compassion for the ten wounds of the "world order" that I enumerate in *Specters of Marx*. It shouts about what is so little spoken of both in political rhetoric and in the discourse of "engaged intellectuals," even among card-carrying champions of human rights. To give a few examples of the form of the macrostatistics we so easily forget about, I am thinking of the millions of children who die every year because of water; of the nearly 50 percent of women who are beaten, or victims of violence that sometimes leads to murder (60 million women dead, 30 million women maimed); of the 33 million AIDS sufferers (of whom 90 percent are in Africa, although only 5 percent of the AIDS research budget is allocated to them and drug therapy remains inaccessible outside small Western milieux); I am thinking of the selective infanticides of girls in India and the monstrous working conditions of children in numerous countries; I am thinking of the fact that there are, I believe, a billion illiterate people and 140 million children who have no formal education; I am thinking of the keeping of the death sentence and the conditions of its application in the United States (the only Western democracy in this situation, and a country that does not recognize the convention concerning children's rights either and proceeds, when they reach the age of majority, to the carrying out of sentences that were pronounced against minors; and so on). I cite from memory these figures published in major official reports in order to give some idea of the order of magnitude of the problems that call for an "international" solidarity and for which no state, no party, no trade union, and no organization of citizens really takes responsibility. Those who belong to this International are all the suffering, and all who are not without feeling for the scale of these emergencies—all those who, whatever civic or national groups they belong to, are determined to turn politics, law, and ethics in their direction.

ASSHEUER: All these reflections ask the question of whether there is still some validity to the categories of the right and the left. What do you think?

DERRIDA: I consider this opposition to be more necessary and more effective than ever before, even if it is true that the criteria and the splits are becoming extremely complex in this regard. For instance: it is true that one part of the left and one part of the right are objectively in alliance *against* Europe and *against* the euro, as they seem to be going to be—sometimes in the name of "national" values, sometimes in the name of a social politics, and even both at once. With the same rhetoric, with a discourse that wants to respect the "national" as much as the "social," there is also another part of the left and another part of the right that are in alliance *for* Europe and *for* the euro. On both sides, the logics and rhetorics are very similar, even if the forms of implementation, the practice, and the interests all diverge. So, to make a brief and elliptical response to a question that would call for long expansions, I would say that the left, for me, the left where I would resolutely want to recognize myself, is situated on the side where today people are analyzing the troubling and new logic of this equivocation and trying to make real changes to its structure; and also to the very structure of politics, the reproduction of this tradition of political discourse.

The starting point for that is a minimal axiomatic principle: the desire to affirm the future, to change, and to change in the direction of the greatest possible justice is on the left. I would not say that any right wing is insensitive to change and justice (that would be unjust), but the right never makes that the first source or the axiomatic principle of its action. To go back to distinctions that are not out of date, despite the far-reaching transformation of the very concept of work, the left will always make the value of "work" superior to the value of "capital." The right will always maintain that the second is the condition of the first. To be "on the right" consists of trying to conserve—but what? Even more profoundly than certain interests, powers, stocks of wealth and capital, social and "ideological" norms, and so on, more profoundly than a politics, the right will always try to conserve a certain traditional structure of the "political" itself, of the relationship between civil society, nation, and state, and so on. If one is holding to this opposition of left and right, it is not easy, I'm sure, to be consistently on the left, to be on the left every day. A difficult strategy.

ASSHEUER: Two of the essential problems of "globalization" are the passing away of the state and the weakness of politics. In your recently published text, "On Cosmopolitanism," you develop some ideas about a new right to asylum and a new separation of powers between the various places of politics, with regard to a possible new status for the city.[3] In what way do you think that philosophy could and should react to the problems mentioned? With a sort of institutional fantasy?

DERRIDA: I'm not sure I understand what you are calling an "institutional fantasy." Like this initiative of cities of refuge, despite its limits and its barely preliminary nature, all political experimentation has a philosophical dimension in itself. It makes it obligatory to ask effective questions about the essence and history of the state. Every political innovation relates to philosophy. "True" political action always engages a philosophy. Every action and every political decision ought to invent their own norms or rules. Doing that goes through or implies philosophy.

Now, at the risk of seeming to contradict myself, I think on the one hand you have to be active against what you call the "passing away of the state" (the state can still, sometimes, set limits to private forces of appropriation, concentrations of economic powers, and it can restrain a violent depoliticization occurring in the name of the "market"). But also, on the other hand, you have to resist the state where it is too often soldered to the nationalism of the nation-state or the representation of socio-economic hegemonies. Every time you must analyze, and invent a new rule: in one case you should challenge the state, in another consolidate it. Politics is not coextensive with states, contrary to what is almost always thought. The necessary repoliticization must not be in the service of a new cult of the state. We have to bring about new dissociations and accept complex and differentiated practices.

ASSHEUER: You often stress that your philosophy proceeds by paradoxes. You show precisely how the familiar philosophies of justice or friendship lead to aporias, but at the same time the claim for an unconditional justice or the idea of a "wholly other" friendship always return in your arguments. Are you not afraid that your philosophy might discourage any political project from the outset, given that the risk of an aporia or a paradox is always being outlined? In relation to your own political commitment: would you say that it is a commitment against or in spite of your philosophy? Or should it be seen as a specifically deconstructive way of doing politics?

DERRIDA: Yes, I do all I can to try to adjust my "commitments" to the unconditional affirmation that runs through "deconstruction." It's not easy, and one is never sure of getting there. This can't ever be an object of knowledge or certainty. You mention discouragement, and like others I do feel that sometimes, but it's also I think a necessary trial to be gone through. If every project was a reassuring object, the logical or theoretical consequence of a knowledge that was guaranteed—euphoric, without paradox, without aporias, without contradiction, with no undecidability to be resolved—it would be a machine functioning without us, without responsibility, without decision, ultimately without ethics, or law, or politics. There is no decision or responsibility without the trial of aporia or undecidability.

ASSHEUER: The notion of "decision" occupies an essential place in your reflections. What is the place of decision in your conception of politics? Is it in some way the replacement for justice?

DERRIDA: It doesn't replace it—on the contrary, it is indissociable from it. There is no "politics" of law or ethics without the responsibility of a decision. In order for the decision to be just, it is not enough for it to apply existing norms or rules, but it must take the absolute risk, in each individual situation, of rejustifying itself, alone, as if for the very first time, even if it enters into a tradition. I can't now—we don't have the space—explain the discourse on the decision that I try to develop elsewhere. A decision, while it remains "mine," active and free, as a phenomenon, must not be simply the deployment of my potentials or aptitudes, of what is "possible for me." In order to be a decision, it has to cut off this "possible," tear up my history, and thus be first of all, in a particular and strange way, the decision of the other in me: coming from the other with regard to the other in me. Paradoxically, it must carry a certain passivity that in no way lightens my responsibility. These are paradoxes that are difficult to integrate into a classical philosophical discourse, but I don't think that a decision, if there ever are decisions, is possible in any other way.

ASSHEUER: If any political engagement runs the risk of falling into aporias, wouldn't it be more logical to say, "Let's forget the aporias and become pragmatic; let's do what has to be done; everything else is a sort of political metaphysics"?

DERRIDA: What you call "a sort of political metaphysics" would in my view be the actual forgetting of the aporias, something we often try to do. But aporias can't be forgotten. What kind of "pragmatics" would it be that consisted in avoiding contradictions, problems that apparently have no solution, and so on? Don't you think that this supposed "pragmatics," realistic or empiricist, would be a sort of metaphysical reverie, taking those words in their most unrealistic and imaginary senses?

ASSHEUER: Should we say that the aporias you observe are tragic? And if so, should it not be recognized that any discourse in a history that is always "tragic" implies connotations that are fairly problematic politically? Isn't this a sort of metaphysics of history?

DERRIDA: It's true, I do often feel these aporias as if they were tragic pains, meaning "tragic" in a slightly vague and everyday sense (terrifying debates, being besieged by a contradiction, the feeling that whatever is done it won't be satisfactory, won't be equal to a demand that is infinite, and that in any case will take a heavy toll). But beneath this "tragic feeling," what you have is the opposite of a "metaphysics of history" and a "tragedy" (in the sense of fatalism and submitting to destiny). Instead what I feel there is rather the enabling condition of questioning, action, and decision—of resistance to fate, providence, or teleology.

ASSHEUER: Your philosophy is manifestly ambiguous toward the hopes of the *Aufklärung* [Enlightenment]. On the one hand, you have contributed to a strong critique of the notions of subject, spirit, and so on, and you extend this to a problematics of the axiomatics linked to these notions. On the other hand, you more and more frequently stress the importance of a certain idea of emancipation that you don't hesitate to attribute to the *Aufklärung*. Do you see an ambiguity of this kind in your thinking? What are the political consequences of such an ambiguity if it exists? Is the idea of democracy also subject to this ambiguity?

DERRIDA: Yes. To be more precise: What is forever ambiguous is at the least the irreducible gap, the always indisputable lack of adequation between the "idea of democracy" and what occurs in reality under that name. This "idea" is not however an "idea in the Kantian sense," at once a governing idea and one that is infinitely distant. It governs the most concrete urgency, here and now. If nonetheless I still cling to this old noun *democracy* and speak so often to the "democracy to come," it is because I see in it the only word for a political regime that, because it carries conceptually the dimension of inadequation and the to-come, declares both its historicity and its perfectibility. Democracy authorizes us in principle to invoke these two openings in public, quite freely, in order to criticize the current state of any so-called democracy.

ASSHEUER: You wrote an impressive book, *Specters of Marx*, with the central point that these specters don't just return, but that they were always among us. If we recognize that at least a part of Marxism consisted in a totalitarian enterprise, then what can specters teach us? Should we not be afraid of those totalitarian specters returning along with the others that we perhaps desire?

DERRIDA: Of course we should be afraid of that—it's one of the lessons to be drawn from the experience of totalitarianism and the terrifying failures of Soviet Marxism. But this vigilance must not become a pretext or alibi for rejecting everything we learned from Marx and that he can still teach us, if we are willing not to yield to what is easy and to age-old repetitions. On this let me again refer to *Specters of Marx* and other books (not only by me). It really is too difficult for a brief response.

ASSHEUER: Since the auto-critique on the part of the left, there has been no more utopian thinking. The conservative critique of culture has done the rest. Your philosophy, we think, doesn't want to give up entirely on utopia, but it doesn't utter the word. Should we see a new name for utopia in the "event" or the "wholly other"?

DERRIDA: Utopia has critical powers that we should probably never give up on, especially when we can make it a reason for resisting all alibis and all "realistic" or "pragmatic" cop-outs, but all the same I'm wary of the word. There are some contexts in which *utopia*, the word at any rate, can be too easily associated with dreams, or demobilization, or an impossible that is more of an urge to give up than an urge to action. The "impossible" I often speak of is not the utopian. Rather, it gives their very movement to desire, action, and decision: it is the very figure of the real. It has its hardness, closeness, and urgency.

ASSHEUER: The question of stateless people and refugees seems to you one of the most urgent of the global problems of capitalism that you analyzed in *Specters of Marx*. In your recent texts, one can find a subject that was also central to the thinking of Hannah Arendt (who in fact appears in *The Monolingualism of the Other* [and in *Of Hospitality*]): the absolute valuation of unconditional hospitality. In what way might such a hospitality lead to responses to the problems of the refugees of global society?

DERRIDA: Unconditional hospitality is inseparable from a thinking of justice itself, but as such it remains impracticable. It cannot be written into the rules or in a piece of legislation. If one wanted to translate it immediately into a policy, it would always carry the risk of having perverse effects. But even as we watch out for these risks, we cannot and must not abandon the reference to hospitality without reservations. It is an absolute pole, outside which desire, the concept, and experience, the very thought of hospitality, would be meaningless. Once again, this "pole" is not an "Idea in the Kantian sense," but the place from which immediate and concrete matters of urgency are dictated. The political task then remains of finding the best "legislative" transaction, the best "juridical" conditions to bring it about that in a given situation the ethics of hospitality are not in principle violated—and are as far as possible respected. For that, you have to change laws, habits, fantasies—a whole "culture." That is what is being looked for at the present time. The violence of xenophobic or nationalistic reactions is also the symptom of it. Today the task is as urgent as it is difficult: everywhere, but especially in a Europe with the tendency to close up on the outside to the extent that it claims to be open on the inside (the Schengen agreements). International legislation is in need of an overhaul. The concept and the experience of "refugees" in this [twentieth] century have undergone a mutation that makes both the policies and the law radically out of date in that connection. The words *refugee, exile, deportee, displaced person*, and even *foreigner*, have changed their meanings; they call for another discourse and another kind of practical response, and they change the whole horizon of what is "political" in citizenship, of what it means to belong to a nation or a state . . .

ASSHEUER: What should be done if the "laws of hospitality" (if there are such things) do not attain the status of actual laws? In such a situation wouldn't there just be an act of grace? Citizens with no civil rights?

DERRIDA: Everything possible must indeed be done to get the laws of hospitality written into actual law. When that is not possible, everyone must judge in their own soul and conscience, often "privately," what must be done (when, where, how, up to what point) without the laws or against them. To clarify: When some of us called for "civil disobedience" in France, on the subject of the reception of undocumented immigrants (and for a small number of us—for instance in my seminars, but in public—this happened more than a year before the press was talking about it and the number of protesters grew spectacularly high), it was not a demand to transgress the law in general, but to disobey laws that seemed to us to be themselves in contradiction with the principles inscribed in our Constitution, with international agreements, and with human rights, and so with a law that we judge higher, if not unconditional. When, under certain restricted conditions, we call for "civil disobedience," it is in the name of this higher law. But I wouldn't reject the word *grace* (a gift with no conditions and no return), which you have just offered me, provided that it is not associated with obscure religious connotations that, however interesting they might sometimes be, would call for other discussions.

ASSHEUER: What is the advantage of a thinking of hospitality compared to other universal moral concepts? Would it be possible to say that it is less abstract and more suitable for thinking a justice that must always address itself to a singular other?

DERRIDA: Yes, I would agree with that formulation. Bearing in mind what I was suggesting just now (the new problems to do with frontiers, the nation-state, the displacements of populations, and so on), today the theme of hospitality is a focus for those matters of urgency that are the most concrete and also the most appropriate for articulating ethics onto politics.

ASSHEUER: If, for reasons of legal security, one did not wish to place confidence in a form of hospitality as moral demand, then in what respect is unconditional hospitality linked to a worldwide juridical order? Do you conceive of a sort of worldwide civic law (Kant's cosmopolitan law) for all humanity? But how can such a law be conceived of without having recourse to a world state, where there would immediately be the question of the authority legitimating it?

DERRIDA: These are problems I have been closely bound up with in my teaching for many years. Reference to Kant is both indispensable and insufficient. A cosmopolitan law (*Weltbürgerrecht*) to govern what Kant called a "universal hospitality" would already, today, constitute the prospect of a huge advance if our authorities for interstate relations wanted to make it real, which is far from being the case. And yet Kant sets plenty of limits and conditions to the exercise of this right (granted only to citizens as such, so from one state to another, and only as a visiting right (*Besuchsrecht*), not a right of residence (*Gastrecht*)—except in the case of individual treaties between states, as with the Schengen European agreements).

We should invent a law (but also a law just beyond the law) to take away these limits. We should invent legitimating authorities that are no longer simply state-based or contracts between states, that are capable of fighting against the hegemony of some states. But definitely not a world state, a single world state! I refer to what we were saying about the state a moment ago. Besides, neither Kant nor Arendt, whom you were citing just now, believed that a single world state was possible or appropriate.

I know, it does seem an insoluble task. But if you had a task whose solution was also the object of a knowledge, a task made accessible merely by knowing it, would that still be a task?

ASSHEUER: In your book *The Other Heading*, you delivered a clear confession of faith for European democracy and yet you sometimes hesitate in relation to the institutions of this democracy. What are the reasons for this hesitation? Are they structural, or are they concerned with a mistaken application of "good ideas"?

DERRIDA: To put it once again too rapidly and too briefly: I am "against" all those who are "against" Europe. As to my anxieties and hesitations, you have already heard the principle of them (against the rush to adjust to what is still a confused and dogmatic concept of what is called globalization; against a form of economism or monetarism too confident in the knowledge of dubious experts; against the reconstitution of large-scale state nationalism, under a demo-Christian hegemony that is sometimes declared and sometimes denied, but deeply embedded in European values; against a Eurocentrism that is not yet sufficiently "thought" or self-reflective; but *for* taking into account this inadequation between existing democracy and a democracy to come, which I was talking about earlier). But I don't think that the process of European unification should be broken off on the grounds of these hesitations. As in democracy, one should fight within the ongoing movement, from the inside, to turn it in other directions.

ASSHEUER: The ethical background of your theory was always recognizable, even if sometimes perhaps rather too well hidden. But why is it that for some time now justice has been in the foreground of your texts as a protagonist? Would it be right to say that the need for a thinking of justice and its implementation has become more serious?

DERRIDA: What you call a "background" was already legible. And always has been. But to know what is legible, you have to read. It is true that in that form and using those words, these themes could only appear in the foreground after a certain "theoretical-critical" passage designed to limit misunderstandings. I don't think these misunderstandings have disappeared, but perhaps they are less easy. At any rate—to say it again—for people who read. No, I don't think that things have "become more serious" in the world, alas. Thirty-five years ago, there were the same troubles, perhaps less immediately mediatized . . .

ASSHEUER: Could you say a few words about the very odd separation that sets you against the thought of the second generation of the Frankfurt School, as it has been elaborated by Jürgen Habermas? It is becoming more and more obvious that there are surprising parallels, at least in your responses, so we are wondering if it is not rather a case of a philosophical or political misunderstanding?

DERRIDA: Once again, a much too brief response for a question that ought to elicit, and will, I hope, elicit, long responses, not only from me. It is true, and I'm delighted by this, that Habermas and I do often turn out to be on the same side and allies in relation to matters of political urgency. We even work together, for instance in international associations such as the Parlement international des écrivains, or CISIA (which is involved with intellectuals, journalists, and others persecuted in Algeria and elsewhere).[4] I think I have always understood and approved of most of Habermas's political interventions in Germany. As to serious and well-known "philosophical" differences that you allude to (whether they are direct or indirect, whether they take place or are "represented" in Europe or elsewhere), on which I explained my position some years ago—does this political solidarity relegate them to the level of straightforward misunderstandings? I'm not sure. I wonder whether an in-depth, detailed, rigorous discussion might not bring up profound political differences, disagreements about the very essence of the "political," the "social bond," and "language"—disagreements on the basis of which there would be new efforts and new tasks to determine.

I hope these discussions will take place, tomorrow or the next day, directly or via others, and that they will be both friendly and demanding.

ASSHEUER: Emmanuel Levinas was one of the most important philosophers for you, it seems to me. At the moment, we are seeing a sort of appropriation of his thought on the part of Catholic and conservative thinking in France. How do you explain this interest from that direction, and how would you situate your own current reflections about Levinas in relation to these attempts at appropriation? Are we dealing with a specifically philosophical issue, or can we see implications that are also instructive as to the political situation of French universities, or at least that of philosophy departments?

DERRIDA: You are right, this "issue" and this "situation" call for vigilant analyses. You know how much I admire and am grateful to Levinas. I consider his thought to be an immense event in this [twentieth] century. But the disturbing "appropriation" you speak of is not only Catholic and conservative, it can also be that of a naive moralism or a simplifying, dumbed-down mediatization. In the texts I devote to him I try to resist this in my own way. I always insist, discreetly but clearly, on reservations of every kind, and especially on political anxieties (for instance on the subject of the nation and Israel, in *Adieu to Emmanuel Levinas*), or on the paradoxes of his concept of the "third" and "justice," on perversions of his ethics that are always possible, on the inevitability of a "perjury" at the heart of "honesty."[5] But here too, so as not to be too vague or unjust, will you allow me to refer to the published texts?

13

"Others Are Secret Because They Are Other"

ANTOINE SPIRE: Preparing for this interview, I wondered whether it was possible to avoid both anecdotes and universalizing philosophical categories. How can one not repeat what has already been said, how can one innovate? In the end don't you think that innovation is just that—repetition to find something new?

JACQUES DERRIDA: Ah, interviews! Yes, I have always suffered from the laws of the interview. After several decades, I really must recognize that I have too often done what I said I didn't like doing. As for "saying again," the logical core of the thing, I've often insisted on that; the point is that there is no incompatibility between repetition and the novelty of what is different. In a tangential and elliptical way, a difference always causes repetition to deviate. I call that *iterability*, the other ([Sanskrit] *itara*) appearing in reiteration. The singular always inaugurates, it even "comes about" unforeseeably, like the new arrival, via repetition.

Recently I fell in love with the French expression *une fois pour toutes*—I think it's untranslatable, but never mind.[1] This expression states in a highly economical way the singular event and the irreversibility of what or who only comes about or comes along once, and thus is repeated no more. But at the same time it opens up onto all the metonymical substitutions that would take it somewhere else. The unprecedented arises, whether we like it or not, in the multiplicity of repetitions. That is what puts on hold the naive oppositions between tradition and renewal, or memory and the future, or reform and revolution. The logic of iterability wrecks in advance the certainties of all sorts of discourses, philosophies, ideologies . . .

What matters is the trajectory, the pathway, the crossing—in a word, the experience. The experience is then the method, not a system of rules or technical norms for supervising an experiment, but the pathway in the process of happening, breaking a way through (*le frayage de la route, via rupta*). In an interview, even if one repeats the same thing, the same "contents"—even so, the situation, the context, the mode of address, the addressees, and the signature are all different every time, and it's the impromptu of this "situation" that is what the reader or listener is waiting for, I suppose. Otherwise, it is always better to read the books—please let me say this once again. And to reread them (that's different every time as well).

SPIRE: When people are talking about you, there are two words that come up: Algiers, the name of the place where you were born; and, in relation to your oeuvre, the philosophy of deconstruction. You define this notion by saying that it's about interrogating the presuppositions, purposes, and modes of efficacy that go with philosophical thinking. But you also claim that at the same time you want to thwart expectations, to play with the programs and institutions and unveil what underlies them, what predetermines them. Basically, to deconstruct is to philosophize?

DERRIDA: Look, in this interview you're repeating and reminding me of the history of the definitions of deconstruction (some of them, not all) that I have been able to venture. So as not to begin again, so as to refer to the books at the same time as putting forward something a bit new, I will clarify two points today.

1. There is a history of "deconstruction" in France and abroad, going back more than thirty years. This pathway—I don't say method—has transformed, displaced, and complicated definitions, strategies, and styles that themselves vary from one country to another, from one individual to another, or from one text to another. This variety is essential to deconstruction, which is neither a philosophy, nor a science, nor a method, nor a doctrine, but, as I often say, the *impossible*, and the impossible as *that which comes about* [*arrive*].

2. Even before this historical sequence (of between thirty and forty years), one must remember the Nietzschean, Freudian, and above all Heideggerian premises of deconstruction. And especially, in relation to Heidegger, that there is a Christian, or more precisely a Lutheran tradition of what Heidegger calls *Destruktion*. Luther, as I describe in my book on

Jean-Luc Nancy and what Nancy calls the "deconstruction of Christianity," was already talking about *destructio* to designate the need for a desedimentation of the theological strata hiding the original nakedness of the evangelical message to be restored. What interests me more and more is to make out the specificity of a deconstruction that wouldn't necessarily be reducible to this Lutheran-Heideggerian tradition. And that's perhaps what differentiates my work from those who are close to me, in France and abroad. Without refuting or rejecting anything at all, I would like to try to make out what separates an ongoing deconstruction from the memory it inherits, at the very instant when it is reaffirming and respecting that memory's inheritance . . .

SPIRE: This deconstruction has been explicated through great texts—by Heidegger, Husserl, Joyce, and Kant. In this act of undoing, desedimentation, decomposition, and deconstitution of sediments, artifacts, presuppositions, and institutions, could one say there is an element of hyper-analysis? There is always a tension there between a demanding reading of the tradition, and what that leads up to, an ethical and democratic responsibility.

DERRIDA: Is it a tension? I'm not sure. Of course, deconstruction busies itself with what we more or less legitimately call the "great texts." Not just the canonical works, from Plato to Joyce. But it performs its exercises on bodies of work that are not literary, philosophical, or religious texts but writings on the law, or institutions, norms, and programs. I have said it too often—the writing that interests deconstruction is not only the writing that libraries protect. Even when deconstruction takes an interest in literary texts, it's also about the *institution* of literature (which is something modern, with a fascinating political history); it is also about processes of evaluation and legitimation, questions of signature, and authors' rights or copyright (you know how unsettled all this is at the moment, because of the "new technologies"); it is about the actual politics of the institution of literature. All that concerns both the content and the form of the literary or philosophical thing.

Yes, I also accept the term *hyper-analysis*. For two reasons. First, you have to push the analysis as far as you can, limitlessly and unconditionally. But secondly, you also have to take yourself *beyond* analysis itself, which, as its name suggests, presupposes regression to an ultimate principle, an element that is simple and indivisible. Now one of the laws that deconstruction responds to, and that it starts off by registering, is that at the origin (thus the origin with no origin), there is nothing simple, but a composition, a contamination, the possibility at least of a grafting and a repetition. All that resists analysis even as it sets it going. This is why the deconstructive operation is not only *analytical* or only *critical* ("critical" meaning capable of deciding between two simple terms), but trans-analytical, ultra-analytical, and more than critical. Critique, the need for critique, for *krinein* [judging] and crisis (*Krisis*) has a history. The deconstruction of this history, like that of the question, of the question-form in general, cannot therefore be simply "critical" in either the Kantian or the Marxist senses of the term, although at the time when I am doing this "other thing," I also want to stay faithful to these legacies. A faithful heir should also interrogate the inheritance, shouldn't he? Submit it to a reevaluation and a constant selection—at the risk, as I said somewhere, of being "faithful to more than one"?[2] To be responsible is both to answer for oneself and for the legacy, before that which precedes us, and to answer, before the others, before that which is coming and remains to come. By definition, this responsibility has no limit. "Deconstruction" must be as responsible as possible. Even if, faced with the infiniteness of responsibility, one can only admit to modesty, if not defeat. One is never equal to a responsibility that is assigned to us even before we have accepted it. We have to recognize this without necessarily developing a culture of the bad conscience. But a culture of the bad conscience is always better than a culture of the good conscience.

I have kept the word *democracy* for the end. It's the most difficult one. I can only use it anxiously. There is certainly a traditional, even current way of defining democracy. No one is against it, even if in France a certain distinction is cultivated between republic (abstract, secular universalism) and democracy (paying more attention, some people say, to community identities and minorities). But beyond this distinction, which I regard as secondary, the originality of democracy is perhaps this. Any democracy is always influenced by the recognition of not being adequate to its model (this is not inscribed in the essence of the other "regimes"—and that's why democracy is not really the name for a type of regime), and so historicity, infinite (and essentially aporetic) perfectibility, and the original link to a promise make it something to-come. This is one of its many aporias (I describe other ones elsewhere, especially in *The Other Heading* and *Politics of Friendship*).[3]

This future, to-come, does not mean the distancing or indefinite delay authorized by some governing idea. This to-come prescribes pressing tasks and urgent negotiations, here and now. However unsatisfactory they are, they do not allow for waiting. To be a democrat would be to act in the recognition that we never live in a (sufficiently) democratic society. This critical work is more than critical, this deconstructive task is indispensable for democratic breathing space, as for any idea of responsibility . . .

SPIRE: Generally, when people are talking about your work, they forget these democratic and ethical aspects and focus on the word *deconstruction*. On this subject, there are some who say that Jacques Derrida is too complicated for them. In fact, the ones who find you unreadable have perhaps not taken the plunge down into your writings and are mainly seeking a beginning way into them. . . . But in *Of Grammatology* and *Margins— Of Philosophy*, you explain that there is no justifiable absolute beginning. To read you, we should seek a strategy rather than a beginning—in other words, we should immerse ourselves in the text and, starting from there, attempt a comprehension exercise with themes that recur frequently and that are ultimately at the heart of your intellectual activity.

DERRIDA:It is also necessary to read the texts that my texts read! It would be absurd to say that they are all "easy," but their difficulty is not of the type that people often object to. There are two categories of "rejection" in this regard, two types of nonreader. First, those who do not work hard enough and think they are entitled to do this; they rapidly run out of steam by assuming that a text must be immediately accessible, without the work that consists of reading, and reading the authors I read, for instance. Then there are the nonreaders who use this supposed obscurity as an excuse for setting aside, really for censuring something that threatens them or makes them anxious—deranges them. So then the difficulty argument becomes a hateful alibi.

Of course, as you were pointing out, there is no beginning—everything began a very long time before us, didn't it? I start by registering the fact that I work here and there, in such and such a more or less French philosophical tradition; I only write in French, a particular kind of French, both very old and very much a living language. I try to assume all my francophone responsibilities, which consist in inheriting in a way that is active, affirmative, transformative, faithful-unfaithful as always, unfaithful through fidelity. But it is not possible to begin everything again at every moment. This would be a form of madness from an economic point of view. Hence the need for the pedagogical links of schools, universities, and the media. Anyone who writes counts on this potential economy and these mediations, and these alliances, and also takes account of these risks. . . . The question of teaching runs through all my work and all my political and institutional engagements, whether to do with schooling, higher education, or the media.[4]

SPIRE: You place a great deal of emphasis on the texts that you work from and that were in existence before you. I am very struck by the importance of this textual reading in your work, which I would like to link to the role of commentary for the Jews. In Judaism, the tradition was constituted through commentary and it only exists in relation to commentary. The Bible is not a sacred text, in that it only exists through and via the commentaries of the people who have read it. One could say that your attitude to the philosophical corpus of civilized people today is the same as that of the Jewish people to the Torah: this wish to comment on a corpus, through time, to say that it is not sacred. That it is only comprehensible today through today's commentary.

DERRIDA: The word *commentary* disturbs me a little. I don't know if what I do is derived from commentary, which is an obscure and overloaded notion, unless you stamp the word with a more active and more interpretive inflection: a countersignature contributes something of its own, during and beyond the passive reading of a text that precedes us but which one reinterprets, as faithfully as possible, leaving a mark behind.

On the Jewish reference, my "belonging" to Judaism, to put it like that, much has been written, as you probably know, for years now, and this always leaves me puzzled. First, because I think that patient, vigilant, micrological, interminable reading is not exclusive to the Jewish tradition. And also I must confess that my familiarity with the Jewish culture you mention is, alas, very weak and indirect. I regret this, of course; it's too late. If what I do reminds people of Jewish annotation, that is not the result of a choice, or a desire, or even of a memory or cultural formation.

You say I don't regard texts as sacred. Yes and no. Of course, I tend to be wary of the procedures of sacralization, or at least I tend to analyze them—their laws and inevitabilities. I try in fact to approach texts not without respect but without religious presuppositions, in the dogmatic sense of religious. Still, in the respect to which I yield there is something that bows before a sacredness, if not before something religious. The text of the other must be read and interrogated without mercy but therefore respected, and initially in the body of its actual words. I can interrogate, contradict, attack, or simply deconstruct a logic of the text that came before me, and is before me, but I cannot and must not change it.

In respect for the actual words, the letter of the text, lies the origin of a process of making sacred. I have tried to show, especially in *The Gift of Death*, that literature, in the strict modern and European sense of the term, preserves the memory of the sacred texts (biblical texts, really) that represent its ancestry; this memory is guilty and repentant, both making sacred and desacralizing.[5] No critic, no translator, no teacher has, in principle, the right to touch the literary text once it is published, legitimated, and authorized by copyright: this is a sacred inheritance, even if it occurs in an atheistic and so-called secular milieu. You don't touch a poem! or a legal text, and the law is sacred—like the social contract, says Rousseau. The origin of this process of making sacred interests me everywhere it happens. The opposition between sacred and secular is naive; it entails a lot of deconstructive questions. Contrary to what we think we know, we have never entered into a secular era. The very idea of the secular is religious through and through—Christian really.

SPIRE: We should question the thematic division between literature and philosophy. When asked why you have not written literature, you have said that literature always does something other than itself. For you, literature would always be something other than itself, and thus it would be philosophy, perhaps. Yet you have held on to philosophy. I think the best way to get beyond this opposition is probably the word *quivering*, or *vacillation*. Reading you, one always feels there is this wish to be as rigorous as possible, like a vacillation of thought while it is being constructed.

DERRIDA: You're right, quivering and vacillation, certainly. That said, when faced by people who suggest that this quivering means I must be taking literature for philosophy and philosophy for literature, I protest, and I ask for proof of it. The same thing for rhetoric and logic. Without mixing them up, I put the question of the frontier between the two of them, and it's not a slight question. There are literary effects in philosophical texts, and vice versa. But determining the meaning and the history and a certain porousness of the frontiers between them is quite the opposite of confusing them and mixing them up. The limit interests me as much as the passage to the limit—going to the limit—or the passage of the limit. That presupposes multiple movements. Deconstruction always consists in making more than one movement at a time, and writing with two hands, writing more than one sentence or in more than one language.

SPIRE: You often mention the fact that Husserl is your first philosophical point of reference. And in your early work on him, you treated the problem of the genesis of that author's philosophy. It would be true to say, wouldn't it, that your work on geometry in Husserl has been the source of a fundamental line that ultimately runs through the whole of your work, taking you to Heidegger and Levinas by way of Sartre? A phenomenological motif seems to accompany your entire oeuvre, a motif that is basically a way of defining objects, ideas, and words, by trying to get them to render everything they can render, by their very identity . . .

DERRIDA: Husserl was not my first love in philosophy, but he left a deep trace on my work. Nothing I do would be possible without the discipline of phenomenology, without the practice of eidetic and transcendental reduction, without the attention given to the meaning of phenomenality, and so on. It is like an exercise that precedes any reading, any reflection, and any writing. Even if, having reached a certain point, I think it necessary to ponder questions about the limits of this discipline and its principles, and the intuitionist "principle of principles" that guides it.

SPIRE: That leads me to the example of the blink, which is absolutely fundamental to Husserl's work. Would it be right to say that you have given that blink a certain depth, by looking both back to the past and forward to the future? The notion of time exists in Husserl, but only in the state of trace. The temporal perspective is something that you have wanted and been able to articulate with phenomenology . . .

DERRIDA: Husserl's major texts on time recognize an absolutely privileged form for what is called the "living present." This is sense, good sense even, at its most indisputable, in appearance: the originary form of experience is the self-presentation of the present; we never leave the present, which never leaves itself, and which no living thing ever leaves. This absolute phenomenological science, this undeniable authority of *now* in the living present—in different styles and with different strategies, it is this that has been the point to which all the major questionings of this kind of time, especially those of Heidegger and Levinas, have been directed.

In a different move, with other aims, what I tried to elaborate using the word *trace* (that is, an experience of the temporal difference of a past without a present past or a to-come that is not a present future) is also a deconstruction, without critique, of that absolute and straightforward evidence of the living present, of consciousness as living present, of the originary form (*Urform*) of the time we call the living present (*lebendige Gegenwart*), or of everything that assumes the presence of the present.

SPIRE: When you say that in Husserl there is a presupposition that explains the thesis of phenomenology, and that this thesis assumes some presuppositions affirmed as such, are you not taking your distance from him, with his return to the things themselves, his rules of intuition, of the datum, and of the thing itself in its presence?

DERRIDA: Phenomenology usually appears as the major reactivation of the philosophical tradition, particularly through its Cartesian and Kantian motifs. It is even said to have revealed the origin of philosophy, metaphysics, or the first philosophy. There is nothing surprising about the fact that Husserl himself is considered a thinker within the tradition. And it is right that that too is thought of as being to his credit. The most forceful philosophical tradition has always, whether directly or not, privileged intuition, the immediate (perceptible or intelligible) relationship with the thing itself. Despite what its name seems to imply (a matter of looking, *intueor*), this intuitionist tradition has not always privileged looking, contrary to what we often think, along with Heidegger or Blanchot. Huge as it seems to be, optical or scopic primacy always, even in phenomenology or Husserlian eidetism, rests on a figure of touch, on a haptic basis. At least that is what I tried to demonstrate, with as much detail as possible, in "Touch."[6] What is more, Husserl must have recognized that in the experience of time and in the experience of the other, his principle of principles, intuitive access to the thing itself, "in person," was held in check. Access to an *alter ego*, for instance, does not offer itself to any originary intuition, only to an analogy, to what is called an analogical "appresentation." We are never on the side of the other, of his originary here-and-now; never inside his head, if you like. This is an essential breach in philosophy. All the "infidelities" to phenomenological orthodoxy went by way of this breach that Husserl opened up himself. The admirable thing with this philosopher is that faced with all these apparently insurmountable difficulties, he never gives up or resigns himself to it; he tries to adjust his analyses scrupulously, maintaining his axiomatics and methodology for the longest possible time, heroically, and marking the places of limit or failure, where an overhaul was necessary. What we have there is a respectable example of philosophical responsibility.

SPIRE: Let's move on from Husserl to Heidegger. I would like to read a trace of his biography in Heidegger's philosophy. For instance, the fact of the articulation between the Greek patrimony and the exclusion of a monotheistic biblical patrimony, his references to the ground and the earth and the critique of technology and progress, in the *Rectoral Address*. I would like to understand this linguistic complexity that distances him from reality and gives the reader the impression of being in a formal and abstract universe, where there is no longer a wish for a link between thinking and the thinking of reality. Do you find that this search for links between Heidegger's philosophy and his biography is meaningless in the end? Do you reject it?

DERRIDA: If you don't mind, I won't respond to the question on Heidegger's politics or his *Rectoral Address*. Not to get out of it, but these things are too complicated for the amount of time and space that we have available. I have published at length what I wanted to say on the topic, in *Of Spirit* and in numerous interviews.[7] The question of "biography" doesn't bother me at all. I am among those few people who have constantly drawn attention to this: you must (and you must do it *well*) put philosophers' biographies back in the picture, and the commitments, particularly political commitments, that they sign in their own names, whether in relation to Heidegger, or equally to Hegel, Freud, Nietzsche, Sartre, or Blanchot, and so on.[8]

You allude to an "exclusion" of the "monotheistic biblical patrimony." Yes and no. There are numerous biblical or theological references and they constantly confirm what we know of Heidegger's deep theological culture (Catholic and Protestant, above all Lutheran, I would say). But it is true that what would be called the Hebraic patrimony seems, let's say, passed over in silence, a heavy silence, as has often been noted (Ricoeur, Zarader). Whence the temptation to include this silence as part of a whole configuration where there wouldn't be only the *Rectoral Address* and a certain motif of the earth that you speak of, but many other indications as well (such as the disdain in regard to all Jewish philosophy, or the "bad treatment," as I think of it, that he inflicted on Spinoza; elsewhere I try to show how Spinoza would have complicated some Heideggerian schemas on the subject of the epoch of representation, and the *cogito* and the principle of reason). I'm not unaware of this configuration, but without wanting to exonerate Heidegger (there has never been any question of that for me, and I even think that Heidegger was not free of the most widespread type of anti-Semitism in his time and his milieu—"We were all a little bit anti-Semitic at the time," Gadamer once said, I think), I still think we have to be attentive to the complexity of things and the nature of texts. There is no anti-Semitic philosophical text by Heidegger (of the sort that, read in a certain way, one could find in Kant, Hegel, or Marx), and while it is true that the statements about technology are marked by strong reactionary or antiprogressive connotations, Heidegger is one of the thinkers of modernity who have taken the issues of modern technology, and the ethical-political vigilance it imposes on us, with the utmost seriousness, in a profoundly meditative way.

SPIRE: In a book on the language of Heidegger,[9] Henri Meschonnic shows that in the philosopher's writings there is an increasing rupture due to a linguistic logic that takes itself as an end, at a distance from the indispensable relationship between language and the thinking of reality. Heidegger's writings are basically a play on words that increasingly cuts itself off from a certain reality . . .

DERRIDA: I long ago learned the lesson of not taking Meschonnic's invectives seriously any more, or what he writes generally, not only on Heidegger. No, there isn't language on one side and reality on the other. If we were cutting ourselves off from reality every time we took account of the folding or subtlety of a language, we would have to burn down all the libraries (Gongora, Mallarmé, Freud, Celan, Lacan, some others too, certainly, in fact almost everyone!), and only Meschonnic's diatribes would survive this. How is it possible to claim seriously that Heidegger shuts himself up in language and flees reality? It's a little bit too simplistic, you see—let's leave it.

SPIRE: Let's now, if you don't mind, approach the question of Paul de Man, literary theorist, linguist born in Belgium, who died in 1983. You were courageous enough to defend him in 1987, after a researcher from a university in Louvain discovered that in 1941 and 1942 he had authored articles in *Le Soir*, a newspaper controlled by the Gestapo and incontestably anti-Semitic. What interested me in the way you dealt with this problem is that you compared his writings to a veiled critique of vulgar anti-Semitism. You showed that his way of approaching the Jewish question, while absolutely anti-Semitic, had at the same time a degree of sharpness and could equally well be interpreted as a way of criticizing vulgar anti-Semitism. In your view, his discourse was split, disjointed, engaged in continual conflicts, and it would be terribly reductive only to characterize it as anti-Semitic. Unlike Heidegger, de Man did nothing else than to reflect on and interpret this past, indeed never refusing to return to it. So he continued to work to understand what had happened to him . . .

DERRIDA: Here too, this whole thing is too tangled up for a simple, short response, one that would at least remain reasonably "responsible." First I am disturbed to see you leap from the "political question of Heidegger" to the "political question of de Man." There is virtually no possible comparison between the two of them, and even less between the two ways I relate to them. There would be plenty to say about the word *affair* around which the press and some academics got themselves very het up [*affairés*]. What connection is there between a great academic philosopher who, made rector when he was over forty, delivers the *Rectoral Address*, and an unknown young man of twenty who earns his living in Belgium, at the start of the war, writing articles of literary criticism of which one seems to be marked by ordinary anti-Semitism (and in need of cautious interpretation, as I tried to demonstrate elsewhere, which we can't do here). Don't say that I "defended" him, even if that was a courageous thing to do. I said clearly, without the least equivocation, that, limited as it was in its duration and to that time, his guilt was undeniable and complete. I even went so far as to write that this wrongdoing was "unpardonable" (and I am not sure I did the right thing, that I wasn't being violent and unjust then; I would give a fuller explanation of this if I had the space).[10] So let's not simplify. It is true that I sought to reconstitute the formidable overdetermination of the texts of that period, and of the "case" and the situation—and I did this at the point when a good proportion of the American academic intelligentsia was seeking to exploit the discovery of these youthful articles, to make it into an atomic weapon against "deconstruction." (De Man had been one of the leading lights of deconstruction in the United States since 1975, first through his references to my work, and then by giving it an inflection of his own—which I have also analyzed in a number of texts.) As to the "discovery" in question, I would like to remind you that it was I who organized the publication of the articles and the public discussion in the weeks that followed, after I had been told about them by the young Belgian researcher. To put it in a nutshell (I have given a lengthy account of this elsewhere), what calls for an analysis is first of all the hypocritical determination of the people who thought they could grab hold of the thing in order to bring a swift trial to a close and thereby, by bringing them into disrepute, get rid of both de Man's writings (forty years of work after the arrival of a young man in the United States!) and also of *all* deconstruction, his and the other kinds, into the bargain. I found this posturing unjust, grotesque, and abject. I said so over and over again, but nor did I ever seek to exonerate this or that sentence from a youthful article by de Man.

SPIRE: I have the impression that whenever a reference or an affiliation seems to circumscribe either you or something that has been the object of your attention, you say it's a trap! Basically, you are extremely sensitive to the diversity of meanings that attach to a word, concept, or orientation. That is of course derived from the rigor that is your own, and I respect that rigor; at the same time, I do ask myself the question of whether there is some sense in synthesis. Especially as the affirmation of synthesis does not exclude contestation. You have shown very well that in the philosophical tradition, a word could sometimes say what it is and also its opposite. When one gets to that point, it is important to consider the question of the spread of knowledge. Isn't it necessary to simplify in order to spread knowledge? And when we simplify, are we absolutely and irreducibly led into betrayal? Do you think that all interviews are betrayals, because they can't enter into the details? That in the end, it will never be possible to define the grain of things? Even if you work at the thing indefinitely, you will never be able to define it sufficiently! That is why, confronted with your precautions which I understand and consider rigorous, I am a bit worried: don't we also have pedagogical responsibilities?

DERRIDA: We do have pedagogical responsibilities, of course that's understood—and shared ones, if you don't mind. Sometimes it is necessary to simplify to transmit a knowledge and to speak in general. But if there must be rules for the best or the least bad simplification, they have to be reinvented in each situation. Whatever precautions I have to take, and however painstakingly detailed I have to be, there comes a moment when, it's true, I do give way to a simplification of some kind. At the same time I am convinced that the task is infinite, that I will always fail to be equal to it, that there is a need to refine arguments ever more scrupulously. But set against this responsibility is the responsibility not to wait, and so at a given moment, here and now, to take the risk (as calculated as possible) of speaking, teaching, and publishing. In agreeing to do this interview, I am prepared to simplify, but I make listeners or readers aware of this by referring them to other speaking and writing situations where I simplify less. I also tell myself that perhaps, perhaps, it is better to simplify a little while letting something get through, like contraband, rather than to be silent with the excuse that one can never be equal to the complexity of things. There are never guarantees, norms of protection, or insurance against the risk that is taken in that way.

If this simplification is a betrayal, let's pause awhile on that word *betrayal.* On the one hand simplification is always disfiguring; we never measure up to a promise, we always betray. But in thus betraying, discourse betrays a truth in spite of itself: unfaithful to a certain truth, it lets through and exhibits another one, at least as an uncontrollable symptom. Across the simplifications, caricatures, and distortions, and across the relentless resistance that we try to oppose it with, the silhouette of a kind of "truth" emerges. The attentive reader or listener, the other in general, will find themselves faced with the truth of someone (me!) who endlessly suffers and struggles in a hopeless resistance to simplification or impoverishment.

I would like to pick up again on another word—you offer it to me—which is "trap." Yes, of course, there are traps, and you set them down where I am going to step. Every time (and it never fails to happen) that someone interviewing me asks me about Heidegger, and not about Heidegger's thought (which is often little known and attracts little attention), but about Heidegger's "Nazism," and then they associate my friend de Man with that (his entire work is generally unknown in France: forty years of a great theorist's oeuvre), these are traps, and traps for me. There is a wish to limit or neutralize my work (very different, by the way, from that of de Man, who in fact only read me, and I only met him, quite late, in the 1970s—since I was not in Belgium in 1940 but expelled from my secondary school at the time, because I was Jewish).

So a trap, yes, and a bit crude. For Heidegger, it is even more outrageous. Not only am I not a disciple of Heidegger's, but for forty years I have never made a reference to him that was not also questioning, not to say critical or deconstructive. It would be sufficient to read a bit to verify that. But it is true that for that reason I do take Heidegger's thought seriously, and that is what appears to be intolerable. The attempt is made not only to make me a Heideggerian but also to reduce Heidegger to the *Rectoral Address*. My work is reducible to a formula, "Heidegger plus a style," to cite a book that some time ago achieved the heights of stupidity and vulgar dishonesty in this field. It was called, if I remember rightly, *La Pensée 68*:[11] an example of the worst simplistic journalism. All this is meant to avoid—and even to prevent—thinking, teaching, and reading, with no respect either for readers or for the thinkers they claim to be writing about. The whole point is to denigrate and hurt—"trap," in fact. But as you know, the handling of traps is sometimes dangerous for the handlers, whether right away or in the long term.

SPIRE: To avoid either trap or betrayal, then, I will base what I say on a concept. When you opposed the two notions of differENce and differANce, thus the differENce of a concept in relation to what it means then the differANce in the time that is necessary for its elaboration, you gradually went from that to an opposition between the written and the oral, showing for instance that the oral sign is fairly differENt from what it means, but differANt in the sense of shorter. According to the same procedure, we can say that the written sign has a greater differANce, and so that it takes longer to elaborate. I came to think about this opposition between differENce and differANce, wondering whether writing spoken out loud is not the synthesis here. An oral utterance prepared by a written text means you have spent some time to define the thing under discussion in the best possible way. Do you accept this idea?

DERRIDA: Absolutely not. The distinction between difference and differance is not what separates oral from written. In differance, it's not just about time but also about space. It's a movement in which the distinction between space and time has not yet come about: spacing, becoming-space of time and becoming-time of space, *differentiation*, process of production of differences and experience of absolute alterity. What I then called "trace" concerns orality just as much, and thus a kind of voice-writing. So it isn't about a hierarchy placing writing before or above speech, either, as some readers in a rush (in a rush not to understand) have wanted to believe or make others believe. Here again, I can only refer to these ancient texts: "Differance" [in *Writing and Difference*] or *Of Grammatology* . . .

SPIRE: I had got to the point of thinking that the difference between a sign and what it signifies is both a differANce and a differENce, in that the

greater the differAnce, the more it takes time—and perhaps space—to explicate the sign, and the closer you get to what you want to signify . . .

DERRIDA: No, on the contrary it's an attempt not to put too much
trust in the concept of sign, and the famous (and indeed incontestable) diacritical difference between signs, the condition of identification for every
signifier or signified. I tried to think the possibility of this differance before
diacritical difference, before a semiotics or a linguistics, even before any anthropology—to put it a bit rapidly. The "trace" is the movement, the
process, really the experience, that both tries and fails to do without the
other in the same. When I say, for instance, that culture is a "differant" nature (I could do this with numerous other conceptual oppositions), that
suggests that culture is and remains nature but in differance, *both* repeated
in its economy and radically altered. That takes us back to what we were
saying above about iterability.

SPIRE: There is a resistance to your work like there is to that of a psychoanalyst. An external resistance that is cultural and political, and an internal resistance to the extent that the trace escapes.

DERRIDA: The trace is never present . . .

SPIRE: . . . So we have to try to find out the nature of the remainder,
what remains once the trace is fixed, what the trace has not left. How can
what remains be defined—how should we approach this remainder?

DERRIDA: A trace is never present, fully present, by definition; it inscribes in itself the reference to the specter of something else. The remainder is not present either, any more than a trace as such. And that is why I
have been much taken up with the question of the remainder, often under
this very name or more rigorously under that of *restance* or remaining. The
remaining of the remainder is not reducible to an actual residue, or to what
is left after a subtraction, either. The remainder *is* not, it is not a being, not
a modification of that which is. Like the trace, the remaining offers itself
for thought before or beyond being. It is inaccessible to a straightforward
intuitive perception (since it refers to something wholly other, it inscribes
in itself something of the infinitely other), and it escapes all forms of pre-
hension, all forms of monumentalization, and all forms of archivation. Often, like the trace, I associate it with ashes: remains without a substantial
remainder, essentially, but which have to be taken account of and without
which there would be neither accounting nor calculation, nor a principle of
reason able to give an account or a rationale (*reddere rationem*), nor a being

as such. That is why there are *remainder effects*, in the sense of a result or a present, idealizable, ideally iterable residue. What we are saying at the moment is not reducible to the notes you are taking, the recording we are making, or the words I am uttering—to what will remain of it in the world. The remains of what remains cannot be calculated in this way. But there will also be remainder effects, sentences fixed on paper, more or less readable and reproducible. These remainder effects will thereby have presence effects—differently in one place or another, and in an extremely uneven way according to the contexts and the subjects that will get attached to it. A dispersion of the remainder effects, different interpretations, but nowhere the substance of a remainder that is present and identical with itself.

SPIRE: Is it right to say that for some years now there has been a more firmly stated political dimension to your work? Do your books have more obvious political consequences?

DERRIDA: I'm sure this dimension is more easily recognizable nowadays in the most conventional of political codes. But it was decipherable in all my texts, even the oldest ones. It's true that in the course of the past twenty years I've thought that after much work I'd sorted out, let's say, for me, the necessary conditions (discursive, theoretical, conforming to deconstructive demands) for manifesting this political concern without yielding, or yielding too much I hope, to the stereotypical forms (which I consider *de*politicizing in fact) of intellectuals' engagement.

When I went to teach clandestinely and got myself imprisoned in communist Czechoslovakia; when I argued actively against apartheid, or for the freeing of Mandela, or against the death sentence, for Mumia Abu Jamal; or when I took part in the founding of the Parlement international des écrivains;[12] when I wrote what I wrote about Marx, about hospitality or undocumented persons, on forgiveness, witnessing, the secret, or sovereignty—just as when I launched the Greph movement and the États Généraux de la Philosophie [States General of Philosophy], then contributed to the creation of the Collège international de philosophie [International College of Philosophy]—I would like to think that these forms of engagement and the discourses that supported them were themselves in agreement (it isn't always easy) with the ongoing work of deconstruction. So I tried to adjust a discourse or a political practice to the demands of deconstruction, with more or less success, but never enough. I don't feel a divorce between my writings and my engagements, only differences of rhythm, mode of discourse, context, and so on. I am more aware of the continuity than of what has been called abroad the "political turn" or the "ethical turn" of deconstruction.

SPIRE: Hearing you speak of a turn, I am wondering whether there isn't a question of rhythm here. I know you are interested in this subject— the heterogeneity of speeds, acceleration . . . Have you been forced, in spite of yourself, to accelerate politically, under a kind of media pressure?

DERRIDA: Differences of speed do seem to be determining. The rhythm differential counts a lot for me; it governs practically everything. It's not very original—when it comes down to it, you only have to be a driver to experience this: knowing how to accelerate, slow down, stop, and start up again. This driving lesson applies just as well to private life and accidents are always possible. The scene of the car accident is imprinted or overprinted in quite a few of my texts, like a sort of premonitory signature, a bit sinister. That said, I don't believe that speeding up on the political highway has been, as you suggest, the result of media pressure. That has always been there, and I didn't give way to it in the period when overhasty readers used to claim that my texts were apolitical.

SPIRE: A pedagogical constraint? Perhaps the world bears down more on you nowadays, because you are well known?

DERRIDA: It bears down differently. In trying not to write under pressure or constraint, I am also responding, necessarily—and I believe I have to do so—to the milieu in which I happen to be living or working: a private or public milieu, primarily French, but also broadly international, academic or otherwise. As soon as you publish and are granted a certain public responsibility, you feel you are under an injunction. You have to reply, even if you maintain the responsibility of responding or not, saying this or that, in this style, at such and such a rhythm, with these particular reasons given, these conditions, and these reservations. How then could you possibly not take any notice of at least the image or the silhouette that you form of a certain type of addressee in order to do, say, or write this or that? The authority you are granted becomes a sort of capital that it is convenient to put at the service of a just cause. But if possible without ever giving up questioning its presuppositions or its axioms. It is often difficult to do both at once, in the same movement, but I always try to.

SPIRE: Very early on there was one cause that rightly mobilized you, the cause of women. Sexual difference is present in many of your texts . . .

DERRIDA: I mostly speak, and this has been true for a long time, of sexual *differences*, rather than of just one difference—dual and oppositional—which, along with phallocentrism, with what I also dub carnophallogocentrism, is in fact a structural feature of philosophical discourse that has been dominant in the tradition. Deconstruction goes by that route in the very first place. Everything comes back to it. Before any feminist politicization (and even though I have often associated myself with that, on certain conditions), it is important to recognize this powerful phallogocentric basis that conditions more or less the whole of our cultural inheritance. As to the specifically philosophical tradition of this phallogocentric inheritance, it is represented—in a different but equal way—in Plato as much as in Freud or Lacan, in Kant as much as in Hegel, Heidegger, or Levinas. At any rate I have applied myself to demonstrating that.

SPIRE: Is what you say a political point of view, one that already inhabited you at that time?

DERRIDA: Yes, to the extent that it is already a political gesture, an opposition or a political resistance, to open the question of this phallogocentrism.

SPIRE: And we have seen how your work on deconstruction continues today. Is this because deconstructing is in one way reconstructing?

DERRIDA: From the outset it was clearly stated that deconstruction is not a process or project marked by negativity, or even, essentially, by "critique" (a value that has a history, like that of the "question"—a history that it is appropriate to keep alive, but which does have its limits). Deconstruction is above all the reaffirmation of an originary "yes." *Affirmative* doesn't mean *positive*. I point this out schematically, because some people think that affirmation is reducible to the position of the positive, and thus that deconstruction's mission is to reconstruct after a phase of demolition. No, there is no demolition any more than there is positive reconstruction, and there is no "phase."

The aporia I say so much about is not, despite its borrowed name, simply a momentary paralysis in the face of the impasse. It is the testing out of the undecidable; only in this testing can a decision come about. So what I do is certainly not very "constructive," for instance when I speak of a democracy to come, and promised, worthy of the name, and to which no existing democracy measures up. There is a kind of despair that is indissociable from the chance given. And from the duty of keeping one's freedom to question, to get indignant, to resist, to disobey, to deconstruct. In the name of this justice that I distinguish from the law and which it is impossible to give up.

SPIRE: Something has always been very present in your writing: friendship. You have a fidelity to the other that crosses various notions, such as gratitude, the debt, tentativeness, the gift . . . And touch, you say, is the exemplary sense.

DERRIDA: It's true—I like to cultivate fidelity in friendship, if possible in a way that is both unconditional and without overindulgence (as in the case of Paul de Man, for instance, where, without turning a blind eye, I did all I could to be just and to bring it about that he would be justly dealt with). None of that is original. But I will quickly add three clarifications (which are more readable and better demonstrated elsewhere, such as in *Politics of Friendship* and *Adieu to Emmanuel Levinas*, or in a text I intend to write on Lyotard).

1. First, *unconditional* fidelity is marked in death, or in the radical absence of the friend, where the author can no longer answer for himself, or answer before us, and can even less exchange or mark some kind of recognition—make return.

2. Second, absolute fidelity to the other goes by way of the test of an originary and fatal perjury, the terrifying possibility of which is no longer only an accident happening to the promise: as soon as there is one, there are two, and thus three, and the third—the possibility of justice, says Levinas—then introduces perjury into the face-to-face itself, into the most straightforward dual relation.

3. Third, the friendship that matters to me involves the "deconstruction" of the models and figures of friendship that are dominant in the West: *fraternal* friendship—a familial and genealogical figure, even if it is spiritual—between two men; no friendship between a man and a woman; the exclusion of the sister; presence; proximity; a whole conception of justice and politics; and so on—just to mention a few themes of *Politics of Friendship*. All that is in fact shot through with another thinking of the impossible and the "may-be," which is at the center of everything I have written on friendship, the gift, forgiveness, unconditional hospitality, and so on.

As for touch, it would be possible to show that from Plato to Husserl or Merleau-Ponty, and especially concentrating on Aristotle, Kant, and others, it constitutes the fundamental sense, even before sight—a sense whose absolute privilege (what I dub haptocentrism—often misrecognized or wrongly interpreted) organizes a sort of intuitionism shared by all philosophies, even those that claim to be nonintuitionist—and even by evangelical discourse. This is what I try to show in this book on Jean-Luc Nancy,[13] which is also a book about the hand—the human hand and the hand of God. This work is also about the Christian body and what becomes of it when, like Nancy, you undertake an interminable "deconstruction of Christianity." A de-hierarchization of the senses displaces what we call the real, that which resists all of appropriation.

SPIRE: What you say here returns us to the limit between what is and what is not . . .

DERRIDA: The internal limit to touch—tact, if you like—means that one cannot (but) touch the untouchable. A limit cannot be touched; it is a difference, an interval that escapes touch or that is that alone which you can touch or think you can. Without being intelligible, this limit is not properly tangible or perceptible. The experience of the limit "touches" on something that is never fully present. A limit never appears as such.

SPIRE: In one of your books you talked about shibboleth—which in Hebrew means river or ear of corn but also password—and here again we are within the limits. And the theme of barriers, interfaces, and passages runs through your entire oeuvre. The theme recurs of the passage to the interior of a man, the theme of something that is him as something that is not him . . .

DERRIDA: As its name suggests, *experience* is a passage: crossing, voyage, breaking through, route, *via rupta*. The shibboleth confers the right to cross a frontier, it's the equivalent of a visa or passport. But it also has the differential, sometimes discriminatory value of a shared secret. It is the mark and sign of recognition of a "between oneself" (community, nation, family, language, etc.). You had to know how to pronounce the word like someone who speaks the language. In *Shibboleth*, my short book on Celan,[14] this motif is linked to the question of interpretation, reading, and teaching as well as to the political problem of discrimination, of frontiers, of belonging to a nation or a language group, the differential mark of circumcision, and so on.

SPIRE: This mark between that which is the body and that which is not the body, between the body and that which is not it—is it invisible?

DERRIDA: The relationship with the world is a relationship between the body and that which is not it all the time—even when we are eating, or when we open our eyes! Visibili*ty* is not visible. That can be said in a very classical, even Platonic way, since it's an old philosopheme. It can also be said differently, with Merleau-Ponty. In "Touch," I propose a reelaboration of this problematic of the visible and the invisible, the tangible and the untouchable. But to limit myself to your question, let's say that the experience of being-in-the-world always exposes the body, its capacity or vulnerability, to its other, to that which is not it—whether it gets suffering or enjoyment from this, or both at once.

SPIRE: This displacement around oneself went as far as a quasi inversion of roles with Safaa Fathy. Around her film *Derrida's Elsewhere*, you became a material—a foreign body from somewhere else. It gave me the impression that you were destabilized, that you were agreeing to take everything up from zero again, as if nothing had been written. You almost passed from the state of subject to the state of object. Doesn't that explain your reluctance or your difficulties when it feels like entering into the logic of another, this other who is interviewing you?

DERRIDA: Yes, there are all the risks and all the gratifications of a game. As if someone were playing the other, the other he also is, acting a part that is his without coinciding with it, a role that is partly dictated by the other and with which you have to play games. A permanent transaction. In this film, and in the book that accompanies it, I am and I also call myself the Actor, or the Artefactor. A play with the signature and substitution, an endless calculation with no basis: to hide yourself, show yourself, and run away or protect yourself, all at once. Run away or protect yourself: both senses of *se sauver*. But anyway, I yielded in front of the camera, in spite of the anxieties or wariness, as here. It really was important to let oneself be seen beyond any control. It's what a little while ago I was calling betrayal, the betrayal of truth, betrayal as truth. So I let this film be shown. At another time, or earlier on, with someone else, perhaps I would have put up more resistance—perhaps I would simply have said no. Perhaps that would have been better. Who will ever know? Too late. The whole thing remains very hazardous . . .

SPIRE: That allows us to consider the cinema. The cinema could be said to be an elsewhere edged with mirrors, but where it's no longer a question of constructing yourself a body, but rather of haunting the screen. So we are back with a notion that is very important in your work, the fact of the specter—we should remember in this connection that one of your books is called *Specters of Marx*. It looks as if the specter of Derrida is drifting about in the film . . .

DERRIDA: Spectrality is at work everywhere, and more than ever, in an original way, in the reproducible virtuality of photography or cinema. And it's one of the themes that Safaa Fathy, who was also aware of my interest in the *revenant*, chose to privilege, along with the themes of the secret, the foreigner, the *elsewhere*, sexual differences, Judaic-Arabic-Spanish, the Marrano,[15] forgiveness, or hospitality. Spectrality also because the film all the time evokes people who are dead—the spectrality of my mother, some family tombs, cats' graves, the burial of the Count of Orgaz, and so on.

SPIRE: Death is present in all your writings. In what way? Simply because everything you write is a manifestation of the value of life, everything you write has an attachment to going on being. Ultimately I wonder whether death isn't what you push further away, the further your work advances?

DERRIDA: In telling yourself that it is not possible to do otherwise, of course, you do have to ask yourself whether this strained effort to push it away as far and for as long as possible doesn't call up, or doesn't recall to us, the attraction of a clinch with the very thing you want to run away from or protect yourself from. The affirmation of life doesn't occur without the thought of death, without the most vigilant, responsible, and even besieged or obsessive attention to this end that does not happen—to happen.

As soon as there is a trace, whatever it is, it implies the possibility of its being repeated, of surviving the instant and the subject of its tracing, and it thereby attests to the death, the disappearance, or at the very least the mortality of that tracing. The trace always figures a possible death; it signs death. As a result, the possibility and imminence of death is not only a personal obsession, it's a way of surrendering to the necessity of what is given for thinking, namely that there is no presence without trace and no trace without a possible disappearance of the origin of the said trace, thus no trace without a death. Which, I repeat, doesn't happen (or manage) to happen, to happen to me; which happens to me, which happens (or man-

ages) not to happen to me.[16] Possibility of the impossible. In *Aporias* I try
to discuss this formulation, with Heidegger, and one or two others . . .

SPIRE: It's both impossible and possible, death, and at the same time,
since it's possible, it's impossible when it's achieved! That does mean something all the same, including when the trace disappears. Isn't there a link
between the living person and the trace? Does the trace change in nature
with death?

DERRIDA: The trace is always the finite trace of a finite being. So it
can itself disappear. An ineradicable trace is not a trace. The trace inscribes
in itself its own precariousness, its vulnerability of ashes, its mortality. I
have tried to draw out all the consequences of this axiom which is basically
very simple. And to do so beyond or before an anthropology and even an
ontology or an existential analytic. What I say about the trace and death
goes for any "living thing," for "animals" and "people."

According to Heidegger, the animal does not die, in the proper sense
of the term, even if it snuffs it or "comes to an end." It's all this system of
limits that I attempt to question. It's not certain that man or *Dasein* has
this relationship fit for death that Heidegger talks about. And inversely,
what we call in the general singular "the animal" (as if there were only one,
and of just one species), can have an extremely complex relationship to
death, marked by forms of anguish, a symbolics of mourning, and sometimes even sorts of tombs, and so on.

SPIRE: When the author of the trace dies.

DERRIDA: The trace is not a substance, a present existing thing, but a
process that is changing all the time. It can only reinterpret itself and always, finally, it is carried away.

SPIRE: We make an inventory of the way in which we preserve the
past, we question the way in which we turn toward it, whether faithfully or
trying to reinterpret it. Your move over the past three years, with your seminars on forgiveness, has been a new way of turning back toward the past,
hasn't it?

DERRIDA: Possible or impossible, forgiveness turns us toward the past.
That's a minimal definition, and a commonsense one, but if there were
time it would be possible to make it a bit more complicated. There is also
some future in forgiveness. Wherever it's a question of forgiveness, in the

"commonsense" meaning of the term, the wrong initially appears irreversible and unchangeable. I first tried to vouch for the idea of forgiveness as an Abrahamic inheritance—Jewish, Christian (Christian above all), and Islamic. That involves intricate structural and semantic analyses which I cannot reconstitute here. In this tradition, and particularly in the Christian tradition, there seem to be two postulations which are contradictory:

1. *On the one hand,* it is not possible to forgive or to ask God to forgive (an enormous question: to know who is forgiving whom or who is forgiving whom for what) unless the guilty person confesses, asks forgiveness, repents, and thus changes, turns along another route, promises to be another person. The person asking forgiveness is always, to some extent, another person. So who—who is forgiven? And for what?

2. *On the other hand,* forgiveness is granted like an absolute grace, without exchange, without change, without repentance or asking for forgiveness. Without condition. These two logics (conditional pardon or unconditional grace granted even to the unpardonable) are in conflict but they coexist in the tradition, even if the logic of the conditional pardon is very much the predominant one, like common sense itself. But this common sense compromises in advance the pure, strict sense of a rigorous concept of forgiveness. Even if nothing ever corresponds to it in actual fact, we are the inheritors of this concept of the unconditional and it has to be taken into account as well. We should vouch for it in a responsible way.

SPIRE: Only the unpardonable can be pardoned. Where does that take you? Behind forgiveness, isn't there a risk of erasure? And thereby of erasing the unpardonable?

DERRIDA: It is right to remember always that to forgive is not to forget. On the contrary, forgiving requires the absolutely living memory of the ineradicable, beyond any work of mourning, reconciliation, or restoration, beyond any ecology of memory. Forgiveness is possible only in recalling, and even in reproducing, without mitigation, the wrong that has been done, what it is that has to be forgiven. If I only forgive what is forgivable or venial, the nonmortal sin, I am not doing anything that deserves the name of forgiveness. Whence the aporia: it is only the unforgivable that ever has to be forgiven.

This is what we call *doing the impossible.* And further, when I only do what is possible for me, I am not doing anything, I am not deciding about anything, I am letting a program of possibilities develop. When what happens is only what is possible, then nothing does happen [*arrive*], in the strong sense of the word. It's not "believing in miracles" to affirm this: an event worthy of the name, the arrival of that which comes about or of the one who arrives, is as extraordinary as a miracle.

Thus the only possible pardon really is the impossible pardon. I try to draw the consequences of this, particularly for our time. And not only, perhaps even not at all in the public or political sphere, because I don't believe that the pardon defined in that way rightly belongs in the public, political, juridical, or even ethical field. Which is why its secret is so serious and important an issue.

SPIRE: So the unpardonable is pardoned, forgiving is no longer forgetting . . . But even so the pardon does still have effects on the trace.

DERRIDA: A pardon that leads to forgetting, or even to mourning, is not, in the strict sense, a pardon. A pardon requires absolute, intact, active memory—of both the wrong and the guilty person.

SPIRE: You also say that forgiveness comes from the fact that we live together in the same society. We do indeed live under the same sky as the Nazi torturers, the Algeria murderers, those guilty of crimes against humanity, and so on.

DERRIDA: To the extent that the criminals you have just mentioned are not condemned to death, we have indeed begun a process of cohabitation, and thus of reconciliation. That isn't the same thing as forgiving. But when you live together, even if you don't live well, a reconciliation is going on.

SPIRE: Let's come back to "who forgives whom for what?" When the unpardonable is crimes against humanity, the victims can no longer speak. But isn't it primarily up to the victims to forgive? Is it possible to forgive in the name of the victims, in their place?

DERRIDA: No! Only the victims might at some point have the right to forgive. If they are dead, or have disappeared in some way, no pardon is possible.

SPIRE: So the victims have to stay alive so as to forgive their torturers—that's the only way it can be?

DERRIDA: Yes.

SPIRE: But in what respect is it unforgivable? In that this has hurt, that it's put to death something in the victim? To forgive the unforgivable can never be death!

DERRIDA: Another aporia: it's all very well for the scene of forgiveness to require the singularity of a face-to-face encounter between the victim and the guilty party, but a third person is active from the start. Even if there are two of you, in the tête-à-tête, forgiveness also implies a third person as soon as it goes by way of a speech or some generally iterable trace. So, for instance, heirs (and the third person is in the position of heir, he preserves the trace) have a sort of right to speech. So the scene of forgiveness can and even must be prolonged after death, contradictory as that appears in relation to the requirement for the face-to-face encounter between two living people, the victim and the criminal.

SPIRE: Let's go from there to the question of the secret. Does the preservation of each person's identity presuppose that we preserve our secrets?

DERRIDA: The secret isn't just some thing, a content that would have to be hidden or kept within oneself. Others are secret because they are other. I am secret, I am *in secret*, like any other. A singularity is of its nature in secret. Nowadays, there is perhaps an ethical and political duty to respect the secret, a certain kind of right to a certain kind of secret. The totalitarian vocation is manifested as soon as this respect is lost. All the same—and this is where the difficulty comes in—there are also forms of abuse in relation to the secret, political exploitations of the "state secret," like the exploitations of "reasons of state," and police or other archives.

I would not want to let myself be imprisoned in a culture of the secret, which however I do rather like, as I like that figure of the Marrano,[17] which keeps popping up in all my texts. Some archives must not remain inaccessible, and the politics of the secret calls for very different kinds of responsibility, according to the situation. Once again, that can be said without relativism but in the name of another responsibility which must each time be singular, exceptional, and thus, as the principle of any decision, itself in some way secret.

SPIRE: And where then is the end of literature's vocation to give an account of the secret?

DERRIDA: Literature keeps a secret that doesn't exist, in a sense. Behind a novel, or a poem, behind what is in effect the richness of a sense to be interpreted, there is no secret meaning to be interpreted. A character's secret, for instance, does not exist; it has no thickness outside the literary phenomenon. Everything is secret in literature and there is no secret hidden *behind* it—there you have the secret of this strange institution *on the subject* of which, and *within* which I never stop wrestling: more precisely and most recently in essays like *Passions* or *The Gift of Death*, but also as far back as a text that is a fiction through and through, *The Post Card*.

Using *secret*, a word of Latin origin that primarily means separation or dissociation, we not quite correctly translate some other semantic forms that are instead oriented toward the interiority of the house (*Geheimnis*) or, in Greek, cryptic or hermetic dissimulation. All of that thus requires slow, prudent analyses. Since the political issues are such burning ones, and more than ever today, with all the advances in police or military technologies, and with all the new problems of cryptography, the question of literature is also becoming more serious again. The institution of literature recognizes, in principle or essentially, the right to say everything or to say without saying, and thus the right to the secret displayed as such. Literature is free. It should be. Its freedom is also the freedom promised by a democracy.

Among all the reasons for asking forgiveness from the point one starts writing or even speaking (I have listed quite a number elsewhere, especially in Safaa Fathy's film), there is also this one: the quasi sacralization of literature appeared at a point in time when an apparent desacralization of biblical texts had begun. Thus literature, as a faithful unfaithful heir, as a perjured heir, asks for forgiveness because it betrays. It betrays its truth.

14 ▓▓▓▓

Fichus

Frankfurt Address

On September 22, 2001, Jacques Derrida was given the Theodor W. Adorno Prize by the city of Frankfurt. This prize was inaugurated in 1977 and is awarded every three years; previous winners include Jürgen Habermas, Pierre Boulez, and Jean-Luc Godard. The prize rewards work which, in the spirit of the Frankfurt School, cuts across the domains of philosophy, the social sciences, and the arts (music, literature, painting, architecture, theatre, cinema, and so on).

The first and last paragraphs of Derrida's address were read in German. It had been written and translated in August. So the references to September 11 were added on the day of the ceremony.

Madame le maire, monsieur le consul général, cher professeur Waldenfels, chers collègues, chers amis: [Mayoress, Consul, Professor Waldenfels, colleagues, and friends:]

I apologize. I am getting ready to greet you and thank you in my language. And language will be my subject: the language of the other, the visitor's language, the foreigner's language, even the immigrant's, the emigré's, or the exile's. What will a responsible politics make of the plural and the singular, starting with the differences between languages in the Europe of the future, and, as with Europe, in the ongoing process of globalization? In what we call, ever more questionably, globalization, we in fact find ourselves on the verge of wars that, since September 11, are less sure than ever of their language, their meaning, and their name.

As an epigraph to this modest and simple expression of my gratitude, I would like to begin by reading a sentence that Walter Benjamin, one day, one night, himself dreamed *in French*. He told it *in French* to Gretel Adorno, in a letter he wrote her on October 12, 1939, from Nevers, where he was in an internment camp. In France at the time this was called a *camp de travailleurs volontaires* ("voluntary workers' camp"). In his dream, which, if we are to believe him, was euphoric, Benjamin says this to himself, in French: *Il s'agissait de changer en fichu une poésie* [It was about changing a poem into a *fichu*]. And he translates: "*Es handelte sich darum, aus einem Gedicht ein Halstuch zu machen* [It was about making a scarf out of a poem]."[1] In a moment, we will stroke this *fichu*, this scarf or shawl. We will spot in it a particular letter of the alphabet which Benjamin thought he recognized in his dream. And we'll also come back to *fichu*, which is not just any old French word for a woman's scarf or shawl.

Do we still dream in our beds? and at night? Are we responsible for our dreams? Can we answer for them? Suppose I am dreaming. My dream would be happy, like Benjamin's.

At this moment, speaking to you, standing up, eyes open, starting to thank you from the bottom of my heart, with the ghostly or *unheimlich*, uncanny gestures of a sleepwalker or even a bandit come to get his hands on a prize that wasn't meant for him—it's all *as if* I were dreaming. Admitting it, even: in truth, I am telling you that in gratefully greeting you, I think I'm dreaming. Even if the bandit or smuggler doesn't deserve what he gets, as in a Kafka narrative—the bad pupil who thinks he has been called, like Abraham, to be top of the class—his dream seems happy. Like me.

What's the difference between dreaming and thinking you're dreaming? And first of all who has the right to ask that question? The dreamer deep in the experience of his night or the dreamer when he wakes up? And could a dreamer speak of his dream without waking himself up? Could he name the dream in general? Could he analyze the dream properly and even use the word *dream* deliberately without interrupting and betraying, yes, *betraying* sleep.

I can imagine the two responses. The philosopher's would be a firm "no": you can't have a serious and responsible line on dreams, no one could even recount a dream without waking up. One could give hundreds of examples of this *negative* response, from Plato to Husserl, and I think it perhaps defines the essence of philosophy. This "no" links the responsibility of the philosopher to the rational imperative of wakefulness, the sovereign ego, and the vigilant consciousness. What is philosophy, for philosophers?

Being awake and awakening. Perhaps there would be a quite different, but no less responsible, response from poets, writers, or essayists, from musicians, painters, playwrights, or scriptwriters. Or even from psychoanalysts. They wouldn't say "no," but "yes, perhaps sometimes." They would acquiesce in the event, in its exceptional singularity: yes, perhaps you can believe and admit that you are dreaming without waking yourself up; yes, it is not impossible, sometimes, while you are asleep, your eyes tight shut or wide open, to utter something like a truth of the dream, a meaning and a reason of the dream that deserves not to sink down into the night of nothingness.

When it comes to this lucidity, this light, this *Aufklärung* of a discourse dreaming about dreams, it is none other than Adorno I like to think of. I admire and love in Adorno someone who never stopped hesitating between the philosopher's "no" and the "yes, perhaps, sometimes that does happen" of the poet, the writer or the essayist, the musician, the painter, the playwright, or scriptwriter, or even the psychoanalyst. In hesitating between the "no" and the "yes, sometimes, perhaps," Adorno was heir to both. He took account of what the concept, even the dialectic, could not conceptualize in the singular event, and he did everything he could to take on the responsibility of this double legacy.

What *does* Adorno suggest to us? The difference between the dream and reality, this truth to which the philosopher recalls us with an inflexible severity, would be that which injures, hurts, or damages (*beschädigt*) the most beautiful dreams and deposits the signature of a stain, a dirtying (*Makel*). The *no*, what one might call in another sense the *negativity* that philosophy sets against the dream, would be a wound of which the most beautiful dreams forever bear the scar.

A passage in *Minima Moralia* recalls this, and I single it out for two reasons. First of all, because in it Adorno talks about how the most beautiful dreams are spoiled, injured, mutilated, damaged (*beschädigt*), and hurt by a waking consciousness that lets us know that they are mere appearance (*Schein*) with regard to actual reality (*Wirklichkeit*). Now the word that Adorno uses for this wound, *beschädigt*, is the very one that appears in the subtitle to *Minima Moralia: Reflexionem aus dem beschädigten Leben* [*Reflections from Damaged Life*]. Not "reflections *on*" a wounded, injured, damaged, mutilated life, but "reflections *from* or *starting from*" such a life, *aus dem beschädigten Leben*: reflections marked by pain, signed by a wounding. The dedication of the book to Horkheimer explains what the form of this book owes to private life and the painful condition of "the intellectual in emigration" (*ausgegangen vom engsten privaten Bereich, dem des Intellektuellen in der Emigration*).

My other reason for choosing this passage from *Minima Moralia* is to mark my gratitude today to those who established the Adorno Prize and who respect his characteristic wit. As always with Adorno, this is his finest legacy, this theatrical fragment makes philosophy stand in the dock before the authority of all its others in a single act, on the same stage. Philosophy has to respond before the dream, before music—represented by Schubert—before poetry, before the theater and before literature, here represented by Kafka:

> Waking in the middle of a dream, even the worst, one feels disappointed, cheated of the best in life. But pleasant, fulfilled dreams are actually as rare, to use Schubert's words, as happy music. Even the loveliest dream bears like a blemish its difference from reality, the awareness that what it grants is mere illusion. This is why precisely the loveliest dreams are as if blighted. Such an impression is captured superlatively in the description of the nature theatre of Oklahoma in Kafka's *America*.[2]

Adorno was haunted by this Oklahoma theater in Kafka's *Amerika*, especially when he recalls his experimental research in the United States, his work on jazz, on something fetishistic about music, on the problems raised by the industrial production of cultural objects—where, as he says himself, his critique is meant as a response to Benjamin's "Das Kunstwerk im Zeitalter seiner technischen Reproduzierbarkeit" [The Work of Art in the Age of Mechanical Reproduction].[3] Whether or not this critique, like so many others, is justified in relation to Benjamin, we have more need than ever to ponder it today. In its analysis of a kind of commodification of culture, it is also the harbinger of a structural mutation in capital, in the cyberspace market, in human reproduction, in global concentration, and in property.

The "worst" nightmare (we can produce numerous historical examples from the start of the twentieth century up to last week): so we would be disappointed to be awoken from it, for it will have shown us how to think the irreplaceable, a truth or a meaning that consciousness might hide from us on waking, even put back to sleep. As though dreaming were a more vigilant state than being awake, the unconscious more thoughtful than consciousness, literature or the arts more philosophical, more critical, at any rate, than philosophy.

So I am speaking to you in the night, *as if* in the beginning was the dream. What is a dream? And dream-thought? And dream language? Could there be an ethics or politics of dreaming that did not yield to the imaginary or to the utopian, and was not an abandonment, irresponsible, and evasive? Once again my excuse for beginning like this comes from Adorno, and in particular from another of his remarks that moves me all the more because—as I do myself more and more often, too often perhaps—Adorno speaks literally of the possibility of the impossible, of the paradox of the possibility of the impossible (*vom Paradoxon der Möglichkeit des Unmöglichen*). In *Prismen* [Prisms], at the end of his 1955 "Portrait of Walter Benjamin," Adorno writes the following passage; I would like to make it a motto, at least for all the "last times" of my life: "In the form of the paradox of the impossible possibility, mysticism and enlightenment are joined for *the last time* in him [Benjamin]. He *overcame* the dream without *betraying* it [*ohne ihn zu* verraten] and making himself the accomplice in that on which the philosophers have always agreed: that it shall not be."[4]

The impossible possibility, the possibility of the impossible this is what Adorno says: *die Möglichkeit des Unmöglichen*. We shouldn't let ourselves be affected by "that on which the philosophers have always agreed," namely the first complicity to break up and the one you have to start by worrying about if you want to do a little thinking. *Overcoming* the dream without *betraying* it (*ohne ihn zu verraten*)—that's the way, says Benjamin, the author of a *Traumkitsch* [Dream Kitsch]:[5] to wake up, to cultivate awakeness and vigilance, while remaining attentive to meaning, faithful to the lessons and the lucidity of a dream, caring for what the dream lets us think about, especially when what it lets us think about is the *possibility of the impossible*. The possibility of the impossible can only be dreamed, but thinking, a quite different thinking of the relation between the possible and the impossible, this other thinking I have been panting after for so long, sometimes getting out of breath over it, running my courses and rushing about—this perhaps has more affinity than philosophy itself with this dream. Even as you wake up, you would have to go on watching out for the dream, watching over it. It is from this possibility of the impossible, and from what would have to be done so as to try to think it differently, to think thinking differently, through an unconditionality without indivisible sovereignty, outside what has dominated our metaphysical tradition, that I try in my own way to draw some ethical, juridical, and political consequences, whether it's to do with the idea of time, or the gift, or hospitality, or forgiveness, or the decision—or the democracy to come.

I have not yet begun to tell you how honored I am, but to justify my-self I have just heard Adorno speaking of Benjamin, those two expatriates; one of them never returned and it's not certain whether the other one ever did. In a moment, I will again speak of a Benjamin turned toward Adorno. As I will often have occasion to quote like this—well, it's another instance of Adorno quoting Benjamin that encourages me to think that my use of quotations here ought to be anything but academic, rule-bound, and con-ventional, but rather, once again, disturbing, disconcerting, even *unheim-lich*. Two pages before that, in the same text, Adorno recalls that Benjamin "meant . . . literally (*wortlich*)" the sentence in *One-Way Street* which said that citations from his works were like highwaymen (*wie Raüber am Wege*), who suddenly descend on the reader to rob him of his convictions."[6] You can be sure of this, the person you are honoring today with a major prize that he is not sure he deserves is also someone who always runs the risk, es-pecially when he is quoting, of being more like the "highwaymen" than a lot of worthy professors of philosophy, even friends of his.

I'm dreaming. I'm sleepwalking. I think I have been dreaming, so as to enable you to hear my gratitude in relation to the great privilege I am being granted today, and probably I am also dreaming of knowing how to speak to you not just as a robber but poetically, as a poet. I certainly won't be capable of the poem I dream of. And then in what language could I have written it or sung it? or dreamed it? I would be divided between, on one side, the laws of hospitality, meaning the desire of the grateful guest who ought to be addressing you in your language, and, on the other, my unshakeable attachment to a French idiom, without which I would be lost, more than ever an exile. For what I most understand and share with Adorno, to the point of compassion, is perhaps his love of language, and even a sort of nostalgia for what will still have been his *own* language. An originary nostalgia, a nostalgia that has not waited for the real loss of lan-guage as a historical event, a congenital nostalgia as old as our bodily close-ness to what is called maternal—or paternal—language. As if this language had been lost since childhood, since the first word. As if this catastrophe were doomed to be repeated. As if it threatened to come back at every his-torical turning point, and for Adorno even with his American exile. In his response to the traditional question "What is German?" in 1965, Adorno revealed that his desire to come back to Germany from the United States in 1949 was primarily because of language. "The decision to return to Ger-many was hardly motivated simply by a subjective need, by home-sickness [*von Heimweh motiviert*]. There was also an objective factor. It is the language (*Auch ein Objecktives machte sich geltend. Das ist die Sprache*)."[7]

Why is it that there is something more than nostalgia in this, and something other than a subjective affect? Why does Adorno attempt to justify his return to Germany by a language argument meant here as an "objective" reason? The case he makes should be exemplary nowadays for all those, throughout the world but particularly in the Europe that is presently being constructed, who seek to define another ethics or another politics, another economy, even another ecology of language: how to cultivate the poeticity of idiom in general, your home, your *oikos*; how to save linguistic difference, whether regional or national; how to resist both the international hegemony of a language of communication (and for Adorno this was already Anglo-American); how to oppose the instrumental utilitarianism of a purely functional language of communication but *without* however yielding to nationalism, state nationalism, or the nation-state's insistence on sovereignty; *without* giving those rusty old weapons to the revival of identities and to all the old ideology—pro-sovereignty, separatist, and differentialist?

Adorno engages, sometimes dangerously, in a complex argument to which, almost twenty years ago, I devoted a long, tormented discussion as part of a course of seminars I was giving on "nationalism," on "Kant, the Jew, the German," on Wagner's "*Was ist deutsch?*" [What is German?] and on what I then called—to give a name to an enigmatic specularity, a large and terrible historical mirror—the "Judeo-German psyche." Let me hold onto just two features of this.

1. The first would be the stress—classically and some might say disturbingly—on the privileges of the German language. A double privilege, in regard to philosophy and in regard to what unites philosophy with literature: Adorno notes that "the German language seems to have a special elective affinity for philosophy (*eine besondere Wahlverwandtschaft zur Philosophie*) and especially for its speculative element which is so easily distrusted in the West as dangerously unclear—and not entirely without justification."[8] If it is difficult to translate advanced philosophical texts, like Hegel's *Phenomenology of Spirit* or *The Science of Logic*, Adorno thinks this is because German embeds its philosophical concepts in a natural language that you have to have known from childhood. Hence a *radical* alliance between philosophy and literature—radical because nourished from the same *roots*, those of childhood. "There has never been a great philosopher," says

Adorno, citing Ulrich Sonnemann, "who was not also a great writer."[9] And how right he is! On the subject of childhood, which was one of his insistent themes—on the subject of one's childhood language, is it by chance that Adorno returns to this right after two famous short aphorisms on the Jews and language: *Der Antisemitismus ist das Gerücht über die Juden* and *Fremdwörter sind die Juden der Sprache* ("Anti-Semitism is the rumour about the Jews" and "German words of foreign derivation are the Jews of language")?[10] Is it then by chance that immediately after his "helpless sadness" (*fassungslose Traurigkeit*), Adorno reveals to us his melancholy (*Schwermut*) in realizing he has spontaneously let the language of his childhood "awaken," as he puts it—or, to be more exact, in realizing that, as if he were pursuing a waking dream, a daydream, a dialectal shape from his childhood, from his mother language, he has let awaken the language he had spoken in the town he came from originally, which he therefore calls *Vaterstadt* [native or "father" town]. *Muttersprache* and *Vaterstadt*?

One evening, in a mood of helpless sadness [*An einem Abend der fassungslosen Traurigkeit*], I caught myself using a ridiculously wrong subjunctive form of a verb that was itself not entirely correct German, being part of the dialect of my native town. I had not heard, let alone used, the endearing misconstruction since my first years at school. Melancholy [*Schwermut*], drawing me irresistibly into the abyss of childhood [*in den Abgrund der Kindheit*], *awakened* this old, impotently yearning sound in its depths [*weckte auf dem Grunde den alten, ohnmächtig verlangenden Laut*]. Language sent back to me like an echo the humiliation which unhappiness had inflicted on me in forgetting what I am.[11]

Dream, poetic idiom, melancholy, abyss of childhood—*Abgrund der Kindheit*—that is nothing other, as you have heard, than the depth of a musical base (*Grund*), the secret resonance of the voice or words that are waiting in us, as at the bottom of Adorno's first proper name, but *impotent* (*auf dem Grunde den alten, ohnmächtig verlangenden Laut*). I stress *ohnmächtig*: impotent, vulnerable. If I had had time, I would have liked to do more than sketch out a reconstruction of the argument; I would have explored a logic of Adorno's thought which attempts, in a quasi-systematic way, to shield from violence all these weaknesses, these vulnerabilities, and these victims *with no defense*, and even to shield them from the cruelty of traditional interpretation, in other words from philosophical, metaphysical, idealist—even dialectical—and capitalist forms of inspection exercise. The specimen exhibit for this defenseless being, this power-deprivation, this vulnerable *Ohnmächtigkeit*, can be the dream, or language, or the unconscious, just as well as the animal, the child, the Jew, the foreigner, or the woman. Adorno was less "undefended" than Benjamin, but he was that too himself, so Jürgen Habermas says in a book in memory of Adorno: "Adorno was defenseless. . . . In the presence of "Teddy" one could play out in an uncircumspect way the role of "proper" adult because he was never in a position to appropriate for himself that role's strategies of immunization and adaptation. In every institutional setting he was 'out of place,' and not as if he intended to be."[12]

2. Another feature of *Was ist Deutsch* counts for more in my view. A critical warning follows this eulogy for "the specific and objective quality of the German language" (*eine spezifische, objektive Eigenschaft der deutschen Sprache*).[13] We recognize in this an indispensable safeguard for the political future of Europe or of globalization: while continuing to contest linguistic hegemonies and what they determine, we should begin by "deconstructing" both the onto-theologico-political fantasies of an indivisible sovereignty and pro-nation-state metaphysics. Adorno does definitely, and how well I understand him, want to go on loving the German language, to go on cultivating that originary intimacy with his idiom—but without nationalism, without the collective narcissism (*kollektiven Narzissmus*) of a "metaphysics" of language.[14] We know the tradition and the temptation, in this country and others, of this metaphysics of the national language, and "vigilance" against it, he says, the watchfulness of the lookout, must be "untiring":

The returning exile, having lost the naive relation to what is his own, must unite the most intimate relation to his own language with untiring vigilance [*mit unermüdlicher Wachsamkeit*] regarding any swindle which it promotes, a vigilance regarding the belief that what I would like to designate the metaphysical surplus of the German language [*den metaphysischen Überschuss der deutschen Sprache*] is itself sufficient to guarantee the truth of the metaphysics it suggests, or of metaphysics in general. In this context I might perhaps admit that this is why I wrote *The Jargon of Authenticity*. . . . The metaphysical character of language is no privilege. One must not borrow from it the idea of depth which becomes suspicious the moment it engages in self-glorification. This is similar to the concept of the German soul. . . . No one who writes in German and knows how much his thoughts are saturated by the German language should forget Nietzsche's critique of this sphere.[15]

This reference to *Der Jargon der Eigentlichkeit* would take us too far afield. I prefer to hear in this profession of faith an appeal to a new *Auf-*

klärung. A little further on, Adorno declares that it is this metaphysical cult of language, depth, and the German soul that has caused the Enlightenment century to be accused of the heresy of being "superficial."[16]

Lady Mayor, colleagues, and friends: When I asked how much time I had to speak, I received three different replies from three different people. These were motivated, I imagine, by legitimate anxiety as much as by desire: the first was fifteen to twenty minutes, then there was thirty minutes, then finally thirty to forty-five minutes. Well, that's the painful economy of a speech of this kind, and I haven't yet begun to touch on my debt to you, to the city and the university of Frankfurt, to so many friends and colleagues (especially Professor Habermas and Professor Honneth)—to all those, both in Frankfurt and elsewhere in Germany, who must forgive me for not mentioning them by name other than in a summary note.[17] There are so many of them: the translators (beginning with Stefan Lorenzer who is here today), the students, and the publishers who have made me so welcome on previous occasions, going back to 1968—at the universities of Berlin, Freiburg im Breisgau, Heidelberg, Kassel, Bochum, Siegen, and above all Frankfurt, three times, last year as well: for a lecture series on the University, for a joint seminar with Jürgen Habermas and, as long ago as 1984, for a big symposium on Joyce.

Before hastening to my conclusion, I don't want to forget either the *fichu* in Benjamin's dream or the contents page of a virtual book on this Adorno Prize, a book and a prize that I no longer hope I may one day achieve or deserve. I spoke to you about language and dreaming, then about a dreamed-of language, then about a dream language, that language you dream of speaking—here now is the dream's language, as we would say since Freud.

I won't inflict on you a lesson in philology, semantics, or pragmatics. I won't pursue the derivations and uses of this extraordinary word, *fichu*. It means different things according to whether it is being used as a noun or an adjective. The *fichu*—and this is the most obvious meaning in Benjamin's sentence—designates a shawl, the piece of material that a woman may put on in a hurry, around her head or neck. But the adjective *fichu* denotes evil: that which is bad, lost, condemned. One day in September 1970, seeing his death approaching, my sick father said to me, "I'm *fichu*." My speech to you today is very oneirophilic, and the reason is that dreaming is the element most receptive to mourning, to haunting, to the spectrality of all spirits and the return of the ghosts (such as those adoptive fathers Adorno and Benjamin—that's what they were for us and others too, in their disagreements as well, and that's what Adorno perhaps was for Benjamin). The dream is also a place that is hospitable to the demand for justice and to the most invincible of messianic hopes. In French we sometimes say *foutu* instead of *fichu*. *Foutu* suggests the eschatological register of death or the end, and also the scatological register of sexual violence. Sometimes irony creeps in. *Il s'est fichu de quelqu'un* means he laughed at someone, he didn't take them seriously or didn't act responsibly in relation to them.

This is how Benjamin begins the long letter he wrote Gretel Adorno, in French, on October 12, 1939, from an internment camp in the Nièvre region: "Last night on the straw bed I had a dream so beautiful that I can't resist the desire to tell you it. . . . It's the sort of dream I have maybe once in five years and which are embroidered around the theme of 'reading.' Teddie will remember the role this theme played in my reflections on knowledge."[18]

So a message meant for Teddy, for Adorno, Gretel's husband. Why does Benjamin tell this dream to the wife, not the husband? Why, four years before, was it also in a letter to Gretel Adorno that Benjamin responded to some slightly authoritarian and paternal criticisms that Adorno had sent him, as he often did, in a letter, and on the subject of dreams— the relationships between "dream figures" and the "dialectical image"?[19] I leave this hive of questions dormant.

The long narrative that follows [in the letter to Gretel Adorno of 1939] brings back into the picture (this is my own selective interpretation) an "old straw hat," a "panama" that Benjamin had inherited from his father. In his dream it had a large crack on its upper part, with "traces of the color red" at the edges of the crack. Then there are women, one of whom is a graphologist and is holding in her hand something that Benjamin had written. He comes up to her and he says:

What I saw was a material covered with images. The only graphical elements in it that I could make out were the upper parts of the letter *d*, whose slender lengths concealed an intense aspiration toward spirituality. This part of the letter moreover had a little sail with a blue border, and the sail billowed out on the design as if a breeze was blowing it. It was the only thing I could "read." . . . The conversation turned for a moment on this writing. . . . At one point I was saying this, *verbatim*: "It was about changing a poem into a *fichu*." [*Es handelte sich darum, aus einem*

Gedicht ein Halstuch zu machen.] . . . Among the women there was one who was very beautiful and was in bed. Hearing my explanation she made a quick movement like a flash. She moved a tiny little bit of the cover that was keeping her safe in bed. . . . And this was not to let me see her body, but the design on her sheet which must have offered an imagery comparable to the one I must have "written," many years ago, as a present for Dausse. . . . After having this dream, I couldn't get to sleep for hours. It was happiness. And it is so that you can share these hours that I am writing to you.[20]

"Do we always dream in our beds?" I asked at the beginning. And so we have Benjamin writing to Gretel Adorno from his internment camp, that he had had the experience of dreaming, in his own bed, of a woman "in bed," a "very beautiful" woman displaying for him the "design on her sheet." Like a signature or initialing, this design bore Benjamin's own writing. We can always speculate about the *d* that Benjamin discovers on the *fichu.* Perhaps it is Dr. Dausse's initial—it was he who had treated him for malaria and who, in the dream, had given one of his women something that Benjamin says he wrote. In his letter Benjamin puts the words "read" and "write" in quotation marks. But the *d* may also be, among other hypotheses, among other initials, like the first letter of Detlef. Benjamin sometimes familiarly signed his letters "Detlef." This was also the first name he used in some of his pseudonyms, like Detlev Holz, which was the political pseudonym he adopted for *Deutsche Menschen* [German Men], another epistolary book, when he was an emigrant in Switzerland in 1936.[21] This was how he always signed his letters to Gretel Adorno, sometimes adding *Dein alter Detlef* [your older Detlef]. As it is both read and written by Benjamin, the letter *d* would then indicate the initial of his own signature, as if Detlef was to be understood as "I am the *fichu* one," and even from his voluntary workers' camp, less than a year before his suicide, and like every mortal who says me, in his dream language: "Me, *d*, I'm *fichu.*" Less than a year before his suicide, a few months before thanking Adorno for having sent him greetings from New York for his last birthday, which was also on July 15, as is mine, Benjamin dreamed, knowing it without knowing it, a sort of poetic and premonitory hieroglyphic: "Me, *d*, from now on I'm what is called *fichu.*" Now the signatory knows it, he says so to Gretel, none of it can be said, written, and read, it can't be signed like that, in a dream, and decoded, other than in French: "The sentence I pronounced [*sic*] distinctly toward the end of this dream also happened to be in French. A double reason for giving you this narrative in the same language." No translation, in the conventional sense of the word, will ever give an account of it, a transparently communicable account. In French, the same person can be, without contradiction and at the same moment, *fichu, bien fichu,* and *mal fichu.*[22] And yet a certain didactic movement respectful of idioms is possible—is even called for, needed, or universally desirable—*starting from* the untranslatable. For instance in a university or in a church on a prize-giving day. Especially if you don't rule out the possibility that the dream also played a part in this throw of the dice—this is what Werner Hamacher has whispered to me—playing the first name of Walter Benjamin's first wife but also that of his sister who was very ill at the time. That name is Dora, which in Greek can mean skin that has been scorched, scratched, or worked over.[23]

In that it leaves Benjamin sleepless afterward, this dream seems to resist the law declared by Freud: "throughout our whole sleeping state we know just as certainly that we are dreaming as we know that we are sleeping [*wir den ganzen Schlafzustand über ebenso sicher wissen, das wir träumen, wie wir es wissen, das wir schlafen*]."[24] The ultimate wish of the system that holds sovereign sway over the unconscious is the *wish to sleep,* the wish to withdraw into sleeping [*während sich das herrschende System auf den Wunsch zu schlafen zurückgezogen hat*].[25]

For decades I have been hearing voices, as they say, in my dreams. They are sometimes friendly voices, sometimes not. They are voices in me. All of them seem to be saying to me: why not recognize, clearly and publicly, once and for all, the affinities between your work and Adorno's, in truth your debt to Adorno? Aren't you an heir of the Frankfurt School?

Within me and outside me the response to this will always remain complicated, of course, and partly virtual. But from now on, and for this I say "thank you" once again, I can no longer act as if I weren't hearing these voices. While the landscape of influences, filiations, or legacies, of resistances too, will always remain craggy, labyrinthine, or abyssal, and in this case perhaps more contradictory and overdetermined than ever, today I am happy that thanks to you I can and must say "yes" to my debt to Adorno, and on more than one count, even if I am not yet capable of responding adequately to it or taking up its responsibilities.

If I had been going to make my gratitude decently measure up to the noble heights of what is given me by you, namely a sign of confidence and the assignation of a responsibility, to respond to it and correspond to it, I would have had to conquer two temptations. In asking you to forgive me a double failure, I will tell you, in the mode of denial, what *I would have liked not* to do or what I *ought not* to do.

It would have been necessary *on the one hand* to avoid any narcissistic complacency, and *on the other* to avoid overestimation or overinterpretation, whether philosophical, historical, or political, of the event with which you are so generously associating me today—me, my work, even the country, the culture, and the language in which my modest history is rooted or from which it takes its nourishment, however disloyal and marginal it remains there. If one day I were to write the book I dream of to interpret the history, the possibility, and the honor of this prize, it would include at least seven chapters. These, in the style of a TV guide, are the provisional titles:

1. A comparative history of the French and German legacies of Hegel and Marx; their joint but so very different rejections of idealism and especially speculative dialectics, before and after the war. This chapter, round about ten thousand pages, would be devoted to the difference between *critique* and *deconstruction*, in particular through the concepts of "determined negativity," sovereignty, totality and divisibility, autonomy, fetishism (including what Adorno is right to call the fetishism, in some *Kulturkritik*, of the "concept of culture"[26]) through the different concepts of *Aufklärung* and *Lumières*,[27] as with the debates and frontiers inside the German field but also inside the French field (these two groupings are sometimes more heterogeneous than one thinks within the national borders, which leads to many errors of perspective). To keep narcissism quiet, I would say nothing about all the differences involved in my not belonging to so-called French culture and especially French academic culture, which I do also know I am part of: this makes things too complicated for the present short speech.

2. A comparative history in the political tragedy of the two countries, in relation to the reception and legacy of Heidegger. Here too, in ten thousand pages or so on this crucial issue, I would go over the similarities and differences between the strategies. And I would be trying to indicate in what way my own strategy, which is at least as hesitant as Adorno's, and at any rate radically deconstructive, goes in a quite different direction and responds to quite different demands. By the same token, we would have to undertake a complete reinterpretation of the legacies of Nietzsche and Freud, and even, if I may go this far, of Husserl, and even, if I may go even further, of Benjamin. (If Gretel Adorno were still alive, I would write her a

confidential letter about the relationship between Teddie and Detlef. I would ask her why Benjamin doesn't have a prize, and I would share my hypotheses on this subject with her.)

3. The interest in psychoanalysis. Generally foreign to German university philosophers, but practically all French philosophers of my generation or the one right before shared this interest with Adorno. Among other things, it would be necessary to insist on the *political* vigilance that must be exercised, without overreaction or injustice, in the reading of Freud. I would have liked to cross a passage in *Minima Moralia*, entitled "This side of the pleasure principle," with what I recently dubbed "beyond beyond the pleasure principle."[28]

4. After *Auschwitz*, whatever this name means, whatever the debates opened up by Adorno's prescriptions on the subject (I can't analyze them here—there are too many of them and they are too diverse and complex), whether or not one agrees with him (and you won't expect me now to present a thoroughly argued position on this in a few sentences)—in each case, Adorno's *undeniable* merit, the unique event which will come to bear his signature, is to have woken up so many thinkers, writers, teachers, or artists to their responsibility in the face of everything of which Auschwitz must remain *both* the irreplaceable proper name *and* a metonymy.

5. A differential history of the resistances and misunderstandings between on the one hand those German thinkers who are also my respected friends, I mean Hans-Georg Gadamer and Jürgen Habermas, and on the other the French philosophers of my generation; for a little while this history has been largely over, but perhaps not yet over with. In this chapter, I would try to show that despite the differences between these two great debates (direct or indirect, explicit or implicit), the *misunderstandings* always occur around interpretation and the very possibility of *misunderstanding*— they turn around the *concept of misunderstanding*, of dissensus as well, of the other and the singularity of the event; but then, as a result, they turn around the essence of idiom, the essence of language, beyond its undeniable and necessary *functioning*, beyond its communicative intelligibility. The misunderstandings on this subject may be past, but they sometimes still pass via effects of idiom that are not only linguistic but also traditional, national, or institutional—sometimes also idiosyncratic and personal, conscious or unconscious. If these misunderstandings about misunderstanding seem to be calming down these days, if not totally melting away, in an atmosphere of amicable reconciliation, we should not only pay tribute to the

work, the reading, the good faith, and the friendship of various people, often the youngest philosophers in this country. We should also take into account the growing awareness of political responsibilities *to be shared* in relation to the future, and not only that of Europe: discussions, deliberations, and decisions that are political, but also about *the essence of the political*, about the new strategies to be invented, about joint positions to take up, about a logic of sovereignty and even the impasses of sovereignty (state sovereignty or otherwise) that can no longer be either endorsed or simply discredited with regard to the new forms of capitalism and the global market, with regard to a new figure, even a new constitution of Europe, which, by faithful infidelity, should be something other than what the various "crises" of the European spirit diagnosed in this past century have represented it—but also something other than a superstate, just an economic or military competitor to the United States or China.

Never before have the responsibilities in this regard been more singular, more acute, and more necessary: being Adorno's birthday, the date of September 11 ought to remind us of this rather than announcing it, as it did in New York or Washington.[29] Never before will it have been more urgent to find another way of thinking of Europe. This different thinking of Europe involves a deconstructive critique that is sober, wide awake, vigilant, and attentive to everything that solders the political to the metaphysical, to capitalist speculating, to the perversions of religious or nationalist feeling, or to the fantasy of sovereignty—through the best accredited of strategies, and the most accepted of political rhetorics, and media and tele-technological authorities, and spontaneous or organized movements of opinion. Outside Europe but in Europe as well. On all sides. I have to say it too swiftly but I venture to maintain this firmly: on all sides. My absolute compassion for all the victims of September 11 will not prevent me from saying: I do not believe in the political innocence of anyone in this crime. And if my compassion for all the innocent victims is limitless, it is because it does not stop with those who died on September 11 in the United States. That is my interpretation of what should be meant by what we have been calling since yesterday, in the White House's words, "infinite justice": not to exonerate ourselves from our own wrongdoings and the mistakes of our own politics, even at the point of paying the most terrible price, out of all proportion.

6. The question of literature, at the point where it is indissociable from the question of language and its institutions, would play a crucial role

in this history. What I shared most easily with Adorno, even took from him, as did other French philosophers—although again in different ways—is his interest in literature and in what, like the other arts, it can critically decenter in the field of university philosophy. Here too one would have to take into account the community of interests on both sides of the Rhine, and the difference between the two literatures but also the difference in the music and the painting and even the cinema, while remaining attentive to the spirit of what Kandinsky, cited by Adorno, called, without hierarchizing, *Klangfarbe*, or "tone color."[30]

This would lead me to a history of mutual reading, before and after the war, inside and outside the academy; and to a politology of translation, of the relations between the cultural market of publishing and the academy, and so on. All this in a style that would sometimes remain very close to Adorno's.

7. Finally I get to the chapter that I would most enjoy writing, because it would take the least trodden but in my view one of the most crucial paths in the future reading of Adorno. It is about what we call, in the singular—which has always shocked me—the *Animal*. As if there were only one of them. By referring to a number of little noticed outlines or suggestions of Adorno's in the book he wrote in the United States with Horkheimer, *Dialektik der Aufklärung*, or in *Beethoven: Philosophie der Musik*, I would try to show (I have already tried to do this elsewhere), that here there are premises that need to be deployed with great prudence, the gleams at least of a revolution in thought and action that we need, a revolution in our dwelling together with these other living things that we call the animals. Adorno understood that this new critical—I would rather say "deconstructive"—ecology had to set itself against two formidable forces, often opposed to one another, sometimes allied.[31]

On one side, that of the most powerful idealist and humanist tradition of philosophy. The sovereignty or mastery (*Herrschaft*) of man over nature is in truth "directed against animals" (*sie richtet sich gegen die Tiere*), Adorno specifies here. He particularly blames Kant, whom he respects too much from another point of view, for not giving any place in his concept of dignity (*Würde*) and the "autonomy" of man to any compassion (*Mitleid*) between man and the animal. Nothing is more odious (*verhasster*) to Kantian man, says Adorno, than remembering a resemblance or affinity between man and animality (*die Erinnerung an die Tierähnlichkeit des Menschen*). The Kantian feels only hate for human animality. This is even his taboo. Adorno speaks of *Tabuierung* and goes a very long way straight off: for an idealist system, animals play a role virtually the same as the Jews in a fascist system (*die Tiere spielen fürs idealistische System virtuell die gleiche Rolle wie die Juden fürs faschistische*). Animals are the Jews of idealists, who are thus just virtual fascists. Fascism begins when you insult an animal, including the animal in man. Authentic idealism (*echter Idealismus*) consists in *insulting* the animal in man or in treating a man like an animal. Adorno twice uses the word *insult* (*schimpfen*).

But on the other side, on the other front, one of the themes of the fragment called "Man and Animal" in the *Dialectic of Enlightenment*, is that one should fight against the ideology concealed in the troubled interest in animals, that the fascists, the Nazis, and the Führer did in fact seem to show, sometimes to the point of vegetarianism.

The seven chapters of this history I dream of are already being written, I'm sure. What we are sharing today certainly testifies to that. These wars and this peace will have their new historians, and even their "historians' wars" (*Historikerstreit*). But we don't yet know how and in what medium, under what veils for which Schleiermacher of a future hermeneutics, on what canvas and on what internet *fichu* the artist of this weaving will be hard at work (the Plato of the *Statesman* would call him or her a *hyphantès* [weaver]). We will never know, not us, on what Web *fichu* some Weber to come will plan to author or teach our history.

No historical metalanguage to bear witness to it in the transparent element of some absolute knowledge.

Celan:

Niemand
zeugt für den
Zeugen.[32]

Thank you again for your patience.

Notes

CHAPTER 2: THE BOOK TO COME

This piece introduced a discussion with Roger Chartier and Bernard Stiegler that took place at the new Bibliothèque nationale de France [French National Library], also known as the Bibliothèque François Mitterrand, on March 20, 1997.

1. Stéphane Mallarmé, *Un Coup de dés* (A Throw of the Dice) (1897), in *Collected Poems*, trans. and with a commentary by Henry Weinfield (Berkeley: University of California Press, 1994), pp. 124–45.

2. Mallarmé, "Le Livre, instrument spirituel" (The Book, Spiritual Instrument) (1895), in *Oeuvres complètes* (Paris: Gallimard: Pléiade, 1979), p. 378.

3. Ibid., p. 379.

4. Maurice Blanchot, *The Book to Come* (1959), trans. Charlotte Mandell (Stanford, Calif.: Stanford University Press, 2003), p. 234; trans. mod.

5. Ibid., pp. 234–35; trans. mod.

6. Ibid., p. 243.

7. Jacques Derrida, *Of Grammatology* (1967), trans. Gayatri Chakravorty Spivak (Baltimore: Johns Hopkins University Press, 1976), p. 16.

8. In French there is a play here on the word *maintenant*, "now," which is literally "hand-holding," from *main* (hand) and *tenir* (hold). *Maintenir* ("maintain"), in the previous sentence, is etymologically the same: to maintain is to hold with the hand.—Trans.

CHAPTER 3: THE WORD PROCESSOR

First published in *La Quinzaine Littéraire* (August 1996) as "Entretien avec Jacques Derrida sur le 'traitement de texte'" (Interview with Jacques Derrida on "Word Processing"). The interview was conducted by Béatrice and Louis Seguin.

1. Derrida, "*Geschlecht* II: Heidegger's Hand," trans. John P. Leavey, Jr., in *Deconstruction and Philosophy: The Texts of Jacques Derrida*, ed. John Sallis (Chicago: University of Chicago Press, 1987).

2. Derrida, "Heidegger's Ear: Philopolemology (*Geschlecht* IV)," trans. John P. Leavey, Jr., in *Reading Heidegger: Commemorations*, ed. John Sallis (Bloomington: Indiana University Press, 1993), pp. 163–218.

3. Derrida, "Freud and the Scene of Writing," in *Writing and Difference* (1967), trans. Alan Bass (Chicago: University of Chicago Press, 1978), pp. 196–231; and *Archive Fever: A Freudian Impression* (1995), trans. Eric Prenowitz (Chicago: University of Chicago Press, 1996).

4. There is a play here on the literal meaning of *maintenant* (now). See Chapter 2, note 8.—Trans.

5. An allusion to Victor Hugo's famous question *De quoi demain sera-t-il fait?* ("What will tomorrow be made of?"). *De quoi demain . . . : Dialogue* is the title of a book of conversations between Derrida and Elisabeth Roudinesco (Paris: Fayard/Galilée, 2001).—Trans.

6. On the discussion of "the end of the book" in *Of Grammatology*, see above, pp. 14–15.—Trans.

CHAPTER 4: "BUT . . . NO, BUT . . . NEVER . . . , AND YET . . . "

This piece was a response to a survey by the journal *Lignes*, in volume 32 (October 1997). The introduction to the survey, given here, spelled out the question being asked, with a view to a reply of "two or three pages."

1. The word *cohabitation* in French is also used of the situation in which more than one party shares government.—Trans.

2. Mgr. Jacques Gaillot is a bishop and human rights activist; the Abbé Pierre is a campaigner on behalf of the poor.

3. A reference to Guy Debord's influential book *The Society of the Spectacle* (1967), trans. Donald Nicholson-Smith (New York: Zone Books, 1992).—Trans.

4. Let's imagine the founding of a new state—on an internet site (with or without the classic institutional authorities: a constitution, the vote, a parliamentary assembly; legislative, executive, and independent judiciary powers, and so on; with or without recognition by the international community, at the end of a more or less traditional process, and so on). So what would be distinctive about this state? The fact that its subject-citizens had never seen or met one another? But we have never seen or met the vast majority of French people; and in fact internet subjects will one day be able to see one another on the screen: they already can, practically. What else? That the "inhabitants" of this virtual state would have no history and memory in common? But no one can guarantee that all the citizens of a country fully share either of these. Except for the history and memory enveloped by a language that is *more or less* a shared one, sometimes not much shared (there is much more to say on this measurement of sharing than there is room for here). That this *virtual* state—virtual in the double sense of the word—would be without territory? Yes, here there presumably is a relevant distinction. It reveals a *constitutive* imaginary or fiction: the supposedly legitimate occupation of a fixed territory, if not the assumption of autochthonous origin, has up till now been a condition of civic belonging, in reality the very being of politics, its link to the nation-state, if not to the state.

This *situation* is in the process of letting itself be overthrown by a shake-up that we would call seismic if this figure didn't still have too much to do with the ground. What we feel is coming is not so much an earthquake as a shake-up *in relation to the ground and to the earth.*

A virtual state whose place is an internet site, a state without ground area — the question that orients us is: will that be an intellectual state? A state whose citizens would essentially be intellectuals—intellectuals *in that they were* citizens? A science-fiction question? I don't think so at all. There are perhaps lots of virtual quasi states of this kind, and have been for a long time. Perhaps it is also written into the concept of the state. An intellectual-state—good thing?

Another mode, another time for the old question: how can one not become, *virtually*, a state intellectual?

CHAPTER 5: PAPER OR ME, YOU KNOW . . .

First published in *Les Cahiers de médiologie* 4 (1997), special issue *Pouvoirs du papier* (Powers of Paper), edited by Marc Guillaume and Daniel Bougnoux.

1. See Derrida, *Dissemination* (1972), trans. Barbara Johnson (London: Athlone Press, 1981), p. 313.

2. The printing connotation—as in "second impression," applied to a reprint—is much more obvious in the French, where *impression* is the ordinary noun for "printing."—Trans.

3. *Chagrin*, a word of Turkish origin, already designates a tanned skin. [In English it is *shagreen*. In French *chagrin* primarily means grief or disappointment.—Trans.] But in the novel that also ends with a scene of burned paper— "the remains of a letter blackened by the fire"—Balzac plays on the word insistently (e.g., "The *chagrin* you inflicted on me would no longer be a *chagrin*"). Even including the "piece of *chagrin*," the "talisman" of this "wonderful skin," it was possible to read "letters encrusted in the cellular tissue," "letters . . . printed or inlaid," "inlaid in the surface," "written speeches." "'There,' he said . . . pointing to the *skin of chagrin*, 'there are To Will and To Have your will, both together.'" And previously: "To Will consumes us, and To Have our Will destroys us, but To Know steeps our feeble organisms in perpetual calm" (Balzac, *The Wild Ass's Skin* [*La Peau de chagrin*, 1831], trans. Ellen Marriage [London: Everyman, 1926], pp. 26–30).

4. *Hypokeimenon* is Greek for "underlying."—Trans.

5. I have dealt with these questions under the heading of the "subjectile" in the wake of Antonin Artaud ("To Unsense the Subjectile," in Paule Thévenin and Jacques Derrida, *The Secret Art of Antonin Artaud* (1986), trans. Mary Ann Caws (Cambridge, Mass.: MIT Press, 2000), pp. 59–157). I mention this here first of all to point out a legal problem that touches significantly on the appropriation of paper. Artaud's nephew saw fit to take the authors of this book to court on the grounds that he had a moral right over the reproduction of graphical works that are in no way his property. It was these works, their material support, their paper

or "subjectile," that his uncle had sometimes indefatigably worked at until he burned or put holes in or perforated the body of them—these are the famous *sorts* (spells) that Artaud cast or cast out. While the trial continues, these "works" on paper, these unique archives of a quasi destruction, cannot be reproduced legally (at least not in color or full-page). The book in which we collected, presented, and interpreted them for the first time has also been banned in its original language. [And the images of the original could not be included in the English translation of the book, cited above and published since this interview.—Trans.]

6. Derrida, *Monolingualism of the Other; or, The Prosthesis of Origin* (1996), trans. Patrick Mensah (Stanford, Calif.: Stanford University Press, 1998), p. 78.

7. Derrida, "Tympan," in *Margins—Of Philosophy* (1972), trans. Alan Bass (Chicago: University of Chicago Press, 1982), pp. ix–xxix; "Circumfession," in Geoffrey Bennington and Derrida, *Jacques Derrida* (1991), trans. Geoffrey Bennington (Chicago: University of Chicago Press, 1991). The other titles mentioned are all books.

8. See above, note 1.

9. I don't know the current figures, but it is worth noting that in 1970, when half the paper produced was for "printing," an inhabitant of the United States consumed 250 kilograms a year, a European less than half that, an inhabitant of the Soviet Union less than a tenth. The figures were vastly lower for Latin America, Africa, and Asia. It seems most unlikely that this tendency has been reversed. But it will be interesting to measure the differential development of this curve during the past decades and especially in the future.

10. See note 3, above.

11. I attempted a reading of this text of Freud's "*Notiz über den 'Wunderblock'*" (A Note on the 'Mystic Writing-Pad'") in "Freud and the Scene of Writing," in *Writing and Difference* (1967), trans. Alan Bass (Chicago: University of Chicago Press, 1978), pp. 196–231.

12. Freud, "A Note upon the 'Mystic Writing-Pad'" (1925), in the *Standard Edition of the Complete Psychological Works of Sigmund Freud*, trans. James Strachey (London: Hogarth Press, 1953–74), 19: 227–28.

13. Ibid., p. 228.

14. *Portefeuille*—literally, a carrier of leaves or sheets—is a wallet; it is a physically smaller but etymologically identical version of the *portfolio*, carrying documents or artworks. Going back to the same roots, the word branches out in both languages into the same metaphor of the professional portfolio or *portefeuille*, including the government minister "without" portfolio [*sans portefeuille*].—Trans.

15. *Pellicule*, meaning literally a "little skin," is the word used in French for a camera film.—Trans.

16. Freud, "A Note," p. 230.

17. Freud, "The 'Mystic Writing-Pad,'" p. 232.

18. Yosef Hayim Yerushalmi, *Freud's Moses: Judaism Terminable and Interminable* (New Haven, Conn.: Yale University Press, 1991).

19. Lacan, "La Science et la vérité" (Science and Truth), in *Écrits* (Paris: Le Seuil, 1966), pp. 856, 861. [This essay is not included in the English translation of *Écrits*.—Trans.]

20. Ibid., p. 864.

21. Ferdinand de Saussure, *Course in General Linguistics*, trans. Roy Harris (London: Duckworth, 1983), p. III. Emphasis mine; Saussure makes the same "comparison" two pages further on.

22. Freud, *Inhibitions, Symptoms and Anxiety* (1926), *Standard Edition*, 20: 90.

23. *Blanc* is both "blank" and "white."—Trans.

24. The series occurs in *The Interpretation of Dreams* (1900), *Standard Edition*, 5: 355.—Trans.

25. Afterward, I wondered what had whispered this word *de-paperization* to me from the shadow of a presentiment or intuition. Presumably its likeness to "pauperization." A law of inversion or historical perversion seems to link the two phenomena. The use of paper in what we can call its "primary" phase or form (what I was earlier on calling inscription, the breaking of a path before mechanical or commercial reproduction) for the time being still remains as dominant as the use of money, most often paper money, as opposed to credit cards, in the poorest societies or social groups. The "rich" have one or perhaps more than one credit card; the "poor," if they are lucky, only have money—and in some places, such as some hotels, they can't even use it to pay any more, assuming that they have enough to do so. At a slightly higher level of wealth, the paper of the banker's check or postal check remains a criterion of relative poverty or limited credit, if we again compare it to the credit card. In all these cases, a residual "paperization" remains an index of poverty, or relative poverty. Paper is the luxury of the poor. Unless the fetishization of its "out of use" status becomes a surplus value for collectors and the object of new speculative investments (collections of long out-of-date manuscripts, banknotes, or stamps).

26. In Latin, there are two words for English *or*, with different logical implications. *Vel* involves alternatives that are not mutually exclusive: "Milk or sugar?" *Aut* implies that they are: "Coffee or tea?"; "Your money or your life?" The *vel* / *aut* distinction is picked up by Derrida again at the end of the interview.—Trans.

27. *Biblion* did not initially mean "book," still less "oeuvre," but a support for writing (in Greek, *biblos* is the internal bark of the papyrus, and thus of paper, just as the Latin *liber* initially designated the living part of the bark). *Biblion* at that time means "writing paper," and not book or oeuvre or opus—only the substance of a support. Metonymically, it then comes to designate any support for writing: tablets, letters, mail. The *bibliophoros* carries letters (not necessarily books or works): mailman, scrivener, secretary, notary, registrar. Metonymies divert *biblion* toward the general meaning of a piece of writing, something "written" (which is no longer reduced to the support, but is inscribed right on the papyrus or tablet, without thereby being a book: not every piece of writing is a book). Then—another displacement—comes the "book" form: of the *volumen*, the roll of papyrus,

the *codex*, the binding of notebooks with pages placed one on top of the other. Will we continue for much longer to use the words *bibliothèque* or *library* for a place which would no longer be essentially a collection of books deposited there? Even if it still harbors every possible book, and even if the number of them does not decrease, as seems likely—even if this number still represents the majority of acquisitions—nevertheless, the governing norms of this kind of space for work, reading, and writing will be set by products no longer corresponding to the "book" form—by electronic texts without paper support, by writings that would no longer be corpus or opus, finite and separable oeuvres. Textual processes will be opened up on international networks, and made available for the "interactivity" of the reader turned coauthor. If we speak of a *bibliothèque* or library to designate this social space, is it only by a metonymic slide comparable to the one which has led to keeping the word *biblion* or *liber* to designate first of all writing, the written thing, and then the book—when in the beginning these words meant the bark of the papyrus or a fragment of *hyle* [wood] taken from the living bark of that kind of tree? [This footnote has been slightly modified to make use of the English *"library"*–Latin *liber* equivalent alongside that of the French *bibliothèque*–Greek *biblion* emphasized in the French text.—Trans.]

28. Derrida, "Faith and Knowledge: The Two Sources of 'Religion' at the Limits of Reason Alone" (1996), trans. Samuel Weber, in Derrida, *Acts of Religion*, ed. Gil Amidjar (New York: Routledge, 2002), pp. 40–101; also in *Religion*, ed. Jacques Derrida and Gianni Vattimo (Stanford, Calif.: Stanford University Press, 1998), pp. 36–78.

29. I had forgotten to come back to the French word *portefeuille* [wallet], which says just about everything on what is *invested* in paper, in the leaf or *feuille* of paper. Current usage: when its "figure" does not designate a set of documents authenticating an official power, a force of law (the ministerial portfolio), *portefeuille* names this pocket within a pocket, the invisible pocket you *carry* [*porte*] as close as possible to yourself, carry on your person, almost against the body itself. Clothing under clothing, an effect among other effects. This pocket is often made of leather, like the skin of a parchment or the binding of a book. More masculine than feminine, let's think about it, a wallet gathers together all the "papers," the most precious papers, keeping them safe, hidden as close as possible to oneself. They attest to our goods and our property. We protect them because they protect us (the closest possible protection: "This is my body, my papers, it's me . . . "). They take the place, they are the place, of that on which everything else, law and force, the force of law, seems to depend: our "papers," in cards or notebooks: the identity card, the driving permit, the business card or address book; then paper money—banknotes—if one has any. Nowadays, those who can also put credit or debit cards in there. These do fulfill a function analogous to that of the other papers, maintaining the comparable dimensions of a card—something that can be handled, stored away, and carried on the person—but they also signal the end of paper or of the sheet of paper, its withdrawal or reduction, in a wallet whose future is metaphorical. First, they are no longer literally made of "paper"; second, they

have lost the relative suppleness and fragility of sheets or "leaves"; third, their use is conditional on a signature to come, and more and more often a numerical signature (guaranteed by the procedures I was mentioning earlier on); and they will not necessarily bear a proper name; fourth, although in theory they are less open to falsification, they are engaged in a process of transformation and substitution that is much faster than for their paper equivalents. One effect among others: the majority of the "rich" often have less cash, less paper money, in their wallets than some of the poor.

During the past two years, I have twice been burgled, the second time in my presence, to put it like that, when I was myself at home. Only two things were stolen, and it was well spotted, admirably targeted: my laptop the first time, my *portefeuille* the second time. So what was taken away was what included or condensed—virtually, *more in less*—less time, space, and weight. What was *carried away* [*emporté*] was what could most easily be *carried* [*porté*] on the person and with the person: oneself as an other, the *portefeuille* and the "portable." Two eras of "carriage," of carriage charges, of the carrying of the head, of the transport or comportment of the self.

No (deconstructive) reflection on *paper* can fail to dwell on every import of the verb *porter* [carry], in more than one language. Think of all the usages, with or without paper, of the word *portable* today; it can be extended to all words, well beyond those technological objects which are the telephone and the computer. [In French, the mobile phone or cell phone is a *portable*.—Trans.] We also say that paper "carries" or "bears" a signature. The whole difficulty gathers together at the point where *porter*, carrying, and the portable—the support and what it carries—belong to the same body.

30. Literally, and originally, *acharnement* means giving the taste of flesh to a dog or falcon in a hunt; in its common metaphorical use with the noun *travailleur*, the adjective *acharné* means to be a worker furiously, passionately, and unremittingly attached to the task.—Trans.

31. For this it is not even indispensable to invoke the multimedia turbulence of the so-called interior monologue, the virtual audiovisuality of the most secret and silent experience. Doesn't this energy of the lack of fit get imprinted on every interview—this one, for instance? Where is it taking place, in actual reality, and at what time, or through what medium? When would its floating virtuality become an act to be formally noted [*prendre acte*] in those archives we call "acts"? Only when it was published on paper in a special issue of *Les Cahiers de médiologie* given over to paper? That would be a bit simple, true and false at the same time. The time of this virtualization and this actualization remains multiple, and forever heterogeneous. Kafka once said this (which I read—an obscure incoincidence and abyss of nostalgia—in a tourist spot near Angoulême, the capital of paper, and not far from Bordeaux, as an epigraph to a novel by François Mauriac, appropriately entitled *Un adolescent d'autrefois* (An Adolescent of Yesteryear): "I write differently from how I speak, I speak differently from how I think, I think differently from how I should think, and so on into the furthest depths of obscurity." [Balzac's

novel *Lost Illusions* begins in Angoulême with a passage on the link between language and technologies in the history of paper and printing.—Trans.]

32. On *chagrin*, both grief and paper (*shagreen*) in Balzac's novel, *La Peau de chagrin*, see above, Chapter 5, note 3.—Trans.

33. I tried to analyze its "ontological" resource, so to speak, in Heidegger. See "*Geschlecht* II: Heidegger's Hand," trans. John P. Leavey, Jr., in *Deconstruction and Philosophy: The Texts of Jacques Derrida*, ed. John Sallis (Chicago: University of Chicago Press, 1987), and "The Word Processor," above, Chapter 3. But it should be made clear that nostalgia (in which Heidegger sometimes places the very impulse of philosophy) is directed more toward handwriting, and not "paper," even if Heidegger speaks of the track or path traced by an artisanal inscription.

34. On this section of *Of Grammatology*, see above, pp. 14–15, 28.—Trans.

35. Marcel Proust, *Time Regained*, in *Remembrance of Things Past*, trans. Scott Moncrieff and Terence Kilmartin, and by Andreas Mayor (London: Penguin, 1981), 3: 1091.

36. P.S. What I am admitting here (but where's the harm?) would be a *desire* (and one that would swear to remain unfulfilled?): the desire no longer to have to write myself, no longer to be relentlessly working, to let the thing get written by itself right on the paper. Nonwork—among many many more, this is one characteristic distinguishing this "fantasy" or bait from the one I have just seen described (and much more beautifully) in *Champ des morts (Fleur de rêve)* (Field of the Dead [Dream Flower]), the title of Jean-Claude Lebensztejn's admirable recent autobiography, if I can call it that, of Nerval (Paris: Éditions du Limon, 1997, p. 79). And I choose this P.S. from it: "P.S. I am adding, some years later, the following sentences found in Théophile Gautier's *Histoire du romantisme* (History of Romanticism): "He worked as he walked, and from time to time he would stop suddenly, looking for a little notebook of paper stitched together, and in it write down a thought, a phrase, a word, a reminder, a sign intelligible to himself alone; and closing the book he would set off on his way again with renewed vigor. That was his way of composing. More than once we had heard him express the desire of trailing all through life an immense strip of stuff that would fold itself up as necessary behind him and on which he would note down the ideas that came to him *en route*, so as to form at the end of the journey a volume of one single line" (p. 71).

In a P.P.S., the author of *Zigzag* (Paris: Flammarion, 1981) further quotes this letter of Ourliac's on Nerval: "It is not possible to be madder than he was on these occasions. He was a miller whose speech was incoherent. I listened carefully to him, studied him closely for entire evenings—not a single straight idea. I reminded him of literature to distract him—he said to me, "Literature! I am holding it, I have defined it [his word for something spoken to him], here it is"—and he tore me off a square of paper all smeared with zigzags. Eight days later he was put away more raving than ever."

37. See note 26 in this chapter on *vel* and *aut*.—Trans.

CHAPTER 6: THE PRINCIPLE OF HOSPITALITY

This interview with Dominique Dhombres was originally published in the newspaper *Le Monde*, December 2, 1997.

1. Derrida, *Of Hospitality* (1997), trans. Rachel Bowlby (Stanford, Calif.: Stanford University Press, 2000).

2. Ibid., pp. 27, 28.

3. Ibid.

CHAPTER 7: "SOKAL AND BRICMONT AREN'T SERIOUS"

This piece first appeared in *Le Monde*, November 20, 1997. [In 1996, the physicist Alan Sokal had sent a spoof article to the journal *Social Text*, which was published and then revealed to be a hoax. The intention was to discredit French theory in its ignorant use of scientific knowledge, and the book subsequently published with Jean Bricmont was meant to substantiate the critique. The occasion of this piece was the publication of the French edition, *Impostures intellectuelles* (Paris: Odile Jacob, 1997), which, as Derrida goes on to explain, exempted him from the list of indicted philosophers. An English edition, *Intellectual Impostures: Postmodern Philosophers' Abuse of Science* (London: Profile, 1998) came out the following year.—Trans.]

1. The conference in question took place at Johns Hopkins University; its proceedings were published in Eugenio Donato and Richard Macksey, eds., *The Structuralist Controversy: The Languages of Criticism and the Sciences of Man* (1970; Baltimore: Johns Hopkins University Press, 1972). Derrida refers here to his answer to a question from Jean Hyppolite on Einstein's theory of relativity (p. 272), following his paper "Structure, Sign, and Play in the Discourse of the Human Sciences."—Trans.

CHAPTER 8: AS IF IT WERE POSSIBLE, "WITHIN SUCH LIMITS"

This essay was published originally in the *Revue internationale de philosophie* 3 (1998), a special number entitled, in English, *Derrida with His Replies*. In it I do indeed attempt to reply to studies [included in that issue of the journal] by Michael Meyer, Daniel Giovannangeli, Karel Thein, John Sallis, Christopher Norris, Arkady Plotnitsky, and Christopher Johnson. [Another translation of this essay, by Benjamin Elwood with Elizabeth Rottenberg, appears in Derrida, *Negotiations: Interventions and Interviews, 1971–2001*, ed. Elizabeth Rottenberg (Stanford, Calif.: Stanford University Press, 2002), pp. 343–70. Within the essay, there are a number of references to "this" volume, meaning the journal issue that included the essays to which Derrida is responding.—Trans.]

1. Maurice Blanchot, "The Last Word" (The Last Word), then "Le tout dernier mot" (The Very Last Word) on Kafka, in *L'amitié* (Paris: Gallimard, 1971), trans. by Elizabeth Rottenberg as *Friendship* (Stanford, Calif.: Stanford University

Press, 1997); and "Le dernier mot" (The Last Word), in *Après coup* (written 1935–36; Paris: Minuit, 1983): "the echo of the word *il y a.* 'That must be the last word,' I thought, as I listened to them" (p. 66).

2. See especially Derrida, *Politics of Friendship* (1994), trans. George Collins (London: Verso, 1997), chaps. 2 and 3, in the wake of that "dangerous perhaps" of which Nietzsche said that it was philosophers' thinking of the to-come. For instance (and so I am italicizing certain words, though with this proviso from the outset: the intention of the quotations I will have occasion to make from my texts is only to open the space of a discussion. I only wish to prolong this beyond certain limits within which it has to remain contained and constrained here, for lack of space. I make myself provide these quotations—against my inclinations, and deliberately running the risk of being accused of complacency. In my mind they are not meant as authoritative arguments or inappropriate displays, nor are they reminders for the authors of the articles discussed. They have no need of them. So all I would like to do, in a brief and economical way, is to use these quotations or references to address a reader who is keen to pursue the exchange that has been begun, and would like to go back to the texts concerned):

> Now, the thought of the "perhaps" perhaps engages the only possible thought of the event—of friendship to come and friendship for the future. For to love friendship, it is not enough to know how to bear the other in mourning; one must love the future. And there is no more just category for the future than that of the "perhaps". Such a thought conjoins friendship, the future, and the *perhaps* to open on to the coming of what comes—that is to say, necessarily in the regime of a possible whose possibilization must prevail over the impossible. For a possible that would only be possible (non-impossible), a possible surely and certainly possible, accessible in advance, would be a poor possible, a futureless possible, a possible already *set aside*, so to speak, life-assured. This would be a programme or a causality, a development, a process without an event.
>
> The possibilization of the impossible must remain at one and the same time as undecidable—and therefore as decisive—as the future itself. (p. 29)
>
> Without the opening of an absolutely undetermined possible, without the radical abeyance and suspense marking a *perhaps*, there would never be either event or decision. Certainly. But nothing takes place and nothing is ever decided without suspending the *perhaps* while keeping its living possibility in living memory. If no decision (ethical, juridical, political) is possible without interrupting determination by engaging oneself in the *perhaps*, on the other hand, the same decision must interrupt the very thing that is its condition of possibility: the *perhaps* itself. (p. 67)

In the French text, quotation marks around the word *living* signal the necessary link between this chancy aporia of the *im-possible possible* and a thought of spectrality (*neither* living *nor* dead, but living *and* dead).

3. See, for instance, J. L. Austin, *How to Do Things with Words* (Cambridge, Mass.: Harvard University Press, 1962). From this impurity, understood differently, I have also tried to draw a number of consequences (in *Limited Inc.* and elsewhere). If I had sufficient time and space allotted for this exercise, I could relate back to it practically everything that I have had occasion to think up till now.

4. J. L. Austin, "A Plea for Excuses," in *Philosophical Papers* (Oxford: Oxford University Press, 1961), p. 133.

5. Ibid., p. 123.

6. Jean-Jacques Rousseau, *Confessions*, trans. Angela Scholar (Oxford: Oxford University Press, World's Classics, 2000), ed. Patrick Coleman, p. 84. [This episode, in which Rousseau describes how he let a servant girl take the blame for his theft when he stole a ribbon as a boy, is further discussed by Derrida in "Typewriter Ribbon: Limited Ink," trans. Peggy Kamuf, in *Without Alibi* (Stanford, Calif.: Stanford University Press, 2002), pp. 71–201; this essay was part of the French version of *Paper Machine*.—Trans.]

7. In the journal issue in which the present piece was first published.—Trans.

8. Regarding Heidegger, one would have to reconstitute and problematize the context in which propositions such as the following appear: "To embrace (*annehmen*) a 'thing' or a 'person' in their essence means to love them, to favor them (*sie lieben, sie mögen*). Thought in a more original way such favoring (*Dieses Mögen*) means the bestowal of their essence as a gift (*das Wesen schenken*). . . . Being is the enabling-favoring (*also Vermögend-Mögende*), the 'may be' (*das Mög-liche*). As the element, being is the 'quiet power' of the favoring-enabling (*des mögende Vermögens*), that is, of the possible (*das heisst des Möglichen*). Of course, our words 'possible' (*möglich*) and 'possibility' (*Möglichkeit*), under the dominance of 'logic' and 'metaphysics,' are thought solely in contrast to 'actuality' (*Wirklichkeit*); that is, they are thought on the basis of a definite—the metaphysical—interpretation of Being as *actus* and *potentia*, a distinction identified with that between *existentia* and *essentia*" ("'Letter on 'Humanism'" (1949), trans. Frank A. Capuzzi, in Martin Heidegger, *Pathmarks*, ed. William McNeill [Cambridge: Cambridge University Press, 1998], pp. 241–42; German words in most cases inserted into Derrida's French text only).

On these problems, see the important book by Richard Kearney, *La Poétique du possible* (Paris: Vrin, 1984). With regard to a thinking of the "more impossible" or the "more than impossible" as possible (*Das überunmöglischste ist möglich*, in the words of Angelus Silesius), see my "Sauf le nom" (Post-Scriptum) (1993), in *On the Name*, ed. Thomas Dutoit, trans. David Wood, John P. Leavey, Jr., and Ian McLeod (Stanford, Calif.: Stanford University Press, 1995), p. 62. All the aporias of the possible-impossible or the more-than-impossible would thus be "lodged," but also dislodging from "within" of what we call with tranquility desire, love, the movement toward the Good, and so on.

9. See, for instance, Pierre Jankélévitch, *Le Pardon* (Paris: Aubier-Montaigne, 1967), p. 204, and "Nous a-t-on demandé pardon?" in *L'Imprescriptible* (1948–71) (Paris: Le Seuil, 1986), pp. 47 ff.

10. "The most rigorous deconstruction has never claimed to be foreign to literature, nor above all to be *possible*. . . . Deconstruction loses nothing from admitting that it is impossible; and those who would rush to delight in that admission lose nothing from having to wait. For a deconstructive operation *possibility* would rather be the danger, the danger of becoming an available set of rule-governed procedures, methods, accessible approaches. The interest of deconstruction, of such force and desire as it may have, is a certain experience of the impossible; . . . the experience of the other as the invention of the impossible, in other words, as the only possible invention." Derrida, "Psyche: Inventions of the Other," trans. Catherine Porter, in *Reading de Man Reading*, ed. Wlad Godzich and Lindsay Waters (Minneapolis: University of Minnesota Press, 1989), p. 36; trans. mod.

11. "We should be more *radical* than deconstruction, and completely leave the realm of propositionalism. Derrida's thought *invites* us to do so." I have just italicized two words. First, I stress the word *invite* for reasons that will I hope become clear later. With regard to unconditional hospitality, hospitality that is both pure and im-possible, should we say that it corresponds to a *logic of invitation* (when the ipseity of home welcomes the other into its own horizon, when it sets its conditions, thereby claiming to know *whom* it wants to receive, expect, and invite, and *how, to what extent, whom* it is *possible* for it to invite, and so on?). Or else to a *logic of visitation* (when the host says *yes* to the coming or the *unexpected and unforeseeable* event of who comes, at any moment, in advance or behind, in absolute anachrony, without being invited, without introducing themselves, without a horizon of expectation: like a messiah so far from being identifiable and possible to anticipate that the very name of messiah, the figure of the messiah, and especially of messianism, would still reveal a hurry to give precedence to invitation over visitation).

How can the meaning of what we call an event be respected, namely the coming that cannot be anticipated of *what* comes and *who* comes, the meaning of the event then being nothing other than the meaning of the other, the meaning of absolute alterity? *Invitation* keeps control and receives within the limits of the possible; thus it is not pure hospitality; it makes hospitality something economic, it still belongs to the order of the juridical and the political; whereas *visitation* appeals to a pure and unconditional hospitality that welcomes what arrives as impossible. How could this im-possible be possible? How would it become so? What is the best transaction—economic *and* aneconomic—between the logic of invitation and the logic of visitation? Between their analogy and their heterology? What then is the experience, if it is this becoming-possible of the impossible as such? I am not sure of having practiced or preferred invitation, rather than the expectation without expectation of visitation, but I won't swear to anything.

Second, I stress the word *radical,* namely the powerful metaphysical motif of radicality whose necessity is indicated by this word. We think of the figure of root, depth, so-called radical origin, and so on; of Aristotle (for whom causes are "roots"); of Husserl—and all those "foundationalisms," as people say in the world of Anglo-Saxon thought in the course of debates to which, I admit, I have never been able to adjust my premises. I feel foundationalist *and* antifoundationalist, from one problematic context to another, from one interrogative strategy to another, and so I don't know how to use this word *in general*: in general I am and remain "*quasi* foundationalist." This figure of radicality, as a figure and as an injunction that cannot be refused—isn't it just what is made to undergo the turbulence of a deconstruction? Deconstruction has never claimed radicalism, or at any rate it has never been a matter of playing the "most radical" card. But it is still true that an excess in this respect can certainly do no harm (radicalism should indeed be recommended to any philosophy, probably it *is* philosophy), but it risks not changing its ground, not changing the ground undergoing the seismic turbulence I mentioned just now. This is why, just above, at the cue for this note, I stress those encumbering "quasis" with which I have so often burdened myself. On the subject of *deconstruction and radicality*, and only out of concern for brevity, "within such limits," let me refer, among my most recent texts, to *Specters of Marx: The State of the Debt, the Work of Mourning, and the New International* (1993), trans. Peggy Kamuf (New York: Routledge, 1994), pp. 88–93.

12. See in particular Rodolphe Gasché, *The Tain of the Mirror: Derrida and the Philosophy of Reflection* (Cambridge, Mass.: Harvard University Press, 1986).

13. For a number of years Giovannangeli's illuminating readings (see especially his book *La Passion de l'origine* (Paris: Galilée, 1995) and his articles in *Le Passage des frontières* (Paris: Galilée, 1994) and *Passions de la littérature* (Paris: Galilée, 1996) have been bringing me back to a Sartrian inheritance that I am able, thanks to him, to interpret. Following this track, I would have liked here to pursue the discussion of the possible-impossible as law of desire or love (in Heidegger and in relation to another thinking of *Ereignis*—whether or not this word is translated as "event"). I would do this, if we had the space and time for it, by taking into account what Giovannangeli develops around the "possibility of an unconscious affect."

14. To speak or write is to take on the inheritance of natural language and ordinary language, *while also formalizing them*, by bending them to that formalizing abstraction, the capacity for which they carry in origin: the use of a word or a phrase, however simple or ordinary, the implementation of their capacity, is already, by the identification of iterable words, a formalizing idealization; thus there is no more a *purely* ordinary language than there is a *purely* philosophical language or a purely formal language or a purely extraordinary language, in whatever sense. In this sense, if it is true that there is no "last word," as Austin says, then it is difficult to say, as he does, that ordinary language is the "*first* word," a word that is simply and indivisibly "first."

15. Derrida, "Passions: An Oblique Offering" (1993), in *On the Name*, p. 137; cf. p. 10. I also examined the Foucauldian concept of "problematization" in "To Do Justice to Freud: The History of Madness in the Age of Psychoanalysis," in *Resistances of Psychoanalysis* (1996), trans. Peggy Kamuf, Pascale-Anne Brault, and Michael B. Naas (Stanford, Calif.: Stanford University Press, 1996), p. 115.

16. See especially Derrida, *Of Spirit: Heidegger and the Question* (1987), trans. Geoffrey Bennington and Rachel Bowlby (Chicago: University of Chicago Press, 1989), particularly the section on the promise, the *yes* before any opposition of *yes* and *no*—and most of all that which comes "before any question," pp. 92–94; and *Politics of Friendship, passim*.

17. On the repetition of this "yes, yes," see also "Ulysses Gramophone: Hear Say Yes in Joyce," trans. Tina Kendall, in Derrida, *Acts of Literature*, ed. Derek Attridge (New York: Routledge, 1992), pp. 256–309; and "Nombre de oui," in *Psyche: Inventions de l'autre* (Paris: Galilée, 1987), 639 ff.

18. Derrida, "Violence and Metaphysics," in *Writing and Difference* (1967), trans. Alan Bass (Chicago: University of Chicago Press, 1978), pp. 79–80. [Derrida has added the emphasis on *invited* and *decision* in the present citation; to show this Alan Bass's *initiated* has here been modified to *invited*."—Trans.]

19. Derrida, *Given Time: I. Counterfeit Memory* (1991), trans. Peggy Kamuf (Stanford, Calif.: Stanford University Press, 1992), p. 29.

20. Derrida, "*Ousia* and *Gramme*" (1967), in *Margins—Of Philosophy* (1972), trans. Alan Bass (Chicago: University of Chicago Press, 1982), p. 55.

21. Ibid., p. 59.

22. Derrida, "Psyche: Inventions of the Other," trans. Catherine Porter, in *Reading de Man Reading*, ed. Wlad Godzich and Lindsay Waters (Minneapolis: University of Minnesota Press, 1989), p. 60.

23. Derrida, *The Post Card: From Socrates to Freud and Beyond* (1980), trans. Alan Bass (Chicago: University of Chicago Press, 1987); see in particular pp. 120–21, 123, 489.

24. Ibid., p. 489. [The Seminar referred to is Lacan's on Poe's short story "The Purloined Letter"; Lacan's text is translated by Jeffrey Mehlman in *Yale French Studies*, 48 (1972): 11–41.—Trans.]

25. *The Post Card*, p. 25.

26. See *Politics of Friendship*, pp. 68–69.

27. *The Post Card*, pp. 403–5.

28. On this impossible possibility, this *im*-possibility as pervertibility, as the permanent possibility of the perversion of a promise into a threat, see Derrida, "Avances," preface to Serge Margel, *Le Tombeau du Dieu artisan* (Paris: Minuit, 1995).

29. I did also, a very long time ago, analyze in an analogous way, in the space of Husserlian phenomenology, an *im-possibility*, the impossibility of full and immediate intuition, the "essential possibility of nonintuition," the "possibility of the crisis" as "crisis of the *logos*." This possibility of im-possibility, I said then, is not simply negative: the trap becomes a chance as well: "this possibility [of crisis] remains linked for Husserl with the very movement of truth and the production of ideal objectivity: this has in fact an essential need for writing" (Derrida, *Of Grammatology*, trans. Gayatri Chakravorty Spivak [Baltimore: Johns Hopkins University Press, 1976], p. 40, trans. mod.; and earlier in *Edmund Husserl's "The*

Origin of Geometry": An Introduction [1962], trans. John P. Leavey, Jr. [1978; Lincoln: University of Nebraska Press, 1989]).

30. "The ultimate aporia is the impossibility of the aporia *as such*" (*Aporias* [1993], trans. Thomas Dutoit [Stanford, Calif.: Stanford University Press, 1993], p. 78). Which is another way of stressing that there is no question without a problem, but no problem that does not hide or protect itself behind the possibility of a reply.

31. On the analogy of the phrase *savoir-faire, savoir-penser* in the section title above is "thinking know-how" or "knowing how to think." Because *savoir-faire* (literally "doing-knowing") is used in English, I have kept the French expression.—Trans.

32. "Différance" (1967), in *Margins—Of Philosophy*, p. 3.

33. Plotnitsky's many admirable studies include: *In the Shadow of Hegel: Complementarity, History, and the Unconscious* (Gainesville: University Press of Florida, 1993); *Complementarity: Anti-Epistemology After Bohr and Derrida* (Durham, N.C.: Duke University Press, 1994); as well as, more recently, some masterly interventions around the so-called Sokal affair. Christopher Norris has just published an important study, written from the same perspective as the one in this collection, which includes a chapter on quantum mechanics. Interested readers will be able to follow a friendly discussion, on the basis of underlying agreement, of some aspects of Plotnitsky's interpretation. Norris regrets that in some places it is "more postmodernist than deconstructive," even though he rightly pays tribute to it (*Against Relativism: Philosophy of Science, Deconstruction, and Critical Theory* [Oxford: Basil Blackwell, 1997], pp. 113ff.). I don't share Norris's reservations, but it seems to me that the space of this problematic and this discussion are today a prime necessity. For my part, I learn much from these places of intersection: between deconstruction and the sciences, certainly, but also between two approaches, definitely very different ones, Norris's and Plotnitsky's, both of which I want to pay tribute to here. No one does more than these two philosophers to dissipate tenacious prejudices (deconstruction as foreign or hostile to "science," or to "reason"; deconstruction—we were pointing this out before—as "empiricist," "skeptical," or "relativist," "ludic" or "nihilistic," "antihumanist," etc.), and no one does it better. No one is better than them at demonstrating the necessity and the fruitfulness of the co-implications between "deconstructive" and "scientific" problematics that are too often kept separated. In discussions but also in institutions.

34. *Of Grammatology*, p. 93.

35. In the following quotation I have italicized the words that refer to these three categories of thought, philosophy, and science: "Derrida's work reflects or mediates aspects of contemporary *science*. It deals of course with only one dimension of his work, but it does show a *thinker* open to the implications of *science*." And Johnson then specifically says what I want to stress for the reason that it does remove the prejudice according to which "science does not think" (Heidegger): "open to the implications of science, of what science gives us to think." How does

science "give" us to think? It's on the subject of this "give" and this "donation" that I would have liked to develop this analysis, beyond "such limits."

36. Derrida, "Faith and Knowledge: The Two Sources of 'Religion' at the Limits of Reason Alone" (1996), trans. Samuel Weber, in Derrida, *Acts of Religion*, ed. Gil Amidjar (New York: Routledge, 2002), pp. 40–101; also in *Religion*, ed. Jacques Derrida and Gianni Vattimo (Stanford, Calif.: Stanford University Press, 1998), pp. 36–78.

CHAPTER 9: MY SUNDAY "HUMANITIES"

First published in [the newspaper] *L'Humanité*, March 4, 1999, on the centenary of its first issue. This was how the newspaper presented its invitation: "For 'Humanity' the newspaper. For humanity *tout court* . . . What is between these two,—in the way that we speak about what is between the lines? This is the question, in the form of a riddle, that we have put to personalities of diverse backgrounds, as a prelude to the appearance of the new '*Humanité*.' A bit like good fairies who are asked to attend at a particularly difficult birth, that of their paper."

Simultaneously, the newspaper published the complete text of the editorial in which Jean Jaurès founded *L'Humanité*.

1. Jaurès was assassinated in 1914. He was a leading figure in the international socialist movement.—Trans.

2. In fact there are *eleven* points: the French text had two fourth points.—Trans.

3. This section alludes to the acrimonious debates in France preceding the passing of legislation, in February 1999, that ratified both the difference and the "parity" of men and women, two groups each entitled to equal access to political office under the French Constitution. Derrida's point—for his French readership—is that France had been somewhat slow to wake up to ideas of sexual discrimination which had been common and influential elsewhere for some time.—Trans.

4. In 1999 a law was passed giving new rights to nonmarried couples, both heterosexual and homosexual, who could choose to register themselves via a "Pacte civil de solidarité"—whence *Pacs*. The law was intended to deal with the problem of the increasing number of gay couples and unmarried heterosexual couples who were not entitled to pensions and other forms of financial security granted only to legally married couples. So here, Derrida mockingly suggests that a way around the problem of the president embodying only one of the two sexes now to be given "parity" under the constitution would be some form of couple arrangement, whether by alternation of male or female occupants of the post, or by cohabitation (old-fashioned marriage or modern Pacs); on the political meaning of *cohabitation* in French, see Chapter 4, note 1.—Trans.

5. See Derrida, *Specters of Marx: The State of the Debt, the Work of Mourning, and the New International* (1993), trans. Peggy Kamuf (New York: Routledge, 1994); "On Cosmopolitanism" (1997), trans. Mark Dooley and Michael Hughes, in *On Cosmopolitanism and Forgiveness* (New York: Routledge, 2001). I apologize for these summary references.

6. The references are to representatives of opposing policies within the then French government on issues of immigration. Derrida mentions the "Pasqua-Debré laws," which imposed restrictions on immigration, in "Not Utopia, the Impossible," Chapter 12 in the current volume.—Trans.

7. See Derrida, *Politics of Friendship* (1994), trans. George Collins (London: Verso, 1997).

8. The word *irredentiste* derives from the Italian nationalist movement of the 1890s, which sought to annex Italian-speaking territories to the newly formed Italian nation-state.—Trans.

9. In French, *mondialisation*, from *monde* meaning "world": hence the following questions. But French also occasionally adopts the term *globalisation*, whence the comparison of the two words. See too Translator's Note.—Trans.

10. Jeremy Rifkin, *The End of Work: The Decline of the Global Labor Force and the Dawn of the Post-Market Era* (New York: Tarcher/Putnam, 1996).

11. See Jacques le Goff, "Temps et travail" (Time and Work), in *Un Autre Moyen Age* (Paris: Gallimard, "Quarto" series, 1999).

CHAPTER 10: FOR JOSÉ RAINHA

This text was published in *L'Humanité* on November 30, 1999, with the introduction given.

1. Movimento dos trabalhadores rurais sem terra (Landless Rural Workers' Movement); MST abbreviates this to Movimento sem terra. In Brazil, 60 percent of farming land is unused. Since 1985, this movement has undertaken group invasions of unused land to pressure the government and speed up the process of agrarian reform in a country where the poorest 40 percent of the people own just 1 percent of the land.—Trans.

2. José Rainha was acquitted in April 2000.—Trans.

3. José Saramago had also offered his support to José Rainha in *L'Humanité* (November 25, 1999).

CHAPTER 11: "WHAT DOES IT MEAN TO BE A FRENCH PHILOSOPHER TODAY?"

An interview with Franz-Olivier Giesbert, published in *Le Figaro Magazine*, October 16, 1999, with the title "Connaissez-vous Derrida?" (Do You Know Derrida?).

1. Derrida and Catherine Malabou, *Counterpath: Traveling with Jacques Derrida* (1999), trans. David Wills (Stanford, Calif.: Stanford University Press, 2004).

2. For Guisbert's *Mondialiste*, I thought it better to avoid coining the word *globalist* here, on the analogy of "globalization." The word does not exist, and it would only exacerbate the existing distinction between the social "world" (*monde*) in the French *mondialisation* and the geographical "globe" of *globalization*: a "globalist" sounds more like a tourist.—Trans.

CHAPTER 12: NOT UTOPIA, THE IM-POSSIBLE

Interview with Thomas Assheuer. A slightly shorter and reworked version was published in *Die Zeit* (March 5, 1998) under the following heading: "'Ich mis-straue der Utopie, ich will das un-Mögliche'": Ein Gespräch mit dem Philosophen Jacques Derrida über die Intellektuellen, den Kapitalismus und die Gesetze der Gastfreundshaft" ("I Am Suspicious of Utopia; I Want the im-Possible": An Interview with the Philosopher Jacques Derrida on Intellectuals, Capitalism, and the Laws of Hospitality).

1. The Parlement international des écrivains (PIE) was founded in 1993; its first president was Salman Rushdie and its current president is Wole Soyinka. Derrida was a vice-president in 1995 when this organization launched an appeal to European cities to set up a network of "cities of refuge" for persecuted writers. "On Cosmopolitanism" (see below, note 3) was written for the PIE conference of cities of refuge held in 1996.

2. Derrida, *The Other Heading* (1991), trans. Pascale-Anne Brault and Michael B. Naas (Bloomington: Indiana University Press, 1992).

3. Derrida, "On Cosmopolitanism" (1997), trans. Mark Dooley and Michael Hughes, in *On Cosmopolitanism and Forgiveness* (New York: Routledge, 2001). See note 1, above.

4. On the Parlement international des écrivains, see note 1, above. CISIA is the Comité international de soutien aux intellectuels algériens (International Committee of Support for Algerian Intellectuals).—Trans.

5. Derrida, *Adieu to Emmanuel Levinas*, trans. Pascale-Anne Brault and Michael B. Naas (Stanford, Calif.: Stanford University Press, 1999).

CHAPTER 13: "OTHERS ARE SECRET BECAUSE THEY ARE OTHER"

An interview with Antoine Spire, published in *Le Monde de l'éducation* 284 (September 2000), in a shorter and slightly different version.

1. Literally, "one time for all (times)"; roughly equivalent to the English idiom "once and for all."—Trans. On *une fois pour toutes*, see further Jacques Derrida and Safaa Fathy, *Tourner les mots—au bord d'un film* (Paris: Galilée, 2000), pp. 82–83.

2. "Fidélité à plus d'un: Mériter d'hériter où la généalogie fait défaut" (Fidelity to More Than One: Deserving to Inherit Where the Genealogy Is Lacking), in *Idiomes, nationalités, déconstructions: Rencontres de Rabat autour de Jacques Derrida* (Idioms, Nationalities, Deconstructions: Rabat Discussions Around Jacques Derrida) (Paris: L'Aube-Toukbal, 1998).

3. Derrida, *The Other Heading* (1991), trans. Pascale-Anne Brault and Michael B. Naas (Bloomington: Indiana University Press, 1992), and *Politics of Friendship* (1994), trans. George Collins (London: Verso, 1997).

4. See especially Derrida, *Du Droit à la philosophie* (Paris: Galilée, 1990); Derrida and Bernard Stiegler, *Echographies of Television: Filmed Interviews* (1996),

trans. Jennifer Bajorek (Cambridge: Polity Press, 2002); "The Right to Philosophy from a Cosmopolitan Point of View" (1997), in Derrida, *Negotiations: Interventions and Interviews, 1971–2001*, ed. and trans. Elizabeth Rottenberg (Stanford, Calif.: Stanford University Press, 2002), pp. 329–42.

5. See Derrida, *The Gift of Death* (1992), trans. David Wills (Chicago: University of Chicago Press, 1995).

6. Derrida, *On Touching—Jean-Luc Nancy* [1998], trans. Christine Irizarry (Stanford, Calif.: Stanford University Press, 2005).

7. See especially "Heidegger, the Philosophers' Hell" (1987), in Derrida, *Points . . . Interviews, 1974–1994*, ed. Elisabeth Weber, trans. Peggy Kamuf (Stanford, Calif.: Stanford University Press, 1995), pp. 181–90.

8. On Hegel, see Derrida, *Glas* (1974), trans. John P. Leavey, Jr., and Richard Rand (Lincoln: University of Nebraska Press, 1986); on Freud, *The Post Card: From Socrates to Freud and Beyond* (1980), trans. Alan Bass (Chicago: University of Chicago Press, 1987); on Nietzsche, "Otobiographies: The Teaching of Nietzsche and the Politics of the Proper Name" (1984), trans. Avital Ronell, in *The Ear of the Other: Otobiography, Transference, Translation*, ed. Christie McDonald (Lincoln: University of Nebraska Press, 1988).

9. Henri Meschonnic, *Le Langage Heidegger* (Paris: PUF, 1990).

10. Derrida, "Like the Sound of the Sea Deep Within a Shell" (1988), in *Mémoires for Paul de Man*, trans. Cecile Lindsay, Jonathan Culler, Eduardo Cadava, and Peggy Kamuf (New York: Columbia University Press, 1989).

11. He does. *La Pensée 68*, by Luc Ferry and Alain Renaut, was published in 1985. In English the book appeared as *French Philosophy of the Sixties*, trans. Mary Schnackenberg (Amherst: University of Massachusetts Press, 1990).—Trans.

12. See Chapter 12, note 1.

13. See note 6, above.—Trans.

14. Derrida, "Shibboleth—For Paul Celan" (1986), trans. Joshua Wilner, in *Word Traces*, ed. Aris Fioretis (Baltimore: Johns Hopkins University Press, 1994), pp. 3–72.

15. Marranos were Sephardic Jews in Spain and (especially) Portugal, forced to convert to Catholicism at the time of the Inquisition in order to escape death or exile, but who preserved their own faith and rituals in secret. Derrida alludes to the figure of the Marrano as keeper of a secret religion, for instance at the end of *Aporias*, trans. Thomas Dutoit (Stanford, Calif.: Stanford University Press, 1993), pp. 74, 77; and in "History of the Lie: Prolegomena," in *Without Alibi*, trans. Peggy Kamuf (Stanford, Calif.: Stanford University Press, 2002), pp. 63–64.—Trans.

16. In French the force of this sentence derives from the multiple senses of the verb *arriver*—"to arrive," but also "to happen" and (before another verb) "to succeed in" or "manage to." Here both "manage" and "happen" translate *arriver*.—Trans.

17. See above, note 15.

CHAPTER 14: FICHUS

1. Walter Benjamin, letter no. 1320, *Gesammelte Briefe*, vol. 6 (1938–40), ed. Christoph Gödde and Henri Lonitz (Frankfurt am Main: Suhrkamp, 2000), p. 343. This letter has twice been published in France (so in French, in its original language: in Benjamin's *Correspondance*, 1929–40, ed. Gershom Scholem and Theodor W. Adorno, trans. Guy Petitdemange [Paris: Aubier-Montaigne, 1979], 2: 307–9; and in Benjamin's *Écrits français* [Writings in French], ed. and trans. J. M. Monnoyer [Paris: Gallimard, 1991], pp. 316–18). Benjamin appears to have noted down this dream for himself, in a version that is essentially identical to the one in the letter to Gretel Adorno, but with the grammar or actual words slightly different in some of its phrasing. This version is published in the *Autobiographische Schriften* (Autobiographical Writings) (Frankfurt am Main: Suhrkamp, 1980), 6: 540–42.

2. Theodor W. Adorno, *Minima Moralia: Reflexionen aus dem beschädigten Leben* (1951; Frankfurt am Main: Suhrkamp, 1973), p. 143; *Minima Moralia: Reflections from Damaged Life*, trans. E. F. N. Jephcott (London: Verso, 1974), p. 111. The phrase in the dedication about "the intellectual in emigration" is on p. 18.

3. Walter Benjamin, "The Work of Art in the Age of Mechanical Reproduction" (1936), in *Illuminations*, trans. Harry Zohn (New York: Schocken Books, 1969), pp. 217–51.

4. Adorno, "A Portrait of Walter Benjamin," in *Prisms*, trans. Samuel Weber and Shierry Weber (London: Neville Spearman, 1967), p. 241.

5. Adorno mentions this article in the same text. It was published in the *Neue Rundschau* and was about surrealism, among other things.

6. Adorno, "A Portrait," p. 239.

7. Adorno, "On the Question: 'What is German?'" trans. Thomas Y. Levin, *New German Critique* 36 (1985): 129.

8. Ibid., p. 129.

9. Ibid., p. 129.

10. Adorno, *Minima Moralia*, pp. 141–42; English trans., p. 110.

11. Ibid., pp. 110–11; emphasis added.

12. Jürgen Habermas, "Theodor Adorno: The Primal History of Subjectivity—Self-Affirmation Gone Wild" (1969), in *Philosophical-Political Profiles*, trans. Frederick G. Lawrence (London: Heinemann, 1983), p. 102.

13. Adorno, "On the Question," p. 130.

14. Ibid., p. 121.

15. Ibid., pp. 130–31.

16. Ibid., p. 131.

17. G. Ahrens, W. S. Bau, H. Beese, M. Bechgeister, U. O. Dünkelsbühler, A. G. Dütmann, P. Engelmann, M. Fischer, Th. Frey, Rodolphe Gasché, Werner Hamacher, A. Haverkamp, F. Kittler, H. G. Gondel, H. U. Gumbrecht, R. Hentschel, D. Hornig, J. Hörisch, K. Karabaczek-Schreiner, A. Knop, U. Keen, B. Lindner, S. Lorenzer, S. Lüdemann, H. J. Metzger, K. Murr, D. Otto, K. J. Pazzini, E. Pfaffenberger-Brückner, R. Puffert, H. J. Rheinberger, D. Schmidt, H. W.

Schmidt, K. Schreiner, R. Schwaderer, G. Sigl, Bernard Stiegler, Peter Szondi, J. Taubes, Ch. Tholen, D. Trauner, D. W. Tuckwiller, B. Waldenfels, Elisabeth Weber, Samuel Weber, D. Weissmann, R. Werner, M. Wetzel, A. Wintersberger, A. Witte, H. Zischler.

I apologize to those whose names I have omitted here.

18. Benjamin, *Gesammelte Briefe*, 6: 341.

19. Adorno, letter no. 39, August 2–4, 1935, in Theodor W. Adorno and Walter Benjamin, *The Complete Correspondence 1928–1940*, ed. Henri Lonitz, trans. Nicholas Walker (Cambridge: Polity Press, 1999), pp. 104–14; Benjamin, letter no. 40, August 16, 1935, pp. 116–19.

20. Benjamin, *Gesammelte Briefe*, 6: 342–43.

21. Benjamin, *Deutsche Menschen* (German Men) (Frankfurt am Main: Suhrkamp, 1962).

22. To be *fichu* is to be nasty; to be *bien fichu* ("well *fichu*") is to have a good body; to be *mal fichu* ("badly *fichu*") is to feel lousy.—Trans.

23. The more usual etymology is from *doron*, gift; Adorno's own name Theo*dor*, from the same root, means "gift of the gods."—Trans.

24. Freud, *The Interpretation of Dreams* (1900), in the *Standard Edition of the Complete Psychological Works of Sigmund Freud*, trans. James Strachey (London: Hogarth Press, 1953–74), 5: 571; *Die Traumdeutung* (Frankfurt am Main: Fischer, 1977), p. 465.

25. Freud, *Die Traumdeutung*, p. 464; cf. *Standard Edition*, 5: 570.

26. Cf. the opening of Adorno's "Cultural Criticism and Society," at the start of *Prisms*, p. 19: "To anyone in the habit of thinking with his ears, the words 'cultural criticism' (*Kulturkritik*) must have an offensive ring."

27. The German and French versions of Enlightenment.—Trans.

28. See Derrida, "Psychoanalysis Searches the States of Its Soul: The Impossible Beyond of a Sovereign Cruelty" (2000), in Derrida, *Without Alibi*, trans. Peggy Kamuf (Stanford, Calif.: Stanford University Press, 2002), pp. 238–80. The passage from *Minima Moralia* is section 37, pp. 60–61.

29. By an odd coincidence, it happens that Adorno was born on a September 11 (1903). Everyone who was in the audience knew this, and according to what had been the usual ritual since the prize was founded, it ought to have been presented on September 11, not September 22. But because of a visit to China (I was in Shanghai on September 11), I had had to ask for the ceremony to be put back.

30. Adorno, "Über einige Relationem zwischen Musik und Malerei" (1965), in *Musikalische Schriften, I–III* (Frankfurt am Main: Suhrkamp, 1997), pp. 628–42; 636–37; trans. Susan Gillespie, "On Some Relationships Between Music and Painting," *Musical Quarterly* 79 (1995): 66–79; 73.

31. See Max Horkheimer and Theodor W. Adorno, *Dialectic of Enlightenment*, and Adorno, *Beethoven: The Philosophy of Music* (1993), trans. Edmund Jephcott (Stanford, Calif.: Stanford University Press, 1998).

32. "No one/bears witness for the/witness" (Paul Celan, "*Aschenglorie*" (Ashaureole), in *Selected Poems of Paul Celan*, trans. John Felstiner (New York: W. W. Norton, 2001), pp. 260–61.

Cultural Memory | in the Present

Stanley Cavell, *Emerson's Transcendental Etudes*

Stuart McLean, *The Event and its Terrors: Ireland, Famine, Modernity*

Beate Rössler, ed., *Privacies: Philosophical Evaluations*

Bernard Faure, *Double Exposure: Cutting Across Buddhist and Western Discourses*

Alessia Ricciardi, *The Ends Of Mourning: Psychoanalysis, Literature, Film*

Alain Badiou, *Saint Paul: The Foundation of Universalism*

Gil Anidjar, *The Jew, the Arab: A History of the Enemy*

Jonathan Culler and Kevin Lamb, eds., *Just Being Difficult? Academic Writing in the Public Arena*

Jean-Luc Nancy, *A Finite Thinking*, edited by Simon Sparks

Theodor W. Adorno, *Can One Live after Auschwitz? A Philosophical Reader*, edited by Rolf Tiedemann

Patricia Pisters, *The Matrix of Visual Culture: Working with Deleuze in Film Theory*

Andreas Huyssen, *Present Pasts: Urban Palimpsests and the Politics of Memory*

Talal Asad, *Formations of the Secular: Christianity, Islam, Modernity*

Dorothea von Mücke, *The Rise of the Fantastic Tale*

Marc Redfield, *The Politics of Aesthetics: Nationalism, Gender, Romanticism*

Emmanuel Levinas, *On Escape*

Dan Zahavi, *Husserl's Phenomenology*

Rodolphe Gasché, *The Idea of Form: Rethinking Kant's Aesthetics*

Michael Naas, *Taking on the Tradition: Jacques Derrida and the Legacies of Deconstruction*

Herlinde Pauer-Studer, ed., *Constructions of Practical Reason: Interviews on Moral and Political Philosophy*

Jean-Luc Marion, *Being Given: Toward a Phenomenology of Givenness*

Theodor W. Adorno and Max Horkheimer, *Dialectic of Enlightenment*

Ian Balfour, *The Rhetoric of Romantic Prophecy*

Martin Stokhof, *World and Life as One: Ethics and Ontology in Wittgenstein's Early Thought*

Gianni Vattimo, *Nietzsche: An Introduction*

Jacques Derrida, *Negotiations: Interventions and Interviews, 1971–1998*, ed. Elizabeth Rottenberg

Brett Levinson, *The Ends of Literature: Post-transition and Neoliberalism in the Wake of the "Boom"*

Timothy J. Reiss, *Against Autonomy: Global Dialectics of Cultural Exchange*

Hent de Vries and Samuel Weber, eds., *Religion and Media*

Niklas Luhmann, *Theories of Distinction: Redescribing the Descriptions of Modernity*, ed. and introd. William Rasch

Johannes Fabian, *Anthropology with an Attitude: Critical Essays*

Michel Henry, *I Am the Truth: Toward a Philosophy of Christianity*

Gil Anidjar, *"Our Place in Al-Andalus": Kabbalah, Philosophy, Literature in Arab-Jewish Letters*

Hélène Cixous and Jacques Derrida, *Veils*

F. R. Ankersmit, *Historical Representation*

F. R. Ankersmit, *Political Representation*

Elissa Marder, *Dead Time: Temporal Disorders in the Wake of Modernity (Baudelaire and Flaubert)*

Reinhart Koselleck, *The Practice of Conceptual History: Timing History, Spacing Concepts*

Niklas Luhmann, *The Reality of the Mass Media*

Hubert Damisch, *A Childhood Memory by Piero della Francesca*

Hubert Damisch, *A Theory of /Cloud/: Toward a History of Painting*

Jean-Luc Nancy, *The Speculative Remark (One of Hegel's Bons Mots)*

Jean-François Lyotard, *Soundproof Room: Malraux's Anti-Aesthetics*

Jan Patočka, *Plato and Europe*

Hubert Damisch, *Skyline: The Narcissistic City*

Isabel Hoving, *In Praise of New Travelers: Reading Caribbean Migrant Women Writers*

Richard Rand, ed., *Futures: Of Derrida*

William Rasch, *Niklas Luhmann's Modernity: The Paradox of System Differentiation*

Jacques Derrida and Anne Dufourmantelle, *Of Hospitality*

Jean-François Lyotard, *The Confession of Augustine*

Kaja Silverman, *World Spectators*

Samuel Weber, *Institution and Interpretation: Expanded Edition*

Jeffrey S. Librett, *The Rhetoric of Cultural Dialogue: Jews and Germans in the Epoch of Emancipation*

Ulrich Baer, *Remnants of Song: Trauma and the Experience of Modernity in Charles Baudelaire and Paul Celan*

Samuel C. Wheeler III, *Deconstruction as Analytic Philosophy*

David S. Ferris, *Silent Urns: Romanticism, Hellenism, Modernity*

Rodolphe Gasché, *Of Minimal Things: Studies on the Notion of Relation*

Sarah Winter, *Freud and the Institution of Psychoanalytic Knowledge*

Samuel Weber, *The Legend of Freud: Expanded Edition*

Aris Fioretos, ed., *The Solid Letter: Readings of Friedrich Hölderlin*